THREE QUESTIONS WE NEVER STOP ASKING

THREE QUESTIONS WE NEVER STOP ASKING

MICHAEL KELLOGG

59 John Glenn Drive
Amherst, New York 14228–2119

Published 2010 by Prometheus Books

Inquiries should be addressed to
Prometheus Books
59 John Glenn Drive
Amherst, New York 14228–2119
VOICE: 716–691–0133
FAX: 716–691–0137
WWW.PROMETHEUSBOOKS.COM

14 13 12 11 10   5 4 3 2 1

Library of Congress Cataloging-in-Publication Data

Kellogg, Michael K., 1954–
    Three questions we never stop asking / by Michael Kellogg.
        p. cm.
    Includes bibliographical references and index.
    ISBN 978–1–61614–186–8 (cloth : alk. paper)
    1. Philosophy—Introductions. I. Title.

BD21.K42 2010
100—dc22

                                                    2010013082

Printed in the United States of America on acid-free paper

For Lucy

—Each morn a thousand roses brings.

So long as man exists, philosophizing of some sort occurs.

—MARTIN HEIDEGGER

CONTENTS

8   CONTENTS

PREFACE

Every New Year's Day for more than twenty years, I have re-read Plato's *Apology*, in which Socrates—on trial for his life—defends his calling as a philosopher. At the age of seventy, Socrates (470–399 BCE) is charged with impiety and corrupting the young. His real "crime" appears to be his close association with some of the architects of Athens's disastrous defeat in the Peloponnesian War (most notably, Alcibiades) and the oligarchic tyranny that followed, which included members of Plato's family. But the official charge is that he has taught the youth of Athens to question the gods and traditional values of the city. It is to that charge that Socrates directs his defense: not as an "apology" in the modern sense of that term, but as a justification for the choices he has made and the life he has lived.

The word philosophy comes from the Greek: *philo–sophia*, the love of wisdom. Apollo's oracle at Delphi proclaimed Socrates to be the wisest man on earth. Socrates, in the first display of his famous irony, concludes that the oracle is correct only in a negative sense: Socrates is wise insofar as he knows that he is not. Others, by contrast, believe they are wise, but are not. Hence, he infers, he is at least wiser than them. To prove his point, Socrates begins questioning those with reputations for wisdom: politicians, prominent citizens, poets. In each instance he examines their beliefs about justice, virtue, and the good

9

life and in each case finds them unable to give a proper account. He shows that those purporting to act with piety or temperance or courage cannot explain the basis for their claims and have not, in fact, given serious thought to the reasons or grounds for their beliefs. They do not really know what piety is or temperance or courage. Is it not a shame, Socrates asks, for men to be concerned with any other matters—particularly with public affairs or with earning money—when they cannot answer such basic questions, when they do not understand virtue or know what the good life is and how to attain it?

In the course of these investigations, Socrates delights the young and offends the powerful, who do not like to be told (and even less have it publicly demonstrated) that they are ignorant of such matters. Socrates compares himself to a gadfly, stinging and irritating and trying to rouse the citizens of Athens to examine their lives and to care, above all else, about virtue. "It is the greatest good," he explains, "for a man to discuss virtue every day and those other things about which you hear me conversing and testing myself and others, for the unexamined life is not worth living for men."[1] In his speech to the jury of 501 male citizens of Athens, Socrates makes clear that he will never stop practicing philosophy and urging each Athenian "not to care for any of his belongings before caring that he himself should be as good and as wise as possible."[2]

Perhaps it is no small wonder that the jury condemns him to death. Certainly, Socrates himself is not surprised at the verdict. Indeed, he almost seems to invite it when he tells the jury he will not, as defendants usually do, beg or plead for his life or put his family on display for sympathy. "I put my trust in the justice of what I say, and let none of you expect anything else. It would not be fitting at my age, as it might be for a young man, to toy with words when I appear before you."[3] To fear death, he argues, is just the ultimate example of man's penchant "to think one's self wise when one is not, to think one knows what one does not know."[4] Far worse than death or any other bodily harm is to act unjustly or to live in willful, selfish ignorance. When he leaves the courtroom, ultimately to drink the hemlock that will kill him, he states: "Now the time has come, and we must go away—I to die, and you to live. Which is better is known to the god alone."[5]

Socrates may be the most important character in Western thought.

I use the word "character" advisedly, because Socrates is primarily a literary creation, akin to Hamlet or Don Quixote or Faust or Don Juan, all founding archetypes of the human spirit. Socrates is a product of Plato's genius and it is difficult (despite additional, more pedestrian sources of information) to penetrate through that genius to the man himself. (To what extent that is possible for any historical figure raises an interesting question, but Socrates is an extreme case.)

The mere fact that there was such a man, who practiced philosophy and was put to death for it by his fellow Athenians, adds a force to Plato's early dialogues that genius alone could not. But had Socrates not existed it would still have been necessary for Western philosophy to invent him. Socrates is the archetype of the philosopher seeking wisdom without rest or compromise, ignoring all material advantage and caring only about virtue and the good life for man. As such, he is both an inspiration and a scourge. Socrates is still a gadfly more than two thousand years after he was condemned by the Athenians. He demands that we account for our lives. He challenges us directly and unequivocally: "are you not ashamed of your eagerness to possess as much wealth, reputation and honors as possible, while you do not care for nor give thought to wisdom or truth, or the best possible state of your soul?"[6]

Socrates compares favorably with those other archetypes: Faust, the restless scholar seeking knowledge; Don Juan, the narcissistic lover seeking conquests; and Don Quixote, the noble knight seeking a half-baked chivalric ideal in a decidedly unchivalric world. Socrates' quest is more fundamental, for he asks how we should live our lives, how we are to distinguish good from bad and right from wrong, and where wisdom is to be found. He believes, passionately, unwaveringly, that such questions have answers, even if he himself is incapable of uncovering them. In that belief, he stands firmly opposed to the principal archetype of the modern spirit, Hamlet, the melancholy skeptic, who cannot make up his mind that there is anything for which it is worth questing.

Still, Socrates himself—despite his belief that the quest for wisdom is the only proper business of man—gives us no assurance or even grounds for hope that the study of philosophy will in fact bear fruit. The early Socratic dialogues—those in which the character

"Socrates" is thought to be closest to the historical Socrates in both method and personality—are almost all aporetic, which is to say without solution or resolution. A problem is posed: what is the nature of piety (*Euthyphro*) or temperance (*Charmides*) or courage (*Laches*)? One person purports to know. Socrates questions him closely, revealing contradictions in his account. At the end, Socrates, the person he questions, and the reader are none the wiser, except in the ironic sense noted above.

Perhaps that is all there is. Perhaps Socrates is correct at his most ironical when he says in the *Apology* that the love of wisdom leads only to the realization that human wisdom is worthless. Ludwig Wittgenstein, who stands at the opposite pole of Western philosophy from Socrates (both temporally and temperamentally), is thought to have concluded something of the sort when he says: "The real discovery is the one that makes me capable of stopping doing philosophy when I want to.—The one that gives philosophy peace, so that it is no longer tormented by questions which bring *itself* in question."[7]

But it is hard to be satisfied with such a non-answer. We are driven to philosophy by a sense of wonder: Why is there something rather than nothing? What can be the meaning of a life that ends in death? What is the best life for man? Philosophers throughout history, starting with Plato, have tried to give actual answers to such questions. They are largely unsatisfactory answers, to be sure. Wonder is the beginning of philosophy; its ends generally lie in the barren ruins of theory. So much so, indeed, that modern philosophy dismisses the eternal questions as naive and not a proper subject for study. There is a lovely anecdote about a cab driver who picked up Bertrand Russell, then the most famous philosopher in the English-speaking world. "I said to him," explained the cabbie, "'Well, Lord Russell, what's it all about,' and, do you know, he couldn't tell me."[8] Academic philosophers report the anecdote as a joke on the layman's (or freshman's) mistaken belief that it is philosophy's job to answer such questions. But I think the cabbie had it about right: what is the point of all your philosophy if it doesn't actually tell you anything worth knowing?

Certainly, that is the feeling that led me, almost thirty years ago, to give up my graduate studies in philosophy and go to law school. The bankruptcy of Anglo-American analytic philosophy left me with an empty feeling of having wasted my time and learned nothing of importance. I decided that experience, not theory, was the road to wisdom. I gathered that experience as a bee gathers pollen, both in government and in private practice, prosecuting mafia dons and street-level drug dealers, arguing cases in the U.S. Supreme Court, and advising private clients while starting and building a law firm with close friends. I gathered even more enriching experience as a husband and the father of three children. But I cannot say that experience—however rewarding spiritually, emotionally, and even financially (which experience tells me is not to be despised)—has made me wiser in a way that I could readily articulate or that a neutral observer would remark upon. If pressed by Lord Russell's cab driver, I could mention family, friends, meaningful work, and persistent interests. But the cabbie's retort—"and do you know, he couldn't tell me"—would still have more than a measure of justice.

Throughout the last three decades, I have never lost the nagging feeling that philosophy still has much to tell us about how we should live our lives and uncover their meaning. Perhaps these are largely negative lessons. But there can be both charm and instruction in the ruins of theories, just as in the ruins of abbeys and castles. The most important point is that we are descendants of Socrates and cannot help listening to his call when he asks for an account of our beliefs, of what we live for and why.

I have written this book in an effort to answer for myself the question why philosophy still matters and what wisdom it has to impart to us. It is not, I think, a wholly negative wisdom. But neither is it embodied in any particular set of doctrines or theories of the sort that are traditionally considered philosophical. Nor, I can say without false modesty, is it likely to satisfy all or most or perhaps any reader other than myself. Indeed, it may not satisfy even myself from day to day. But failing to accept any answer as final and definitive is itself part of Socratic wisdom.

My book is structured around what Immanuel Kant considered the three core questions of philosophy: What can I know? What may I hope? What ought I to do? These are questions that—however much we immerse ourselves in the whirl and concerns of everyday life—we cannot, in the end, escape. They intrude themselves, not just in times of personal crisis, but at odd moments and in varied ways. Even those who are not inclined to the discipline of philosophy or are not even particularly reflective will feel their force on occasion. Whether we develop satisfactory answers or not, wrestling with such questions is part of what it is to be human.

I proceed by juxtaposing a pair of thinkers on each of these three questions. In a sense, but only a very loose one, the first member of the pair is a builder, the second a destroyer. One explores the promise of a theory; the other the consequences of its ruin.

The first pair deals with the possibility of philosophical knowledge: Plato (427–347 BCE), whose theory of forms provides both an answer to Socrates' aporetic dialogues and a job description for all future philosophers; and Ludwig Wittgenstein (1889–1951), who fatally undermines the Platonic quest and dismisses philosophical theories as "language on holiday."

The second pair deals with the existence of God: Immanuel Kant (1724–1804), who limits reason to make room for faith; and Friedrich Nietzsche (1824–1900), whose madman in the marketplace brashly announces the death of God as the fundamental fact of modern life.

The third pair deals with virtue: Aristotle (384–322 BCE), who explores the practical ethics of public life; and Martin Heidegger (1889–1976), who dismisses public ethics as an artificial, external constraint on man's freedom and authenticity.

These pairs, and the questions they address, are not intended to be self-contained. There is a continuous narrative line that extends through Wittgenstein back to Kant and through Nietzsche back to Aristotle. Not only do the modern thinkers deepen our understanding of, and our interest in, the older ones. But reading Kant and Aristotle can actually develop and extend ideas later clarified by Wittgenstein and Nietzsche. As Nietzsche explains, "I live as if the centuries were nothing."[9] All six thinkers are engaged in a continuous dialogue with one another on issues that touch our lives directly and profoundly. I have arranged them in an order that I believe unveils an ever deepening understanding of the shape of the intellectual, spiritual, and moral space in which our lives unfold.[10]

I will not apologize for tackling questions that have occupied the greatest minds through the centuries, nor for purporting as an amateur to provide an exposition of thoughts studied with the greatest care and over many years by experts. As Leo Strauss noted, "We cannot define our tasks by our powers, for our powers become known to us through performing our tasks; it is better to fail nobly than to succeed basely."[11] I know that my book, measured against its aspirations, is a failure; I only hope that it is a noble one. Socrates would ask no more.

ACKNOWLEDGMENTS

With few exceptions, I have not attempted to document in the notes my many debts to the extensive secondary literature on each author. Instead, in a separate section on "Suggestions for Further Reading," I list the books and articles that I have found most helpful, as well as the most important of each author's works. I also list there the books or materials from which I have derived the biographical details in text.

My friend and colleague, Mark Evans, and my brother, Peter Kellogg, read through the entire manuscript in its early stages. Their many insightful comments and suggestions made this a much better book. Peter Pesic of St. John's College, Sante Fe, was also a perceptive reader and tireless correspondent as the chapters evolved.

The following people read portions of the manuscript and I benefited greatly from their comments: James Edwards, Harry Kellogg, Brian Leiter, Alexander Nehamas, and Julius Moravcsik. The late Professor Moravcsik and my Oxford advisors—P. M. S. Hacker and the late P. F. Strawson—instilled in me a lifelong love and appreciation of Plato, Wittgenstein, and Kant, respectively.

I would also like to thank my law partners and in particular, Mark Hansen, who gracefully accepted the fact that I was missing in action during much of the period when this book was written.

Bernadette Murphy, Darrin Leverette, and my longtime, indispensable assistant, Marilyn Williams, put the book in its final form.

Finally, my greatest thanks to my wife, Lucy, and to my three children—Baird, Cole, and Camille—who may not have quite understood my continued fascination with six dead philosophers but who gave me their unequivocal and good-humored encouragement and support. Their value is beyond words.

PART ONE
WHAT CAN I KNOW?

P hilosophy, as Wittgenstein notes, constantly calls itself into question. Philosophers ask about the nature of truth, the existence of God, and the meaning of life. Yet no two philosophers would agree on the answers, or even on how to get the answers, to such questions. The history of philosophy is in many ways a history of changing self-conceptions of philosophy's pretensions to knowledge. Philosophy is a subject that repeatedly devours and then reinvents itself.

Philosophy originated in speculation about nature and our place within it. The great pre-Socratic philosophers—Thales (624–546 BCE), Pythagoras (582–496 BCE), Heraclitus (535–475 BCE), Parmenides (510–440 BCE), Democritus (460–370 BCE)—were protoscientists and mathematicians. The science and math provided grounding and context for otherwise wild speculations. Yet, as the mathematical and empirical sciences advanced, they spun off into their own disciplines with their own criteria for knowledge. So, too, did the social sciences, such as psychology, sociology, and economics. Philosophy—called the Queen of the Sciences because of its supposed ability to knit them all together into a unified vision—was left without any clear criteria of its own for what constitutes knowledge on the overarching issues about which it is concerned.

To what sort of knowledge does philosophy aspire? Put another way, what, if any, knowledge does philosophy have to offer that either transcends or provides a foundation for the knowledge available in individual disciplines such as physics or economics or history?

The history of philosophy divides roughly into three approaches to this question: the metaphysical, the epistemological, and the linguistic. The metaphysical approach seeks to go "beyond physics"— beyond what we can learn through everyday experience and scientific experiments—to knowledge of reality acquired through reason and thought alone. Metaphysicians believe that, just as we can puzzle out the theorems of geometry with paper and pencil, so too we can puzzle out the mysteries of the universe simply by thinking them through with the utmost care. The greatest of the metaphysicians is Plato, whose theory of forms we will study in the next chapter.

The epistemological approach, begun by the French philosopher and mathematician René Descartes (1596–1650), focuses on the inquiring subject, the "I" that seeks knowledge. Epistemologists think it is premature to lay claims to knowledge in any discipline until we first meditate on how it is that man learns and can know anything. The greatest of the epistemologists is Kant, whose critique of pure reason seeks to place the natural sciences on a firm foundation and banish metaphysical speculation. We will study Kant in the third chapter, in the context of his view that we must recognize the limits of knowledge in order to make room for faith.

Finally, the linguistic or analytic philosophers believe that the only secure method of philosophy is to analyze the concepts used in other disciplines in order to clarify and sharpen their meaning. Philosophy has no independent subject matter; it is merely a handmaiden of subjects in which real knowledge is sought. The greatest of the linguistic philosophers is Wittgenstein, whom we will study in the second chapter. Yet Wittgenstein, although he says that all philosophical problems dissolve when the language used to state them is clarified, dismisses linguistic analysis of the sort practiced today as a waste of time and a disguised reversion to Platonic metaphysics.

Neither Plato nor Wittgenstein is easy to understand. Plato's prose is beautiful, his intellect is unrivaled, and his vision is compelling. But his constant resort to metaphors and myths at critical points makes his thought difficult to pin down. Wittgenstein's austere style has a beauty of its own, and his thought burns with an almost demonic intensity. But his constant focus on concrete examples and the elusiveness of his broader points render his writings as cryptic as Plato's.

Yet no one can understand modern thought without grappling with the juxtaposition of these two thinkers. Plato establishes our aspirations and expectations from philosophy. He promises a comprehensive understanding in which every piece of the puzzle falls into place. Wittgenstein, by contrast, deliberately seeks fragmentation and dismisses the false comfort of theories that oversimplify and distort our everyday practices, robbing them of their richness and resonance. Whether we have read them or not, we live in a post-Wittgenstein age with Platonic longings.

CHAPTER ONE
PLATO AND THE
TASK OF PHILOSOPHY

The European philosophical tradition . . . consists of a series of footnotes to Plato.[1]

Plato was born in Athens in 427 BCE, the scion of an aristocratic, wealthy, and influential family. In his youth he was an accomplished wrestler and aspired to be a poet. By all accounts, his early poems showed great promise.

But, like many of the wellborn youths of Athens in this era, Plato fell under the spell of Socrates. He was completely captivated by the Socratic insistence that a man must be able to give a reasoned account of his beliefs and his actions, and that he must place virtue and wisdom before all other pursuits. He began to haunt the agora (marketplace) and lyceum (gymnasium) where Socrates engaged in his withering cross-examinations of those who claimed to understand and practice virtue. Poetry was cast aside as at best a distraction from the serious business of philosophy and at worst a dangerous and corrupting illusion.

Plato was twenty-three when the Peloponnesian War (431–404 BCE) ended in a disastrous defeat for Athens, and he was twenty-eight when his fellow Athenians—pushed beyond limit by the war and the tyranny that followed—condemned Socrates to death. Plato's reaction was not surprising: disgust with the city and its politics. He established a school in the sacred grove of Academus, outside Athens, and taught and wrote there for much of the rest of his life, dying in 347 BCE at the age of eighty-one and leaving behind a body of work that has inspired readers and bedeviled professional philosophers ever since.

All of Plato's surviving writings (aside from a handful of letters, most of dubious authenticity) take the form of dialogues. They begin (insofar as one can group them chronologically based on internal evidence) with idealized, exquisitely crafted encounters between the quasi-historical Socrates and various Athenian citizens with pretensions to wisdom. In the course of the dialogues, those pretensions are punctured, but no competing claims to wisdom are put in their place. The early dialogues end in confusion and doubt, a state of mind superior only to thinking one knows what one does not know.

But Plato transcends his teacher. In a series of transitional dialogues, still using Socrates as his interlocutor, he begins to put in place the positive doctrines and theories that reach full flower in *The Republic*. To resolve the core Socratic question of how one can know virtue and lead a good life, Plato develops a full-scale metaphysics (theory of being), he places the good life for man in the context of the good society and fashions an educational system, including a restrictive theory of the arts, designed to mould ideal citizens. In the process, Plato sets the agenda for future philosophers. Metaphysics, ethics, aesthetics, and political theory are all established as parts of a single, interconnected enterprise.

To say that Plato is the greatest of all philosophers does little justice to his work. He is the greatest thinker in the Western tradition, as well as a writer of uncommon subtlety and power. His dialogues belong on the same narrow shelf as Homer's and Dante's epics, Shakespeare's plays, and Montaigne's essays. I had a teacher in college who liked to say: No man can consider himself educated who has not read *The Republic* with understanding. Complete understanding may be too high a benchmark. But repeated readings are definitely a requisite.

THE EARLY DIALOGUES

Euthyphro is not the earliest of Plato's dialogues, but it is generally presented first in editions of his work, and for good reason. It forms a natural unit with the *Apology* and two related dialogues (*Crito* and *Phaedo*) dealing with the trial and death of Socrates. It is also a perfect introduction to the sort of philosophy practiced by Socrates and the challenge that he posed to Plato.

In *Euthyphro*, Socrates is on his way to face the charges of impiety and corrupting the young that will eventually lead to his conviction and death. He meets Euthyphro, who expresses surprise at seeing Socrates in the vicinity of the courts. Socrates explains his mission. Euthyphro in turn says that he is there to pursue murder charges against his own father. One of his father's household servants killed another servant when drunk. The father had the offending servant bound hand and foot and thrown into a ditch, while he sent to the priest for instructions on what to do with him. Meanwhile, the servant died of hunger and cold.

It is important to recognize that Euthyphro's actions in prosecuting his own father are startling and would seem impious to Socrates' contemporaries. Euthyphro himself recognizes this and is proud of his singular stand: "They say it is impious for a son to prosecute his father for murder. But their ideas of the divine attitude to piety and impiety are wrong, Socrates."[2] Socrates himself presses this point: "'Certainly, Euthyphro, most men would not know how they could do this and be right. It is not the part of anyone to do this, but of one who is far advanced in wisdom.' 'Yes, by Zeus, Socrates, that is so.'"[3] Euthyphro adds, speaking of himself in the third person, "Euthyphro would not be superior to the majority of men, if I did not have accurate knowledge of all such things."[4]

Euthyphro is so pompous and sure of himself that he does not even recognize Socrates' irony, which is laid on very thick in this dialogue. Indeed, Socrates openly mocks Euthyphro, but Euthyphro never notices, and the mockery might make the reader uncomfortable were Euthyphro not insufferable.

Since Euthyphro is so confident of his own wisdom and his knowledge of piety, Socrates proposes to become his pupil and to learn the true nature of piety so that he can respond properly to the charges brought against him. Euthyphro readily agrees. But when Euthyphro tries to explain "what is the pious, and what is the impious," all he does is cite his own example. "The pious is to do what I am doing now, to prosecute the wrongdoer, be it about murder or temple robbery or anything else, whether the wrongdoer is your father or your mother or anyone else; not to prosecute is impious."[5]

Socrates is hardly satisfied with this response, and he makes a critical move characteristic of all the early dialogues: he refuses to accept mere examples as an explanation of the virtue in question. "Bear in mind then that I did not bid you tell me one or two of the many pious actions but that form itself that makes all pious actions pious.... Tell me then what this form itself is, so that I may look upon it, and using it as a model, say that any action of yours or another's that is of that kind is pious, and if it is not that it is not."[6] In other words, Socrates asks Euthyphro for an account of piety ("this form itself") that will enable him to distinguish truly pious actions from actions that are not pious, an account that will withstand challenge and questioning.

Euthyphro fails miserably at this task. He begins by appealing to authority: "the pious is what all the gods love, and the opposite, what all the gods hate, is the impious."[7] Through his questioning Socrates forces Euthyphro to admit that the gods only love piety because it is pious; it is not pious because the gods love it. Describing an affect or quality of piety (that it is loved by the gods) does nothing to advance our understanding of what piety actually is.

Euthyphro's alternative definitions fare no better. He argues that piety is the care and service of the gods. Socrates presses him on this definition to determine just what sort of "care" he has in mind. Through examples of horse breeders, hunters, and cattle herders, he establishes that care in each of those cases aims at the good and benefit of the object cared for. Horses, hunting dogs, and cattle are all benefited and become better through expert care. But Euthyphro is forced to admit that the gods are not made better by our piety. So he tries a different tack, noting that the sort of "care" he has in mind is the care of servants for their masters, so that piety is a sort of service to the gods. Socrates then gets Euthyphro to admit that service is directed at a goal: doctors promote health, shipbuilders build ships, farmers aim at producing food from the earth. What excellent aim, Socrates asks, do the gods achieve using us as their servants? Euthyphro insists that the service to the gods is merely pleasing to them, rather than aimed at some separate end, and to the extent it is pleasing to them, the gods benefit us, we do not benefit the gods. The argument has, accordingly, come full circle. Piety is "what is pleasing to the gods," yet they had both already concluded that piety could not be defined that way. "Either we were wrong when we agreed before," Socrates says, "or, if we were right then, we are wrong now."[8]

Euthyphro expresses his frustration with this mode of proceeding: "Socrates, I have no way of telling you what I have in mind, for whatever proposition we put forward goes around and refuses to stay put where we establish it."[9] Socrates says, by contrast, that it is Euthyphro's propositions that move around in a circle, like the famous statues of Daedalus (reputed to be so lifelike that they would step down from their pedestals and run off). Socrates insists that he would "rather have your statements to me remain unmoved [that is, stand up to analysis] than possess the wealth of Tantalus as well as the cleverness of Daedalus."[10]

Socrates accordingly proposes that they start again from the beginning. But Euthyphro dismisses him: "Some other time, Socrates, for I am in a hurry now, and it is time for me to go."[11] At this point, Socrates' irony reaches its height: "What a thing to do, my friend! By going you have cast me down from a great hope I had, that I would learn from you the nature of the pious and the impious and so escape Meletus' indictment by showing him that I had acquired wisdom in divine matters from Euthyphro, and my ignorance would no longer cause me to be careless and inventive about such things, and that I would be better for the rest of my life."[12]

Socrates has revealed through his questioning that Euthyphro has no idea what piety is. He cannot define it. He has no model or form to guide his actions. He has no basis for distinguishing true piety from false. He cannot even defend a single proposition about piety without running head-on into some other proposition that he admits to be the case. But he presses ahead with his prosecution nonetheless, convinced that he is in the right. He will not even stop to consider further. Socrates, on trial for his life, will stop on his way to court to discuss the true nature of virtue and the good life for man. He does not claim to have any answers, and he would certainly never prosecute another based on an assumed knowledge that he does not possess. But he will ceaselessly inquire into the one truly important issue for man.

We as readers are appalled at Euthyphro's arrogant and unjustified assurance, and are wholly at one with Socrates' ironic response to it. Yet we as readers are the targets of Plato's deeper, and more bitter, irony.[13] We smugly sympathize with Socrates' disdain of Euthyphro without realizing that an equal disdain is directed at the reader who finishes the dialogue, as Euthyphro finishes the discussion, and goes on about his life, unchanged, still making judgments about matters as to which he has no knowledge and about which he has not even tried to consider critically and seriously. Plato's immediate readers, after all, include the very men who condemned Socrates to die for impiety without ever having a firm sense, or being able to give an account, of what piety is. We are all complicit in that crime insofar as we live and act without knowledge of virtue.

Euthyphro provides the model for all the early dialogues. Socrates challenges someone (often a prominent Athenian, such as a general or politician) to give an account of a particular virtue or excellence, such as justice (*Crito*), temperance (*Charmides*), courage (*Laches*), friendship (*Lysis*), or beauty (*Greater Hippias*). The prominent citizen is often only too happy to oblige. Socrates then proceeds, through a series of questions and homely examples, to dismantle that account, a process known as *elenchus* (or refutation).

But it is refutation of a peculiar sort. Socrates does not match proposition for proposition. He does not defeat one position by arguing more persuasively for a different position. Since Socrates denies possessing any knowledge he declines to rely on any beliefs of his own. That is not to say that Socrates does not have beliefs; as we shall see, he has some very important ones. But he does not *know* whether those beliefs are true and hence is unwilling to rely upon them. His only method of proceeding therefore is to extract admissions from his subjects that can serve as premises from which to prove that the subject's thesis is incorrect.

Accordingly, Socrates elicits a general statement concerning the nature of, say, courage. He then explores the implications of that statement through a process of questioning. The implications invariably turn out to be inconsistent with each other or with something else the speaker believes. That is to say, one of the logical consequences of the general statement turns out to be unacceptable. A contradiction is established, but whether the original statement or the contradicting statement or both need to be abandoned is generally left unresolved at the end of the dialogue.

In this way, Socrates is able to reject or refute pretensions to knowledge without claiming to have knowledge of his own. But that is not to say that Socrates does not consider some beliefs to be true and others not. Socrates rather draws a sharp distinction between knowledge and mere opinion. It is a premise of Socrates' mode of proceeding that if you possess a virtue (such as temperance) you must have some sense of its nature, and, "since you know how to speak Greek,"[14] you should be able to articulate that nature or at least to express opinions and impressions about it. Socrates assumes that each person he questions holds some true beliefs about the virtue at issue, and these are the admissions that Socrates seeks to extract with his questions and then use to show that the general statement put forward at the outset cannot be correct.

So the interlocutors may well possess true beliefs about virtue. What they do not possess is knowledge. Without knowledge, beliefs (even true beliefs) are not firmly rooted. Without knowledge, our beliefs are like the Daedalus statues. They will not stand still and cannot provide a certain guide for our behavior. We have no criteria for distinguishing between true and false beliefs, and true and false beliefs will accordingly collide with one another and create contradictions. Only knowledge provides a solid, immovable foundation and a crystalline consistency that will withstand even Socrates' questioning.

Thus, a courageous man confronted with a dangerous situation may well choose the courageous course of conduct. He will have an intuition of what courage requires. But if he is unable to give a general account of what courage consists—an account that will cover not just this or that case, but provide a clear line of demarcation between courageous conduct, on the one hand, and cowardly conduct, on the other—then he will not know that his action is correct. In such a state, he cannot be certain that he has not been swayed by pleasure or self-interest into a false belief and hence a wrong course of conduct.

An inability to give an account of virtue is not only an intellectual failing, but a moral one as well. Ethical judgments must have an objective, articulable basis; otherwise they are arbitrary and unmoored. That is why Socrates repeatedly refuses to accept specific examples as satisfying his request for a definition of the virtue under discussion. "I wanted to include not only those who are courageous in warfare but also those who are brave in dangers at sea, and the ones who show courage in illness and poverty and affairs of state; and then again I wanted to include not only those who are brave in the face of pain and fear but also those who are clever at fighting desire and pleasure, whether by standing their ground or running away." What, Socrates asks, "is the courage that is the same in all these cases"?[15]

Socrates is not interested in individual intuitions of piety or courage or justice except insofar as those are useful in testing a more general account. He wants to know what it is that makes each example share in the essence of piety or courage or justice. He wants a clear, unambiguous, self-sufficient standard for judging whether individual actions or persons are pious, courageous, or just. Socrates takes it as an article of faith that "a man who has knowledge would be able to give an account of what he knows."[16]

Yet the Socrates of the early dialogues has no idea how to come by such an account. A later dialogue (written to show the limitations of the Socratic approach and pave the way for the Platonic solution) illustrates this point. The question in *Theaetetus* is the nature of knowledge. Theaetetus answers that knowledge is geometry and astronomy and music and arithmetic and "the crafts such as cobbling, whether you take them together or separately." "That is certainly a frank and indeed a generous answer," Socrates responds. "I asked you for one thing and you have given me many; I wanted something simple, and I have got a variety.... You were not asked to say what one may have knowledge of, or how many branches of knowledge there are. It was not with any idea of counting these up that the question was asked; we wanted to know what knowledge itself is."[17] But *Theaetetus*, like the aporetic dialogues, reaches a dead end. Socrates not only has no knowledge; he does not even know in what knowledge itself consists.

So what is it that Socrates is seeking to accomplish in these early dialogues? Why does he consider refutation ending in doubt a worth-while endeavor?

I think there are three reasons. First, Socrates repeatedly cites his "fear of unconsciously thinking I know something when I do not."[18] The refutation of false beliefs has an independent, if largely negative, value. "I count being refuted a greater good, insofar as it is a greater good for oneself to be delivered from the worst thing there is than to deliver someone else from it. I don't suppose there's anything quite so bad for a person as having false belief about the things we're discussing right now."[19] Doubt fosters humility, and humility is precisely what Euthyphro and those who condemned Socrates lack.

Second, the process of inquiry is itself a moral act. In the *Apology*, Socrates asserts that "the unexamined life is not worth living."[20] The best way to examine one's life, in Socrates' view, is to examine one's beliefs about virtue and the good life. Anyone who "knows Greek" (that is, anyone who shares human language) can talk about such issues and test his own and others' opinions. He thereby engages not in an abstract discussion but in a test of his way of life and the choices he has made. To conduct such an investigation sincerely will require great courage as well as mental acumen and careful reasoning.

Finally, the Socratic inquiry is aspirational. By eliciting contradictions and false premises, by constantly testing assertions and forcing interlocutors to choose among inconsistent beliefs, Socrates moves toward an ideal of a harmonious set of beliefs. This will never be a stable, fully realized ideal. Because belief rather than knowledge is in question, everything is up for grabs in further discussions and subject to further investigation. Consistency in one's beliefs is not knowledge; indeed, in theory at least one could hold consistent false beliefs. But the elimination of contradiction and inconsistency is a step in the right direction, particularly when grounded in the moral intuitions in which Socrates himself places such great stock.

On a less modest level, the aspiration is to transcend mere belief altogether. For mere belief will, under pressure, yield to pleasure and passion and false arguments. Only knowledge provides an unassailable mooring for virtue. Despite eschewing any personal pretensions to knowledge of virtue, Socrates nonetheless displays a perfect faith in the power of reason to achieve understanding and, through under-

standing, goodness and the proper life for man. Socrates does not
know how to do so. He does not believe anyone in his experience has
in fact done so. Yet he retains as an article of faith that such understanding is possible. All his inquiries are conducted against the background of this faith.

Indeed, the reason we know that a particular early dialogue has
failed, that it has fallen short of the ideal, is that Socrates has an
implicit standard for what would constitute success. He wants an
account of the form or essence of the virtue in question. He does not
want to know whether this or that person or object is beautiful. He
wants to know what beauty is by virtue of which individual objects are
beautiful. He wants to know what justice is by virtue of which persons
and societies are just. He wants to know what courage is by virtue of
which individual actions are courageous. Socrates believes that there is
an essence or "form" of each virtue and individual examples are
instances of that virtue insofar as they partake of the form. Once we
understand and can give an account of these forms, Socrates believes,
we will be impervious to pleasure and passion as well as to the
sophistry of false argument. We will know the good and do the good.

Socrates was, by Plato's account, "of all the men of his time, the
best, the wisest, and the most just."[21] But he never did claim to know
the good; at least, not in his own right. That was left for his most
famous student in a series of dialogues in which, although Socrates is
still the nominal protagonist, the doctrines are decidedly Plato's.

THE TRANSITIONAL DIALOGUES

There are several dialogues in which Socrates begins a transition from
gadfly (worrying the citizens of Athens because they do not sufficiently care for virtue) to midwife (bringing forth affirmative statements about the nature of virtue and the good life for man). Of these
"transitional" dialogues, *Meno* is the most significant because it high-
lights so clearly the way in which the Socratic paradoxes will lead,
ultimately, to a Platonic solution.

Meno begins by following the pattern of the early dialogues discussed above. Meno, a young man from an aristocratic family, asks

Socrates whether virtue can be taught. Socrates, naturally, professes not to know even what virtue is, much less whether it can be taught. "If I do not know what something is, how could I know what qualities it possesses?"[22]

Socrates accordingly turns the tables on Meno and presses him to give an account of virtue. Meno first offers a litany of examples, describing the virtues of men, women, children, slaves, and the elderly. Socrates, right on cue, chides Meno for giving him many virtues when he is looking for one. Even if virtue manifests itself in different ways among different groups so that it appears there are "many and various" virtues, he explains, "all of them have one and the same form which makes them virtues, and it is right to look to this when one is asked to make clear what virtue is."[23] Meno then lists various different virtues from the standard Greek list, which includes moderation, justice, courage, and wisdom. But Socrates again insists upon "one description to fit them all," the form of virtue "in which they are all the same and do not differ from one another."[24]

Meno makes a couple attempts at such a description and is easily refuted by Socrates. Meno then expresses his frustration at the manner in which Socrates is "bewitching and beguiling" him: "I have made many speeches about virtue before large audiences on a thousand occasions, very good speeches as I thought, but now I cannot even say what it is."[25] Socrates, of course, professes to be "more perplexed than anyone"[26] and proposes that they start again.

This is where the dialogue changes dramatically from the early pattern. Meno does not decline and walk off. Nor does he offer yet another definition for refutation. Instead, he questions the entire enterprise by means of a paradox. How can we even look for virtue, he asks, when we don't know at all what it is? And if we do meet it, how will we know that we have found it? In other words, even if Meno is able to offer a proposition about virtue that happens to be true, how will either of them know the difference between truth and falsity?

These are exactly the questions we asked about the early dialogues. But now Plato's Socrates has a somewhat different answer from the one we reconstructed for the historical Socrates. Socrates cites an account of "divine matters" about which he has heard wise men and women speak. According to this account, which he considers "both true and beautiful,"[27] the soul of man is immortal but undergoes many births. There is nothing the soul has not seen and does not know, and thus the soul contains within itself the imprint of all knowledge, including knowledge about virtue. The process of learning then is in fact a process of recollecting what is already in the soul, and nothing prevents a man from discovering everything for himself "if he is brave and does not tire of the search." "We must, therefore, not believe [Meno's] argument," Socrates says, "for it would make us idle, and fainthearted men like to hear it, whereas my argument makes them energetic and keen on the search."[28]

Taken in a purely metaphorical sense, this argument is akin to the less modest "aspirational" point discussed above. We continue to inquire because we believe as an article of faith that there are answers and a possibility of knowledge, even if we do not know how to attain them. But Meno rightly challenges Socrates to explain how learning can be recollection and how we can know this to be the case. A mere appeal to authority (what "wise men and women" say) will obviously not suffice.

There follows one of the most extraordinary and important passages in all of Western philosophy, a quite magical moment in which Socrates, through a series of simple questions (designed to guide but not teach), shows that a slave boy, with no education in geometry, somehow knows within himself a basic proof of geometry (which is that you can double the area of a square by forming a new square using, as one of the sides, the diagonal of the original square).

Socrates allows Meno to choose at random one of his many attendants, the only requirement being that he "speak Greek." Socrates asks the boy if he knows what a square is and establishes that it is a figure with four equal sides and that the lines joining the middles of these sides are also equal. Socrates then elicits from the boy that if each side is two feet long, there are four square feet in the square (one square foot in each of the four smaller squares created by the lines joining the middles of the sides).

Socrates then asks the boy how long the sides would need to be if the square encompassed eight square feet rather than four square feet. The boy, not surprisingly, answers four. But through a series of questions Socrates gets the boy to recognize that if the sides are each four feet long, then the square will contain sixteen square feet, not eight.

There is an important point to illustrate here applicable to the standard Socratic inquiry. The boy thinks he knows the length of the required line, but he does not know. Through a series of questions Socrates makes the boy realize he does not know; he makes him realize that four is not the correct answer. But the boy still does not know how to reach the correct answer. "Even now he does not yet know," Socrates stresses, "but then he thought he knew, and answered confidently as if he did know, and he did not think himself at a loss, but now he does think himself at a loss, and as he does not know, neither does he think he knows."[29]

So the boy is in the same position as Meno with respect to the question of virtue. He has been cured (perhaps more than Meno) of thinking he knows something that he does not know. Not only has that not done him any harm, Socrates notes, but "we have probably achieved something relevant to finding out how matters stand, for now, as he does not know, he would be glad to find out, whereas before he thought he could easily make many fine speeches to large audiences about the square of double size and said that it must have a base twice as long."[30] The Socrates of the transitional dialogues has not lost his mocking irony, and Meno takes it in good sport.

But Socrates goes on now to elicit the correct answer from the slave boy. Through a series of questions he helps the boy figure out for himself how to double the original square (from four square feet to eight square feet). He does so by using the four-foot-sided square the boy originally thought was the correct answer, dividing it into four smaller squares through lines (A to C, and B to D in the figure below) joining the middle of the sides, and then drawing diagonals that cut in half each of the smaller (four-foot-square) squares. The diagonals join A to B, B to C, C to D, and D to A. These diagonals in turn form a square of their own, a square that combines half of each of the four square-foot squares. It follows, as the slave boy recognizes, that the internal square is twice as big (eight square feet) as the square with which they started.

Meno acknowledges that the slave boy has not expressed any opinion that was not his own and hence that these opinions were somehow "in him" all along. "So the man who does not know," Socrates explains, "has within himself true opinions about the things

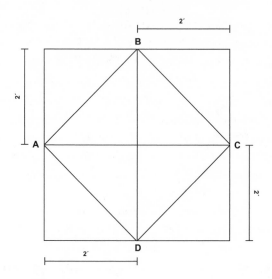

that he does not know. ... These opinions have now just been stirred up like a dream, but if he were repeatedly asked these same questions in various ways, you know that in the end his knowledge about these things would be as accurate as anyone's. ... And he will know it without having been taught but only questioned, and find the knowledge within himself."[31]

Socrates accordingly draws the conclusion that "the truth about reality is always in our soul"[32] or at least that we must believe that to be the case, so that we will search ceaselessly for it. Just as Euclid (circa 325–270 BCE) would later systematize and expand our knowledge of geometry, Socrates believes that philosophy can chart the geometry of the soul and with it the true nature of reality and the good life for man.

Meno, however, rightly pulls Socrates back to the question at hand. Can virtue be taught or is it a natural gift? Socrates proceeds to argue that all knowledge can be taught and that virtue is a form of knowledge. He points out that the various qualities of the soul are good if guided by wisdom and understanding, but bad if not. Courage can become recklessness if not guided by understanding. The same is true for moderation, justice, intelligence, generosity, and the like. These qualities are neither harmful nor beneficial in themselves. All require wisdom for their proper application. Socrates concludes that virtue is accordingly "as a whole or in part" wisdom and thus that the "good are not good by nature" but rather due to knowledge.[33] It follows, he says, that virtue can be taught.

It is important to recognize that the argument here is quite dubious. It may well be true that qualities of the soul are rendered good or bad by wisdom: courage can easily become recklessness; caution can become cowardice; generosity can become ostentation; thrift can become avarice; even a longing for justice can be cold and tyrannical if not tempered with understanding. Wisdom may well be required to strike the appropriate balance. But wisdom in this sense does not necessarily equate to knowledge. Indeed, wisdom has often been considered quite distinct from knowledge, as an indefinable product of experience and judgment that can perhaps be imparted through parables or by examples, but that bears no resemblance to the ideal of geometric knowledge presented in the dialogue. Thus, although it may well be true that the wisdom that brings virtue is not "by nature," it still does not follow that it can be taught—certainly not in the way that geometric propositions can be taught.

Socrates himself seems to recognize the weakness of his argument, because he promptly undercuts it by asking why, if virtue can be taught, there are no recognized teachers. If someone wants to become a physician, we send him to learn from good physicians. Good shoemakers can also teach their craft, as can musicians. We know where to send the students of these crafts, and the results of the teaching are both recognizable and verifiable. Those with knowledge can impart their knowledge to others. Yet Socrates notes his own unsuccessful efforts to find proper teachers of virtue. "I have often tried to find out whether there were any teachers of it, but in spite of all my efforts I cannot find any."[34] The Sophists in particular, who were itinerant teachers for a fee, are singled out for special scorn (and linguistic history, at least, bears out this verdict, since the term sophist has come to mean, in essence, one who uses specious reasoning).

But even past men of virtue, recognized masters of that particular "craft," have proved unable to pass on to their children the virtue they themselves possessed. Socrates gives repeated examples of good and worthy men who had wicked and corrupt sons. The fathers taught these sons, or paid to have them taught, many useful skills, sparing no expense on their educations. Yet the one thing that mattered most they could not impart. "It is surely clear," Socrates says of one such example, "that if virtue could be taught he would have found the man who could make his sons good men, be it a citizen or a stranger, if he himself did not have the time because of his public concerns."[35]

Thus, we are left with another paradox. If virtue is knowledge and knowledge can be taught, how can it be that virtuous men are unable to teach virtue to their children? How can it be that there are no recognized and acknowledged teachers of virtue?

Socrates resolves this paradox by reference to the distinction between knowledge and true belief discussed above. He concludes that those conspicuous for virtue do not have knowledge, but rather right opinion that leads them to follow the right course. They are akin to soothsayers and prophets who may also say many true things when inspired but have no knowledge of what they are saying. "That is the reason why they cannot make others be like themselves, because it is not knowledge which makes them what they are."[36]

Virtuous men may be divine and inspired, but they have no solid foundation in knowledge. Virtue "comes to those who possess it as a gift from the gods which is not accompanied by understanding,"[37] and hence cannot be taught. Even true beliefs are unstable and easily upset and always open to challenge. But when tied down with a true account, through the process of recollection, true opinions become knowledge and remain in place. Such knowledge is unassailable, and men who possessed it would be like living beings among the flitting shadows of the underworld.

The key point, Socrates thus concludes, is to attain knowledge of "what virtue in itself is."[38] Only then can we determine how virtue is acquired and can best be taught. In a sense, then, at the end of *Meno* we are in the same position we were in at the end of one of the early dialogues: without any clear sense of the object of our inquiry or how to uncover it. We do at least have an ideal of what knowledge would look like and how, through the process of dialectic (questioning and refining), it might be obtained. We have a model of geometric knowledge and inquiry, but no sense of how to apply that model to the question of virtue and the good life for man.

Thus, *Meno* like the early dialogues is aporetic; it ends in doubt and uncertainty. But there is a surprising twist. After posing the question that they must continue to investigate, it is Socrates, not Meno, who ends the dialogue. We must "try to find out what virtue in itself is," he explains. "But now the time has come for me to go."[39] This is shocking. Socrates has always been prepared to inquire further until he exhausts the patience of his interlocutor. But Socrates must go because his method of elenchus cannot determine what virtue in itself is. Socrates must give way before a new form of inquiry. It is a sad moment to have him ushered off the stage, particularly with the same words he uses at the end of the *Apology* when he goes to his death. Socrates has posed the questions that must be answered. He has set the standards that any acceptable answer must meet. But, like Moses, he is dismissed short of the promised land.

THE REPUBLIC

Although he bears a definite resemblance to the Socrates of the early dialogues, the Socrates of *The Republic* is a very different character. His agenda is the same: "to determine which whole way of life would make living most worthwhile for each of us."[40] His irony is intact. He even makes a few perfunctory disclaimers as to knowledge. And he proceeds in dialogue form, questioning his interlocutors. But in fact his questions are now pregnant with theories and hypotheses for which he seeks assent. Socrates is no longer testing the views of his interlocutors. He is testing his own positive doctrines. And, rather than dealing with a single moral issue, such as the nature of virtue or courage, Socrates tackles a series of interrelated issues that extend far beyond the scope and concerns of the early dialogues.

There is nothing dogmatic in Socrates' approach. He stresses the tentative nature of his views and the need for a fuller account of them. Indeed, he often relies on metaphors, rather than logical proofs, on critical points. But at the end of this dialogue, we have been presented with an integrated vision of man's place in a just society, the path to true knowledge, and the ultimate nature of reality. Most important, we have been presented with a description of the best life for man, which (unsurprisingly or perhaps the ultimate in Socratic irony) turns out to be a job description for future philosophers, whose quest is to know the truth and to bring their lives and their souls in harmony with it.

The Republic begins as a traditional dialogue, in which Socrates probes standard and not-so-standard views on the nature of justice. In the standard Greek view, to do justice is to benefit one's friends and harm one's enemies or, more simply put, to give to each what is owed to him (good to those who are good and bad to those who are bad). Socrates rather quickly disposes of that view, arguing that it is never just to harm anyone. Then he confronts the more radical proposal put forward by Thrasymachus that "justice is nothing other than the advantage of the stronger."[41] By this statement, Thrasymachus appears to mean that justice is a purely conventional label applied by those in power to serve their own interests at the expense of others. The ruling faction will always make laws that favor its own advantage, and anyone who violates those laws will be punished as lawless and unjust.

Through his standard questioning, focusing on the nature of medicine and horse-breeding (each of which seeks the advantage of its subjects), Socrates forces Thrasymachus to admit that the just ruler seeks not what is advantageous to himself but what is advantageous to his subjects. But Thrasymachus doesn't really care about the labels "justice" and "injustice." He cares about the reality of power. He believes that justice, in the ordinary sense of that term used by Socrates in his questioning, is in fact a hindrance to obtaining and maintaining power. "A just man," he says, "always gets less than an unjust one."[42] He considers true justice to be a "very high-minded simplicity,"[43] whereas injustice on a grand scale (sufficient to impose one's will on others) makes one happy and blessed. "Injustice," he concludes, "if it is on a large enough scale, is stronger, freer, and more masterly than justice."[44]

Socrates states his firm belief that injustice is not more profitable than justice, "not even if you give it full scope and put no obstacles in its way."[45] Socrates manages to refute Thrasymachus fairly easily, by getting him to admit that each thing has a virtue or excellence by which it is made better and a corresponding vice by which it is made worse. He again uses homely examples: horses, pruning shears, eyes, ears. In each case the particular virtue of the thing in question is what makes it function best and provides its highest use. He then argues that justice is the particular virtue of the soul and hence that only the just man will live well and be happy.

But the reader is hardly convinced by this exchange. Nor is the reader meant to be convinced. Indeed, the flimsy nature of the argument is intended to underscore the limits of Socratic inquiry and the need for a deeper analysis of the questions posed in the dialogue. Other participants in the discussion chide Socrates for appearing to persuade rather than truly convincing them that it is better to be just rather than unjust. They note that justice is at best an "onerous" virtue that must perhaps be practiced in order to maintain a proper reputation for justice, but that in reality injustice is more to the advantage of each individual. In a comment that resonates for contemporary, as well as ancient, politics, they argue that as long as one creates a "facade of illusory virtue," while in fact ruthlessly seeking one's own advantage at every turn, one can live "the life of a god."[46] Anticipating Nietzsche, they argue that only the weak praise justice because they fear injustice and hope to persuade the strong to spare them. In practical affairs, injustice often triumphs over justice. Accordingly, if Socrates believes that injustice in fact has a bad effect on a person and justice a good effect, regardless of practical consequences, he must show that to be the case rather than offer "only a theoretical argument that justice is stronger than injustice."[47]

He does so by changing the subject, or at least by changing the object of the inquiry. They had been discussing justice in the individual. But Socrates (now more properly understood, though not without qualifications, to represent Plato himself) suggests that they first inquire into justice in a city (the *polis*, or city-state, which was the standard unit of governance in Greece at the time). Socrates notes that just as larger letters will be easier to read from a distance than smaller letters, so too it may be easier to discern the true nature of justice in a city than in an individual. The transposition makes perfect sense given the Platonic assumption that justice is a single thing and thus will be the same in a city as in an individual. That is, both a city and an individual will be just insofar as they partake in the same form of justice.

We will not enter here into a full account of Plato's controversial vision of the just society. Its basic outlines are well known. He argues for a very modern division of labor, which is at the same time a very ancient sort of caste system. Men differ from one another by nature, he believes, and society as a whole will be better off "if each person does one thing for which he is naturally suited."[48] The city will need craftsmen and farmers and retailers of various sorts, as well as hunters, artists, nannies, and cooks—an entire array of job descriptions filled by the persons most suited to, and best trained for, those jobs. But there is no flexibility, no ability to respond to market circumstances, no freedom even to choose. In Plato's ideal city-state, children follow the same path as their parents and (with extremely limited exceptions) are allowed neither to rise nor to fall in the world. Indeed, Plato proposes that the people be told a myth (a "noble lie") that the gods have predestined them for their place in society.

There will also be a race of warriors (bred particularly for this task) who will act as the guardians of the city. They will live in common, eschew all personal possessions, and be trained from childhood in the military arts. Men and women alike—Plato makes no distinction here—will live in barracks, train in the gymnasium and on the battlefield, and be carefully schooled in music and poetry to make them martial in spirit, disdainful of material possessions, and fiercely loyal to and protective of their city. Plato proposes to practice eugenics, in which the bravest and strongest men and women are coupled together most frequently, and their children will be raised in common, not knowing who their actual parents are, so that all guardians feel a sense of family loyalty and devotion and respect for one another. In exchange for their preservation and protection of the city, the guardians will escape the "obvious and ignoble" troubles that men endure in making money, dealing with debt, organizing their households, and raising their children. Plato praises this life as "blessedly happy."[49]

Plato spends considerable time on the proper education of the guardians. Because they will hold the power in the city, a power they could easily use to advance their own interests rather than those of the city as a whole, they must be molded from a very young age. They will be told only approved stories that will "shape their...souls"[50] and promote the required virtues, "leading them unwittingly, from childhood on, to resemblance, friendship, and harmony with the beauty of reason."[51] To this end, the city will lay down "the patterns on which poets must base their stories and from which they mustn't deviate."[52] Artists who depart from those patterns, even great artists such as Homer—who portray heroic figures acting in fearful or selfish ways, or unjust people as happy, or the gods as quarrelsome and false—will be expelled from the city. "It is in music and poetry," Plato says, "that our guardians must build their bulwark."[53] For "lawlessness easily creeps in there unnoticed" and "flows over little by little into characters and ways of life" and from there "makes its insolent way into the laws and government, until in the end it overthrows everything, public and private."[54]

Plato's vision of the just society will inevitably, and probably correctly, strike the modern reader as appalling.[55] He seems to combine a desire for rigid, military rule with a cranky insistence that cultural change will lead to social disintegration (think rock-and-roll or rap). Yet three things must be said in his defense. First, the open democratic society of Athens (the society that had condemned Socrates) has recently suffered a complete defeat at the hands of Sparta, resulting in a violent tyranny that served only the interests of the tyrants. Plato believes that democratic regimes are inherently unstable and, after lurching back and forth under the influence of this or that persuasive speaker, will inevitably collapse into tyranny. Plato accordingly looks to Sparta—a far more austere, military regime, in which individual interest is rigidly subordinated to the public good—as a model for his just society.

Second, it is a premise of modern, liberal, democratic capitalism that individuals should be free to shape their lives by making their own choices in accordance with their own desires and their own vision of the good life. (Two thousand years after Plato, Adam Smith demonstrated that the aggregate of such self-interested choices, when circumscribed by the rule of law, in fact results in the most efficient and productive economy.) Yet Plato is surely correct that human desires are not a fixed quantity.[56] Our desires and our vision of the good life are heavily influenced by our culture. Human nature is indeed malleable and, while it may go too far to say that, when young and tender, the soul "takes on *any* pattern one wishes to impress on it,"[57] it would be willful ignorance to suggest that movies, music, and the latest cultural icons do not have a tremendous influence in shaping the character and desires of the young. Thus, insofar as it is legitimate at all for society to debate the proper education of the young, it cannot simply ignore the effect of the arts. Perhaps it is alarmist to suggest that changes in the arts will "in the end...overthrow everything, public and private." But Plato is trying to construct what he envisions as the best society for man and hence wants to ensure a stability that changing cultural norms would surely undermine. (The Egyptians strictly forbade any innovations in their highly stylized art forms, and Egyptian society lasted largely unchanged for three thousand years.)

Finally, we must remember that our ultimate quarry in the dialogue is the just individual. We examine the just society in order to discover justice writ large so that we can transfer that account to the individual. But Plato's view of justice in the individual seems to dictate his version of the just society rather than vice versa. That is perhaps most apparent in his account of the virtues. As previously noted, the four standard Greek virtues were thought to be wisdom, courage, moderation, and justice. Plato locates wisdom in the ruling class. He locates courage in the warrior class. He identifies moderation mostly with the class of tradesmen, but also with the warriors, since both groups must allow themselves and their passions to be governed and guided by their betters. "Moderation is surely a kind of order, the mastery of certain kinds of pleasures and desires."[58] Finally, Plato locates justice in the harmony of the whole. It consists in each of the three groups contentedly doing its own particular work and not that of any other group. (The difference between moderation and justice is subtle, but it appears that moderation could exist even if the tradesmen and the warriors chafe under the yoke of the rulers, provided that they follow orders; justice is found only where there is true harmony—in Orwellian terms it would not occur until the tradesmen and warriors "learn to love Big Brother.")

This account of the virtues of the city seems contrived and artificial and, as my reference to Orwell would suggest, totalitarian. But when it is transferred to the individual it yields stunning insights. Plato develops a tripartite account of the soul, corresponding to the three parts of his city: the rational part, which learns and calculates; the irrational part, which "lusts, hungers, thirsts, and gets excited by other appetites"; and the spirited part, which "is wholly dedicated to the pursuit of control, victory, and high repute."[59] Wisdom is to be found in the rational part, which exercises foresight on behalf of the whole soul. Courage is to be found in the spirited part. Moderation is to be found in the control that reason exercises over the appetites and the spirit, to ensure that they are directed at proper objects. And justice is to be found in the harmony of the whole.

We are of course familiar with tripartite accounts of the soul—most notably, Freud's id, ego, and superego—but Plato's account achieves a comparable degree of psychological insight at least two centuries ahead of his time. It leads to a dramatic twist in his conception of justice, which is concerned less with a man's relation to others, with what he does externally, than "with what is inside him, with what is truly himself and his own."[60] In very modern-sounding terms, Plato explains that the just man "puts himself in order, is his own friend," and "from having been many things he becomes entirely one, moderate and harmonious."[61] Only then does he act, and when he does so he acts in a way that preserves and promotes this inner harmony.

According to Plato, then, injustice is a kind of civil war between the various parts of the soul, a rebellion in which parts intended to be ruled by reason instead seek to rule, and "the turmoil and straying of these parts are injustice, licentiousness, cowardice, ignorance, and, in a word, the whole of vice."[62] A disordered soul, a soul in turmoil, allows itself to be governed by its passions and appetites and acts accordingly. An ordered soul, by contrast, acts according to the dictates of wisdom, and with appetites and spirit governed thereby. Justice then is the health and well-being of the soul, whereas injustice is disease and weakness and a shameful condition.

This is a compelling account. And it provides at least the beginnings of an answer to the question of why justice is always better than injustice. But our ordinary conception of justice focuses on a man's public actions, on how he treats his fellow men and how he conducts himself in public affairs. It is not immediately clear how Plato expects to bridge the gap between internal harmony and these external actions. Plato notes that the actions of a just man will be governed by wisdom. But we do not yet have an account of how such wisdom is to be obtained or in what it consists.

A similar gap mars his account of the just society. In a just society the tradesman class and the warrior class are in harmony with the dictates of the ruling class. But how are we to guarantee that the ruling class will itself act justly and in the interests of the city as a whole? Plato's answer to this question is the most surprising of all: until philosophers rule as kings or those who are now called kings and other leading men genuinely and successfully philosophize, "cities will have no rest from evils."[63]

Philosophers as kings? Only a philosopher could think that was a good idea, at least if one considers the academics in today's universities, who are not known for their practical judgment or political acumen and who often seem out of touch with mainstream views. (William F. Buckley famously remarked, "I would rather be governed by the first 2,000 names in the Boston phone book than by the 2,000 members of the faculty of Harvard University.")

But Plato has a very specific conception of philosophy. He believes that the rational part of the soul is capable, through long practice and training, of knowing the good and ordering the soul (and society) in accordance with it. Put modestly, Plato believes that there is such a thing as wisdom in human affairs and that the whole point of being a philosopher is to try to grasp that wisdom and act accordingly. Put more dramatically, he believes that the universe is so arranged that the good society and the good life for man are already predetermined and that it is the philosopher's job to grasp these eternal forms and bring himself and the world into harmony with them. It is to this conception of universal order that Plato devotes the core books (the latter part of V, and all of VI and VII) of *The Republic*.

The standard caricature of the philosopher (presented by Aristophanes in *The Clouds*) is of someone who is dreamy and impractical. But Plato believes that, in fact, all of us live in the equivalent of a dream world. The physical world is a world of appearances, constantly in flux. Things come to be, things pass away. Appearances can deceive us (e.g., a straight twig looks bent when placed partially under water). Objects appear different in different lights, and they change over time, losing some qualities, gaining others. We can form opinions about such phenomena; we can construct hypotheses and build theories that help explain them. But we can never have knowledge about them.

Knowledge, for Plato, follows the model of mathematics, and particularly geometry. Knowledge proceeds not from particular instances to generalizations. Knowledge proceeds from demonstrable first principles (e.g., the four sides of a square are equal; the three angles of a triangle add to 180 degrees) and builds on those first principles. Knowledge concerns matters that are intelligible rather than perceptible. We may draw lines on paper to illustrate the principles of geometry; but those principles exist independently of (and in a far more perfect form than) the lines. The lines on paper are inevitably crooked and inexact; they get erased or fade with time. But the truths of geometry are fixed and immutable and perfectly exact. The claims of geometers are about the "square itself and the diagonal itself, not the diagonal they draw."[64]

Plato offers a metaphor of a line divided into two unequal sections: one representing the intelligible world and one the visible world. He divides the visible world in turn into images (shadows, reflections in water, appearances caused by changing light, and all the perceptions of our senses) and the originals of these images (the earth, the animals around us, all the plants, and the whole class of manufactured things). We use the images, he says, to form beliefs and hypotheses about the originals. That is the method of "the so-called sciences, for which their hypotheses are first principles."[65] In the intelligible realm, by contrast, we use thought to obtain understanding: direct, demonstrable knowledge of the immutable first principles from which we can reach conclusions "without making use of anything visible at all, but only of forms themselves, moving on from forms to forms, and ending in forms."[66]

Plato's distinction between the truths of mathematics and those of the natural sciences is perfectly acceptable in its own right. The principles of geometry are grasped by the intellect, not by the senses; they are susceptible of rigid proof and they do not change over time. (The fact that non-Euclidean systems of geometry were later developed does not alter the point: Euclidean geometry is strictly correct given its premises.) Scientific theories, by contrast, must account for physical data and are falsifiable by further data. No theory of the physical world, however basic and seemingly well founded, is immune to revision. But two plus two will always equal four. Thus, mathematics and the sciences have different paradigms of knowledge and Plato is certainly within his rights to reserve the label of "true knowledge" for mathematics, while characterizing scientific theories as "beliefs."

The key article of faith for Plato, however, is that the model of mathematical knowledge can be extended to moral issues. In our own hierarchy of knowledge, we would agree to place mathematics at the top, followed by the natural sciences, followed (perhaps a distant third) by the "social sciences" (including economics, psychology, and sociology). But most would then be inclined to place ethics and political theory, the traditional subjects of philosophy, on a much lower rung (if not a different ladder altogether), as matters of intense importance but also of intense and never-ending dispute and, hence, as susceptible only of belief, not knowledge.

But Plato places philosophy with mathematics, as offering a purer, better, and more certain knowledge than the changeable sciences. He feels that this must be so if discourse is to be possible. We are able to talk about beauty, courage, justice, wisdom, and moderation. We distinguish these virtues in words and the words have meaning. But the meanings of the words cannot be tied to specific instances. Beauty is not just a particular sunset or person or piece of music. The sunset will fade; the person will age; sonatas are transitory and may be badly played. Yet beauty as an ideal persists. Thus, the beautiful must be something separate and apart from these particular instances. The particular instances, however imperfect and transitory, are beautiful insofar as they partake in this abstract ideal of beauty. Beauty must therefore correspond to something fixed and immutable, which is intelligible rather than perceptible to us. It is our dim apprehension of this form of beauty that gives meaning to our ordinary discourse about it and that allows us to distinguish particular instances.

We are "lovers of sights and sounds," Plato notes.[67] We focus on beautiful sounds, beautiful colors, and beautiful shapes, but our thought is unable to see and embrace the nature of the beautiful itself. As a consequence, we have no true knowledge. Yet just as the geometer can proceed from imperfect lines on paper to a comprehension of the truths of geometry, so too the philosopher can proceed from individual imperfect instances of beautiful things to a contemplation and understanding of the beautiful itself. This will in turn give the philosopher a greater apprehension as to which things in the world partake of the form of beauty and which do not. The same is true for courage, justice, moderation, and wisdom.

This is Plato's theory of forms. The forms are eternal, immutable, and nonphysical. They underlie and give structure to the visible world, in much the same way that Plato thinks geometry does. The forms are apprehended by thought alone through a process of abstract reasoning that Plato calls "dialectic." Plato's dialectic bears a strong resemblance to the Socratic elenchus: a probing and testing of concepts to ensure that the interlocutor can give a true and consistent account of the virtue in question. But Plato, unlike Socrates, believes that the end result of that probing is knowledge, not doubt. He believes that there is a solid irreducible core to each concept (a form) that is intelligible to us and that, through dialectic, we can proceed from particular instances to a direct apprehension of that form. Dialectic accordingly entails an intellectual slicing and dicing of concepts—or, to change the simile, the cutting and polishing of a perfect, translucent diamond—so that the exact contours and full brilliance of each form are directly apparent to our reason. Once we have such a grasp of the form itself, we can proceed to give an account of it, and to distinguish particular instances, in a way that will stand up even to Socratic inquiry. Having grasped this "unhypothetical first principle," reason "reverses itself and, keeping hold of what follows from it, comes down" to understand for the first time and with a clarity hitherto impossible the particular instances of that form in the world.[68]

This notion of ascending and descending is captured perfectly in Plato's celebrated metaphor of the cave. He likens all of us to prisoners in a cave, with necks and legs fettered. The only light is provided by a fire burning above and behind the prisoners. Between them and the fire is a low wall, and objects of all shapes and materials are carried above the wall so that they cast shadows that the prisoners (who cannot turn their heads to look at the objects themselves) see projected on the wall in front of them. For the prisoners, these shadows are reality and they "would in every way believe that the truth is nothing other than the shadows of those artifacts."[69] Indeed, they would honor and accord power to those among them who were sharpest at discerning and remembering the shadows and the order in which they pass.

The philosopher is the one who can break those fetters, stand up and turn around, accustom his eyes to the light of the fire, and recognize that what he has been seeing, what he has taken for reality, are mere images and shadows. Yet he must go further, up the steep path and out into the sunlight where he will at first be blinded by the dazzling light but will gradually come to know not images of things, dimly perceived, but the things themselves, and even the sun itself. He will then recognize how inconsequential are the shadow images known to the prisoners and he will prefer any fate on earth rather than to share their opinions and live as they do.

The entire visible realm, Plato says, and the whole of our ordinary existence should be likened to this prison dwelling. The upward journey is the journey of the soul in its study of intelligible things, and the equivalent of the sun in that intelligible realm is the form of the good, which orders all things and is the ultimate source of "all that is correct and beautiful in anything" and that "provides truth and understanding, so that anyone who is to act sensibly in private or public must see it."[70] Plato acknowledges that he does not know whether or not his account is true. But it is for him a basic article of faith that, for life to be intelligible, it must be so ordered that our words have meaning, not in virtue of transitory, changeable appearances, but because they are tethered to fixed and immutable forms. It is this proper moral order and the ultimate intelligibility of reality that he terms the form of the good.

Returning to his vision of the just society, Plato then explains how the rulers will single out from an early age those who show a love of learning, who are high-minded, without pettiness, and good at remembering, and most of all who are always guided by the truth and pursue it in every way. These chosen few, with the best minds and the strongest characters, will receive extensive training in mathematics and dialectic. They will learn to know and to love the good above all. Such men, Plato notes, will not want to rule. They would prefer to stay in the realm of the forms, in contemplation of the good, and will be very reluctant to descend again into the darkness of the cave.

Indeed, when they do so they will at first stumble badly, since their sight will not be accustomed to the darkness and to the disputes over shadows that preoccupy most lives. But they will follow their duty to the city and their fellow citizens, they will work their way back from the realm of the forms down to clear-eyed discernment of public affairs and "the city will be governed, not like the majority of cities nowadays, by people who fight over shadows and struggle against one another in order to rule—as if that were a great good—but by people who are awake."[71] Having seen the good, having made it their sole and exclusive aim and study, they will "in turn put the city, its citizens, and themselves in order, using it as their model."[72]

We may still be skeptical that philosophers can become rulers. But it is difficult to fault Plato's belief, whether applied to today or to his own time, that "hardly anyone acts sanely in public affairs,"[73] and that the struggle for power as an end in itself is destructive of good order and sound government.

It is even more difficult to fault Plato's belief that philosophy is properly concerned with "knowing what always is, not what comes into being and passes away."[74] Over the entrance to his Academy, Plato had emblazoned: "Let no man ignorant of geometry enter here." Plato's choice of mathematics as the model of obtainable truth seems apt, for it promises knowledge that is qualitatively different from what the sciences can tell us about the world. It promises true understanding of the underlying structure that seems to order our world. If comparable knowledge is possible about moral issues then there can certainly be no greater occupation for man. If there is a moral structure and order to the world, if there is meaning in human life, and if there are answers to moral questions (real answers, not just endlessly debatable opinions), then how could anything be more important than this inquiry?

The alternative, at any rate, is bleak indeed. Without any grounding in truth, we will yield day by day to the desire at hand. Our values will have no mooring and our lives no fixed purpose. Plato gives a very modern description of this ungrounded existence:

> Sometimes he drinks heavily while listening to the flute; at other times, he drinks only water and is on a diet; sometimes he goes in for physical training; at other times, he's idle and neglects everything;

and sometimes he even occupies himself with what he takes to be philosophy. He often engages in politics, leaping up from his seat and saying and doing whatever comes into his mind. If he happens to admire soldiers, he's carried in that direction, if money-makers, in that one.[75]

There is neither order nor necessity in such a life. And because desires are insatiable there is no genuine satisfaction either; we are trying to fill a vessel full of holes. Like cattle, we "feed, fatten, and fornicate," and to outdo others in these things we kick and butt and sometimes even kill.[76]

Yet, if we are at all reflective, we cannot escape a nagging sense that we are living our lives among the shadows, and that there is something more, some deeper meaning and reality if only we could perceive it steadily and clearly. It is the job of philosophy, Plato tells us, "to awaken the best part of the soul" and rescue it from the "barbaric bog" in which it is buried.[77] By directing our thoughts upward, by loving truth and justice and the good above all, we can escape from the shadows and give order and clarity to our lives. We can avoid the civil war within ourselves that occurs when reason is overthrown and we are governed by passions and desires we were meant to control. Such is the proper life for man, a life that corresponds with the philosopher's quest for knowledge and understanding. The man who pursues such a life will have his soul purified and rekindled by its contemplation of the truth and will thus far stand outside human concerns and draw closer to the divine.

THE PHILOSOPHER'S QUEST

There is obviously a strong current of mysticism in Plato's theory of the forms. A long period of study and discipline may be required, but ultimate enlightenment (i.e., contemplation of the "pure, ever existing, immortal and unchanging"[78] forms) seems more a matter of grace than of rational thought. His dialogues are intended to lead the reader in the right direction, but he does not convey his doctrines in treatise form, as propositions to be learned. "There is no writing of mine about these matters," he explains in the only letter of his considered authentic (or at least accurate in portraying his views), "nor will there ever be one. For this knowledge is not something that can be put into words like other sciences; but after long-continued intercourse between teacher and pupil, in joint pursuit of the subject, suddenly, like light flashing forth when a fire is kindled, it is born in the soul and straightaway nourishes itself."[79]

There is also in Plato a corresponding tendency, evident most clearly in the *Phaedo*, to denigrate the body and the physical world (a denigration that found a strong echo in Christianity). "While we live, we shall be closest to knowledge if we refrain as much as possible from association with the body and do not join with it more than we must, if we are not infected with its nature but purify ourselves from it until the god himself frees us."[80] The philosopher must approach the forms with thought alone, "freeing himself as far as possible from eyes and ears, and in a word, from the whole body, because the body confuses the soul and does not allow it to acquire truth and wisdom whenever it is associated with it."[81] Indeed, it is only when we are dead and exist as pure souls, unencumbered with the body and the physical senses, that we will truly attain wisdom. Plato goes so far in this dialogue as to call philosophy a preparation for death, and death itself the ultimate cure for the disease of life.

We are a long way from Socrates, who wants to use rational thought to know how to live his life as a man. It is hardly an answer to his inquiry to suggest that wisdom will be obtained only when we go beyond both reason and life itself. But, despite the undeniable strands of mysticism, Plato does keep faith with the more earthly, practical Socrates. Plato's primary criterion for apprehension of the forms is not a wholly personal and unverifiable mystical experience; it is the ability to give a true account and to stand up to Socratic-style questioning. "Unless someone can distinguish in an account the form of the good from everything else," Plato explains, and "can survive all refutation, as if in a battle, striving to judge things not in accordance with opinion but in accordance with being, and can come through all this with his account still intact, you'll say that he doesn't know the good itself or any other good."[82]

Cutting through the trappings of metaphor and mysticism, Plato's challenge is a simple one. Like Socrates he asks us to give an account of our lives and our values that will bear the most intense scrutiny. Unlike Socrates, however, he believes it can be accomplished. He believes, that is, that the study of dialectic can lead us to refine and modify our current beliefs with sufficient clarity and precision that we will come to see and understand the bedrock principles that give justice and the other virtues their content. He believes that these first principles are consistent with one another and form an ordered whole. And he believes that from these first principles we can determine whether particular acts and institutions are or are not just. He believes in short that justice and courage and wisdom and goodness are objects of genuine knowledge and inquiry, and that we have no more important business than to know and understand them and to order our lives accordingly.

As an article of faith, Plato's account is an admirable one. It may ultimately rely on metaphor and analogy to convey how it is that we can come to know the forms and, even more so, how it is that physical objects can participate in those forms. But something similar is needed even in geometry, where metaphors of seeing with the mind's eye and sudden flashes of understanding are perfectly at home. At any rate, Plato tells us, dialectic is the only inquiry that travels this road toward moral understanding. It is the only alternative to a complete moral relativism.

Plato sees a simple and compelling dichotomy. Either "each thing has a being or essence privately for each person," or "things have some fixed being or essence of their own."[83] In other words, either justice is a purely subjective and manipulable judgment (which was the view put forward at the beginning of *The Republic* by Socrates' interlocutors) or it has a content independent of our individual needs and desires. If the latter—if justice and goodness and other such terms have objective content—then "they are not in relation to us and are not made to fluctuate by how they appear to us. They are by themselves, in relation to their own being or essence, which is theirs by nature."[84] And it is the job of the philosopher to understand that nature.

With this basic dichotomy—between purely subjective judgments and objective concepts—comes a series of other distinctions: becoming versus being; things in flux versus those that are immutable;

the perceptible versus the intelligible. Philosophers, he tells us, are properly concerned in each case with the latter. And Plato goes even further. He argues that unless there are "pure, ever existing, immortal and unchanging" forms, then discourse itself is impossible because our words will have no grounding; there will be no objective meanings to correspond to them, but only the purely subjective meaning that each person assigns to them.[85]

Plato is not ignorant of the difficulties of his theory of forms. In the *Parmenides*, he himself anticipates and explores many of the most serious of them. And he recognizes that his responses to those difficulties invariably take refuge in analogy and metaphor. But he is still confident that some such account must be correct. And he poses a direct and forceful challenge to those who disagree with him. "If someone," he says, "having an eye on all the difficulties we have just brought up and others of the same sort, won't allow that there are forms for things," "he will not have anything on which to fix his thought... and in this way he will utterly destroy the power of discourse."[86]

Plato then asks future philosophers to choose: they must either accept some theory such as the theory of forms, or they must explain how discourse can be possible when our words have no objective anchors, no intelligible meanings to which they correspond. Twenty-three hundred years later, an Austrian philosopher named Ludwig Wittgenstein, living and working in England, will take up that challenge and break the hold of Plato's dichotomy. In the process, he will announce the end of philosophy as conceived and practiced since Plato.

CHAPTER TWO
WITTGENSTEIN AND THE END OF PHILOSOPHY

Philosophy simply puts everything before us, and neither explains nor deduces anything.[1]

Ludwig Wittgenstein was born in Vienna on April 26, 1889. Although of Jewish descent, his paternal grandfather had assimilated to Protestantism, and his mother was a Roman Catholic. Wittgenstein's family was extremely wealthy, having built their fortune by providing the iron and steel used to fuel the Austro-Hungarian empire. They lived in a highly cultured environment, and the composers Johannes Brahms and Gustav Mahler were close family friends, as was the painter Gustav Klimt. Ludwig's brother, Paul, became a concert pianist and, after losing his arm in the First World War, continued his career by commissioning pieces from Ravel and others to be played with the left hand alone. His sister, Gretl, was analyzed by Freud and helped him escape to England after the *Anschluss.*

Ludwig was the youngest of eight children and was initially considered the least gifted of the group. He was fascinated with mechanics and studied engineering in his youth (overlapping at the same school for one year with Adolf Hitler). He eventually traveled to the University of Manchester in England, where his interests strayed from aeronautics to applied mathematics to the foundations of mathematics. This last field led him in 1911 to Cambridge University and the thirty-nine-year-old Bertrand Russell, whose works, *The Principles of Mathematics* and volume one of *Principia Mathematica* (written with Alfred North Whitehead), had already made him world famous.

To his credit, Russell immediately recognized Wittgenstein's particular genius. He cultivated and even indulged the intense and often difficult young man who would displace him as the most important philosopher of the twentieth century. Wittgenstein studied with Russell for several terms before retreating to an isolated farm in Norway to work on the thoughts that would be incorporated into his first book. Wittgenstein was also in contact with Gottlieb Frege (1848–1925), a German logician, mathematician, and philosopher. Both Russell and Frege were engrossed in trying to uncover the hidden structure of language. The early Wittgenstein extended and deepened their work and brought it to what he thought was its final form.

At the outbreak of the First World War, Wittgenstein volunteered to serve in the Austrian army. He lobbied to be sent to the eastern front and, once there, repeatedly volunteered for the most dangerous forward observation posts. He received the Silver Medal for valor under fire. In his backpack, he kept his notebooks and a small copy of Tolstoy's *Gospels*. Somehow, he managed to complete his book in the trenches. He was later captured and sent as a prisoner of war to a camp near Monte Cassino, Italy, but was able to send the completed manuscript to Russell and another copy to Frege. This work, known as the *Tractatus Logico-Philosophicus*, was ultimately published in 1921, and translated into English in 1922.

When he returned from the war, Wittgestein was wealthier than ever due to his father's pre-war decision to put the family money in American bonds. But Wittgenstein insisted on giving away his entire fortune, mostly to his sisters and to Paul. (His other three brothers had by then committed suicide.) With no money, and in the belief that he had already solved all the problems of philosophy, the thirty-one-year-old Wittgenstein left Vienna to teach school in various Austrian villages. He later designed and supervised the building of a house for his sister, a severe and austere building, free of all ornament. And he worked for a time as a gardener at a monastery.

But Wittgenstein was eventually lured back to philosophy and, indeed, became convinced that his earlier work was in critical respects completely mistaken. In 1929, he returned to Cambridge, where he submitted the *Tractatus* as his doctoral thesis and became a fellow at Trinity College. Russell and G. E. Moore were his examiners and Moore wryly reported, "It is my personal opinion that Mr. Wittgenstein's thesis is a work of genius; but, be that as it may, it is certainly well up to the standard required for the Cambridge degree of Doctor of Philosophy."[2]

Wittgenstein lived in England until his death from cancer on April 29, 1951, interspersed with periods of complete isolation in Norway, where he built a small cabin, and on the coast of Ireland, where he rented a remote cottage. He became a British subject after the *Anschluss.* His brother Paul had by then left Austria for America. Wittgenstein's sisters transferred a large portion of the family fortune from Swiss banks to the Third Reich for certificates guaranteeing that their Jewish heritage, and that of their children, would be ignored. During the war, Wittgenstein left Cambridge and worked, first, as a porter at a hospital in London and later in a medical laboratory in Newcastle.

Wittgenstein never published another book. Aside from a single short article, he never published anything at all after the *Tractatus.* But he wrote constantly and carefully prepared the manuscript of his masterpiece, *Philosophical Investigations,* before deciding he was dissatisfied with it. His views largely became known through a devoted circle of students who would meet regularly in his rooms. Wittgenstein did not lecture so much as think aloud about the problems that concerned him, using his students as sounding boards and props, and sometimes standing silent in the middle of the room for long periods while he wrestled with a particularly knotty issue.

He was a remarkably ascetic man. His furnishings consisted of a cot, a card table to write upon, and a couple of camp chairs. He never wore a tie, and his only forms of relaxation appear to have been detective stories and movies, especially westerns, where he would sit in the front row, munching on a pork pie, seeking refuge from the philosophical conundrums that tormented him most of his waking hours.

The *Investigations* was published two years after his death. There followed a great number of books culled from his voluminous notebooks by his executors, and many of his students published sets of lecture notes and reminiscences. Wittgenstein's "books" now fill a substantial shelf. But the two great works, the works that embody Wittgenstein's most finished thoughts and by which he should be judged, are still the *Tractatus* and the *Investigations*. Both books are beautifully austere, consisting of short, numbered paragraphs, sometimes of a single sentence. They are clearly, even elegantly, written and yet astoundingly difficult to understand because Wittgenstein made little effort to provide the context of his thoughts or even a sustained argument. It takes repeated readings and considerable background in the history of philosophy for the reader to get his or her bearings.

The two books deal with the same question that Plato posed in *Parmenides*: how is meaningful language possible? Plato thought that language must be tethered to a realm of intelligible and unchangeable forms and that the goal of the philosopher is to clarify his language and put his thinking (and his life) in order by means of his direct apprehension of these forms. Absent some such external mooring, Plato felt, language would be impossible. Words would have a purely private meaning and we could not communicate with one another at all. Unless a philosopher accepts some such theory as the forms, for all its difficulties, he will have nothing on which to "fix his thought," which will "utterly destroy the power of discourse."

It is a measure of Plato's genius that, in both his early and late philosophy, Wittgenstein was still struggling with precisely the dilemma that Plato posed more than two thousand years earlier. But in his two books Wittgenstein proposed radically different answers to that dilemma, answers that spawned two completely different schools of philosophy (logical positivism and ordinary language philosophy). Wittgenstein himself repudiated both of those schools, however. He was not interested in schools of thought or the construction of theories. His passionate desire was to clear the ground of all theory to make way for ethics and religion, understood not as bodies of doctrines or even objects of rational inquiry, but as particular ways of viewing and appreciating the world and our fellow human beings.

Wittgenstein was not a modest man; geniuses seldom are. He was in his early twenties when he wrote, in the preface to the *Tractatus*, that "the *truth* of the thoughts that are here communicated seems to me unassailable and definitive. I therefore believe myself to have found, on all essential points, the final solution of the problems [of philosophy]."[3] He continued to so believe throughout his life. The nature of his "final solution" changed radically, but the fervent conviction—that philosophy, as traditionally practiced, is at an end—remained.

THE TRACTATUS

Wittgenstein seeks in the *Tractatus* to chart the limits of language and, thereby, of thought and reality. He does so from the inside, so to speak, by focusing as Plato did on how language acquires meaning. The *Tractatus* is full of oracular sayings such as "The world is all that is the case"; "Logic is a mirror image of the world"; and "We cannot think what we cannot say." It also contains a fair amount of logical notation that most readers will find difficult if not impossible to follow. Fortunately, the essence of what Wittgenstein is saying can be explained fairly simply.

The driving concept in the *Tractatus* is that language pictures or models reality. A sentence must have something in common with the world it depicts, just as a courtroom diagram of an accident, insofar as it is accurate, must have the same elements (car, pedestrian, stop sign, crosswalk) in the same relation to one another as in the accident itself. The elements of the proposition (picture or model) must stand for the elements of reality that are being depicted.

Like Plato, Wittgenstein feels that language has to be moored in an external reality that gives meaning to our words. Like Plato, Wittgenstein believes in "the determinacy of sense"—that is, that our concepts have sharp boundaries so that any proposition is either true or false. This is the law of the excluded middle. There is no grey area in which meaning collapses or truth is ambiguous. Since language gets meaning from its description of possible states of affairs in the world, and since those states of affairs either exist or do not exist, there can be no ambiguity in language or reality.

Wittgenstein recognizes, however, that our ordinary language appears far from precise. He feels that this is attributable to a misleading surface grammar that disguises the true logical form of our sentences. Through logical analysis, the philosopher can lay bare a sentence's underlying logical structure and hence the way in which the sentence depicts a given state of affairs in the world.

The bedrock of any such analysis, Wittgenstein thinks, must be *elementary propositions*, which depict the simplest possible states of affairs. The words in an elementary proposition name objects and the objects provide the meaning for the words. These elementary propositions cannot be broken down further; neither can the state of affairs that they depict. An elementary proposition is as simple as the Xs and Os of elementary computer code; the switch is either on or off; the state of affairs either obtains or it does not obtain. Thus, elementary propositions are either true or false; there is no excluded middle, no ambiguity. And every possible state of affairs is independent of any other possible state of affairs; there is no necessity other than logical necessity.

Wittgenstein does not explain the nature of the "objects" named in these elementary propositions; nor does he give examples of the states of affairs they depict. Whether the objects are sense data (as some later argued) or material particles of physics, Wittgenstein doesn't feel he needs to say or even could say. The key point is that bedrock must be reached: language must be anchored to the world through the simplest possible propositions describing the simplest possible states of affairs. The sense or meaning of each elementary proposition is given by its truth conditions: the conditions under which it is true or false. One can, so to speak, hold the elementary proposition up against the world to determine if the state of affairs it depicts either exists or does not exist.

More complex propositions, he concludes, are *truth functions* of elementary propositions. That is to say, they are constructed out of elementary propositions and their truth is a function of the truth of each of the elementary propositions that compose them. (Wittgenstein made some substantial and lasting innovations in logic, here, by building up truth tables to show how elementary propositions can be charted into composite propositions.) Ordinary propositions also picture states of affairs, although of a more complex type. Since there is no ambiguity in elementary propositions—they are either true or false—more complicated propositions (which are truth-functions of elementary propositions) must also be unambiguous.

Logic thus plays a critical role in Wittgenstein's analysis. Even elementary propositions have a logical structure or form that must mirror the reality they depict. Composite propositions add another layer of logical structure by using logical constants, such as "or," "and," "not." These logical constants are not themselves the names of any objects; rather, they function as the connective tools or scaffolding of language. This scaffolding shows the formal properties of the world governing the ways in which simple states of affairs can combine into more complex states of affairs. Logic, which is prior to experience, sets forth the limits and structure of possible states of affairs. Logical propositions are necessarily true (they are "tautologies"). They tell us nothing about the world as it actually is, but they show us the limits and structure of that world. They show us the boundaries of what is expressible and of what is possible.

There is, thus, a congruence between language and reality at three levels: names (simple signs) go proxy for objects (simple things); elementary propositions picture possible states of affairs; and the formal properties of language mirror the formal properties of the world. An interesting by-product of this view of language is that all languages, no matter how varied in surface appearance (German, Chinese, Sanskrit), must have the same underlying elements and the same logical structure. Propositions in any language have a precise sense because they are truth-functions of elementary propositions. It follows that every language can be translated precisely into every other language (a thesis known as the determinacy of translation).

It also follows that our thoughts must have the same logical and composite structure, and the same determinacy, as language and reality. It is in thought that we make the connection between elementary propositions and the possible states of affairs that give them their sense. In order to make that connection, our thoughts must mirror both propositions and the states of affairs that propositions depict. This is how we are able to speak and think about the world: through a one to one correspondence (and shared logical form) between the elements of language (simple names), the elements of the physical world (simple objects), and the elements of thought. This is how the world, thought, and language *must be* if we are to think and speak about the world.

So far, Wittgenstein seems simply to be proposing a traditional philosophical answer, using modern tools of logical analysis, to the Platonic question of how language is tethered to reality. But Wittgenstein's approach has radical implications for ethics and religion—for questions of value and the meaning of life—which he explores in the last portion of the book. For Wittgenstein, as for Plato, such questions are the whole point of philosophy. They give purpose to the entire enterprise.

But in Wittgenstein's view of the relation of language to the world, there is no room even to pose such questions, far less to answer them. Language describes only contingent states of affairs. It deals with facts (what is "accidental"), not values. "In the world everything is as it is, and everything happens as it does happen: *in* it no value exists."[4] Propositions have meaning only insofar as they describe possible states of affairs. All propositions, therefore, are of equal value. "Propositions can express nothing that is higher."[5] "It is impossible for there to be propositions of ethics," because such propositions would not describe possible states of affairs.[6]

That is not to say, however, that questions of value are unimportant. Wittgenstein has used philosophy to chart the limits of language. "*The limits of my language* mean the limits of my world."[7] Within those limits, there is no value, no meaning. Even with a complete description of the world (all true propositions) the question of the meaning of life will be untouched. Thus, he concludes, "the sense of the world must lie outside the world."[8] Ethics, which Wittgenstein merges with religion, must be transcendental. We cannot talk meaningfully about value. But we can experience it. Even more important, we can will it.

Wittgenstein makes the point that we do not experience ourselves as objects in the world. Our consciousness seems rather to envelop the world. We have thoughts that, as discussed above, are congruent with language and with possible states of affairs. But the subject having those thoughts is separate from them. This subject, which Wittgenstein describes as an indivisible point, "does not belong to the world: rather, it is a limit of the world."[9] This subject is the bearer of good and evil, through the exercise of will. This subject can also experience the world as a limited whole, *sub species aeternitatis*, under the guise of, or in light of, eternity. It is this admittedly mystical experience—of seeing the world, the entire sphere of the natural sciences, as limited and incomplete—that Wittgenstein considers the source of both ethics and religion. "The solution of the riddle of life in space and time lies *outside* space and time."[10]

But outside space and time our thoughts have no purchase. We cannot articulate the experience in any meaningful way. Thus, the meaning of the world lies outside meaningful thought and meaningful language. It can only be experienced. It can only be willed. Herein, Wittgenstein thought, is the solution to the problems of philosophy. A proper logical point of view shows those problems to be nonsensical. Philosophy sets limits to what can be thought and to the sphere of the natural sciences. But when everything is properly represented the problems of philosophy disappear. Once philosophy shows the relations between language, thought, and the world, there is nothing left for philosophy to do. Philosophy has the merely negative, therapeutic task of restricting discourse to what can legitimately be said by pointing out that what purport to be philosophical propositions are disguised nonsense.

The result, of course, is that the *Tractatus* itself is full of nonsense. Wittgenstein does not shrink from this conclusion. But he considers the *Tractatus* at least to be illuminating nonsense because it shows the relationship between language, thought, and reality and hence it shows the limits of our world. The *Tractatus* leads the reader to a correct logical point of view. "My propositions," he explains, "serve as elucidations in the following way: anyone who understands me eventually recognizes them as nonsensical, when he has used them—as steps—to climb up beyond them. (He must, so to speak, throw away the ladder after he has climbed up it.)"[11] Once the reader has climbed that ladder, "he will see the world aright," and he will no longer need to try to express what cannot be expressed, but only experienced.

The parallels with Plato's metaphor of the cave and the philosopher's ascent are wonderful; the differences equally so. In Plato, the philosopher leaves the shadows behind and ascends to the realm of the forms, a higher reality, which gives meaning to life and an anchor for language. The philosopher's experience of those forms is a mystical one but it leads to a direct, intuitive knowledge of the good that will order his soul and guide his conduct. In Wittgenstein, language is already anchored in the world, but the philosopher ascends to a viewpoint from which he can survey that world as a limited whole and find meaning in that perspective. That perspective can be said to correspond in a sense with Plato's contemplation of the form of the good. But for Wittgenstein, the philosopher does not achieve new knowledge, but rather a new understanding, a new sort of experience that transforms himself and his world.

In this way, Wittgenstein fulfills a Platonic need while avoiding a Platonic pitfall. In *Parmenides*, Plato poses the question whether there are forms for dirt and hair and other trivial objects. He assumes there must be (otherwise the inability to fix our thoughts will destroy the power of discourse about such objects), but thereby risks trivializing the theory of forms and the realm of virtue and the good. Ethical concerns—concerns about value—are what drove him to the theory in the first place. Wittgenstein takes care of that problem by letting ordinary, contingent propositions deal with dirt and hair—indeed, with the entire realm of contingent facts in which no value is to be found. Like Plato, Wittgenstein believes that if our focus is on the world of contingent facts (what Plato calls the realm of shadows), the state of our souls will be imperiled. Even if we know all true propositions of science, we will still not be one jot closer to what is truly important in life. Like Plato, therefore, Wittgenstein finds value in the transcendental. But for Wittgenstein the transcendental is not an anchor for thought and language; it lies beyond thought and language. The philosopher who attains this perspective will not become a master of dialectic, able to give an account of virtue and the meaning of life that will withstand all Socratic challenges. There is nothing to say about such matters. They are objects of experience, not knowledge. Wittgenstein accordingly ends the book with the words, wonderfully resonant in German: Wovon man nicht sprechen kann, darüber muß man schweigen. "What we cannot speak about we must pass over in silence."[12]

THE PHILOSOPHICAL INVESTIGATIONS

By the time he returns to philosophy in 1929, Wittgenstein is well on his way to rethinking the model of language that informs the *Tractatus*. By the time, fifteen years later, he has crafted the 693 short sections that constitute part I of the *Investigations*, he has turned that worldview inside out, and with it the main tradition of Western philosophy since Plato. Language is no longer a mirror of reality— whether conceived in terms of ideal forms, sense experiences, or other metaphysical simples—but an autonomous, organic growth, loosely grounded in the forms of life that constitute our natural history. Although he still feels that the surface grammar of language is misleading and inclines us to philosophical errors, he believes that the cure for such errors is not to penetrate through language to some underlying logical structure, but rather to get a perspicuous overview of the actual ways in which we use expressions in daily life. When one does so, he believes, the philosophical problems are revealed as confusions and simply disappear.

The *Investigations* accordingly deals with a series of problems in philosophy of language, epistemology, metaphysics, and the philosophy of mind, but, interestingly enough, not in ethics or religion. Wittgenstein demonstrates a method by which such problems can be dissolved. But "the real discovery," he explains, "is the one that makes me capable of stopping doing philosophy when I want to."[13] This "real discovery" is the recognition that so-called philosophical problems constitute "the bewitchment of our intelligence by means of language,"[14] and, although philosophy can eliminate such bewitchment, it does not explain anything or provide any foundations for our existing practices. Philosophy "leaves everything as it is."[15] Where that leaves ethics and religion—and whether philosophy itself can, on this view, be seen as a worthwhile activity—remains to be seen.

THE AUGUSTINIAN PICTURE

Wittgenstein opens the *Investigations* with a quotation from St. Augustine, a thinker he reveres. The passage from Augustine's spiritual autobiography, *The Confessions*, describes how Augustine learned (or assumes he learned) language. It is an unremarkable passage at first glance. Augustine simply reports that he learned the words for things by watching and listening to his elders name and point to objects. "As I heard words repeatedly used in their proper places in various sentences," he explains, "I gradually learnt to understand what objects they signified; and after I had trained my mouth to form these signs, I used them to express my own desires."[16]

Wittgenstein believes that this account reflects "a particular picture of the essence of human language," which is that "individual words in language name objects" and that "sentences are combinations of such names."[17] That picture contains the germ of the idea that the meaning of a word is the object for which the word stands, and we learn the meaning of a word by becoming acquainted with that object. This idea will obviously sound familiar to readers of the *Tractatus* or *The Republic* or any of dozens of other texts in the history of Western philosophy. But those are highly refined, fully developed theories. The point Wittgenstein wants to make here is that this pretheoretical "picture" has a powerful hold upon us and infects our every attempt to think philosophically. Indeed, in a basic sense "to think philosophically" is to be in the grip of the Augustinian picture.

Accordingly, one could well say that the entire point of the *Investigations* is to break the Augustinian picture's hold upon us. That is not to say that Wittgenstein thinks the picture is incorrect. It is just a picture, not a thesis. For some words it seems appropriate enough. "If you describe the learning of language in this way," Wittgenstein explains, you are "thinking primarily of nouns like 'table,' 'chair,' 'bread,' and of people's names, and only secondarily of the names of certain actions and properties; and of the remaining kinds of words as something that will take care of itself."[18] But the picture is misleading even for paradigmatic examples of "object words." Elaborate theories are required to make the remaining kinds of words fit the required model. These theories increasingly ignore the actual ways in which words are taught and used.

Wittgenstein asks us to imagine a language for which this "primitive idea of the way language functions" works best, which would be "a language more primitive than ours." He imagines a builder and his assistant. The only words in the language are "block," "pillar," "slab," and "beam." When the builder calls them out, the assistant brings the building stone that he "has learnt to bring at such-and-such a call." He asks us to "conceive this as a complete primitive language."[19]

One thing should immediately strike the reader.[20] Not only is this imagined language more primitive than our own, but also the speakers themselves would have to be more primitive than ourselves—so primitive indeed that they would seem more like zombies than humans. In explaining how he observed his elders, Augustine notes that "their intention was shown by their bodily movements, as it were the natural language of all peoples: the expression of the face, the play of the eyes, the movement of other parts of the body, and the tone of voice which expresses our state of mind in seeking, having, rejecting, or avoiding something."[21] But one cannot imagine the builder and his assistant, with their limited vocabulary and the carrying back and forth of slabs and beams and the like, with much variation in expression, or tone of voice, or play of the eyes. If these creatures were more expressive, we intuitively feel, that would be reflected in a more expressive language and vocabulary. Herein lies a critical point for Wittgenstein: "to imagine a language means to imagine a form of life," and "the *speaking* of language is part of an activity, or of a form of life."[22] He puts the same point slightly differently when he says: "commanding, questioning, recounting, chatting, are as much a part of our natural history as walking, eating, drinking, playing."[23] The builder commands and the assistant responds; but creatures who did not also question, recount, and chat would be very far from us indeed. Their natural history would have to be altogether different.

A second thing to notice about this limited language is that the meaning of even these basic words is more complicated than might first appear. The word "slab" as spoken by the builder does not just indicate the object in question; it is a command to bring the slab to the builder. The word "slab" is something like a label that applies to the object, but the critical thing for the assistant is to understand that he is to bring a slab when the builder utters the word. The point Wittgenstein is making here is that words themselves are like tools, and the teaching of language is not so much explanation, as training. Wittgenstein also likens words to chess pieces. The significance of a chess piece is not the piece of wood that a player happens to have in front of him. It is given, rather, by the rules of the game that governs its use. Similarly with words, we show that we understand them by using them and responding to them in appropriate ways. Meaning, then, is given by use and not just by a correlation of word and object. "To understand a language means to be master of a technique."[24] To emphasize this point, Wittgenstein refers to his primitive language as a "language game." The rules according to which we use words, according to which we play various "language games," Wittgenstein calls "grammar" (a term he gives a much broader application than the rules of proper usage studied in school).

A third thing to notice is that the "object words" in this highly simplified language game are themselves simple. The slabs and beams of the builder are presumably uniform. There is no real variation between the different slabs and hence it is relatively uncomplicated, once the assistant has learned which building stone is a slab, to recognize other items of the same sort. Accordingly, the term "slab" seems to have a determinate sense, which can be learned through "ostensive" teaching (that is, by someone pointing to the object and saying "slab"). This object and objects like it are "slabs" and nothing else. But such words are actually the exception rather than the rule. Consider a word like "game." There are many kinds of games: board games, card games, ball games, Olympic games, all varieties of children's games (hopscotch, kick-the-can, tag). We even talk of "the games people play" in relationships. To what single "object" does one point in order to teach the word "game"? What do all these games have in common that makes them "games"? What are the necessary and sufficient conditions for being a game?

Wittgenstein's point here is absolutely critical. "These phenomena have no one thing in common which makes us use the same word for all."[25] We are strongly inclined to say, but there *must* be something in common or they would not be called games. If you look at them, however, you will see similarities and relationships, but you will not see something that is common to all. "Don't think, but look!" Wittgenstein cautions.[26] When you do so, and when you pass from games of one type to games of another type, you will find correspondences, but some characteristic features drop out and others appear. When you

really look, you see "a complicated network of similarities overlapping and criss-crossing: sometimes overall similarities, sometimes
similarities of detail."[27] Wittgenstein characterizes these similarities
as "'family resemblances'; for the various resemblances between members of a family: build, features, colour of eyes, gait, temperament,
etc. etc. overlap and criss-cross in the same way."[28] Thus, learning to
use such concepts is far more complicated than simply having a single
game pointed out to one or being given a precise definition that covers
each and every game.

From an initial contemplation of the Augustinian picture, we are
thus introduced to many of the key coinages that help us survey
aspects of our language that we are inclined to overlook when doing
philosophy and that are critical to understanding the *Investigations*,
including "family-resemblance concepts," "language games,"
"grammar," and "forms of life." These terms will enable us to deal
with the three most important insights in Wittgenstein's later philosophy: the indeterminacy of sense, the impossibility of a private language, and the autonomy of grammar.

I use the word "insights" here advisedly. These are not theses that
Wittgenstein is putting forward. He is not constructing a new philosophical theory about the relationship between language and the
world, on the one hand, and language and thought, on the other. He
is, rather, using grammatical insights—insights about the way words
are actually used and taught—to dissolve certain philosophical problems that seem to arise when we extract our language from its
everyday use and, under the grip of the Augustinian picture, construct theories about the essence of language, thought, and reality.
Rather than suggesting that Wittgenstein argues for, or has a theory of,
the indeterminacy of sense, a more accurate account would be that he
shows how standard philosophical assumptions about the determinacy
of sense ignore the way that language actually works. So, too, with the
notion that we learn the meaning of sensation words and other
mental states through a kind of private ostensive definition. And so,
too, with the idea that our language and the form of life in which it is
embedded stands in need of a justification or grounding that philosophy can provide.

Each of these insights paves the way for Wittgenstein's announcement that Western philosophy has finished its run and reached a dead end. This is, one might say, Wittgenstein's one genuine philosophical thesis, or at least assumption, but it is a wholly negative one. All his other remarks are provisional and grammatical. He demonstrates a piecemeal method by which particular philosophical problems can be dissolved by obtaining a perspicuous overview (*übersicht*) of the actual way in which a particular language game functions. His one bold leap is in saying that the series of examples can be broken off and one can stop doing philosophy secure in the knowledge that philosophy can explain nothing; it leaves everything as it is.

THE INDETERMINACY OF SENSE

As we saw, the standard first move in the Socratic dialogues is to reject any attempt to offer a definition of justice or virtue or courage in terms of examples. Socrates always wants to know what is common to each example that makes an action just and that distinguishes it from an unjust action. "I didn't ask you whether this or that thing was just," he says, "but rather what justice is by virtue of which each of these individual things is just." Socrates wants an exact definition that will allow one to say precisely of any action whether or not it is just and why. That is what Socrates considers "doing philosophy," and he categorically refuses to accept as "being able to give an account" of a concept anything that falls short of this ideal. Thus, for any proffered account (e.g., it is just to pay your debts), any counter-example, however bizarre (e.g., it cannot be just to return borrowed weapons to a deranged man), is sufficient to defeat that account. An inability to give an exact definition—a definition that will cover all instances of justice and only those instances—is considered a sure sign that the interlocutor has no idea what justice is; that he has never even thought seriously about the most important matters concerning his own soul.

It is hardly an exaggeration to say that Socrates' first false step leads philosophy on a wild goose chase for the next two thousand years. He creates an ideal of what constitutes a philosophical explanation that many if not most of our concepts simply will not support. He assumes that all concepts must have precise boundaries—such that, for any real world example, it is either within or without those boundaries—and therefore anyone who understands that concept must be able to describe the boundaries exactly. This ideal or assumption is intimately related to, and a product of, the Augustinian picture. If words stand for objects, and the meaning of a word is the object for which the word stands, then words must exactly represent or mirror those objects. Since objects have clear boundaries, the meanings of the words that represent those objects must be equally precise.

In its crudest form, this view of language is easily repudiated. To say that all words signify objects is to turn all words into names. To further assert that the meaning of these names is the objects correlated with each of them is to confound the meaning of a name with its bearer. It is an inadequate account of meaning even for that limited group of words that we ordinarily classify as names. "When Mr. N. N. dies one says that the bearer of the name dies, not that the meaning dies,"[29] and if the sword Excalibur is broken in pieces it does not follow that the meaning of the word is broken in pieces or that the word ceases to have meaning because the sword ceases to exist.[30] Thus, meaning and bearer cannot be equated (in this simplistic fashion) even in what appears to be the most plausible case of proper names.

Plato's solution to this problem, of course, is to make the forms—the "objects" named by our words—eternal and unchangeable. Later philosophers, such as Locke, turn the objects into ideas in our minds. Wittgenstein, in the *Tractatus*, makes them into metaphysical simples. In each case, the ideal of the determinacy of sense is retained by correlating a precise object with the word in question. And, in each case, we are said to learn the meaning of the word by becoming acquainted with that object. In other words, we are somehow able to give an exact account of all possible uses of the word through a direct apprehension of the object for which it stands.

The later Wittgenstein thinks this approach is exactly backward. We don't learn the use of a word by somehow apprehending its hidden essence, the abstract object for which it stands. Rather, meaning is a function of use. We learn the meaning of words through particular examples of their use and by mastering the rules according to which they are used. There is no underlying metaphysical essence at which these examples point and from which they derive their correctness. If we peel back all the layers of the onion, we are left with nothing. The onion *is* the layers, just as the meaning of a word is a function of its various uses in the language. That is not to say that words like "table," "chair," and "bread" don't refer to objects in the world. But the words are part of our language; their meaning is a function of the role they play in that language. There is nothing mystical (or even particularly precise) about the many homely or exotic varieties of tables, chairs, and loaves to which they refer.

The problem with all the earlier theories, Wittgenstein feels, is that, under the grip of the Augustinian picture of language, they look at language as a form of words rather than the use made of a form of words. That is, a sentence is extracted from its context in human life and activity and regarded merely as a static combination of words. Then the philosophical "problem" arises of how this combination of words, this mere series of marks or sequence of sounds, can have meaning and serve as a mode of communication between men. This is seen as a problem because the very thing that gives the words their meaning (i.e., their use, the role they play in human life) is ignored. Viewed statically rather than dynamically it appears amazing that a word or sentence can have meaning. As a result one tends to look for meaning in something lying outside language, in something which breathes life into the lifeless series of marks or sequence of sounds. But that is simply to push back the "problem" of how we can use words to another, quasi-mystical level. No one is ever able to explain how the rules for use of a word can somehow be "read off" a direct apprehension of the object for which it stands.

To counteract this picture of language—to demystify it— Wittgenstein repeatedly returns words to their context in human life and activity. He constantly asks how words are taught and learned. "Every sign *by itself* seems dead. *What* gives it life?—In use it is *alive*. Is life breathed into it there?—Or is the *use* its life?"[31] Wittgenstein doesn't particularly care which formulation we use, as long as we recognize that our understanding of a concept is a function, not of our apprehension of some hidden essence, but of how we teach and explain and use that concept in everyday experience. "Let the use *teach* you the meaning."[32]

Once we reorient our thinking in this way, the demand for determinacy of sense simply disappears and with it a whole host of confusions, most notably the Socratic insistence that in order to know what a concept means you must be able to give an exact account of all its possible uses.

> Compare *knowing* and *saying*:
>   how many feet high Mont Blanc is—
>   how the word "game" is used—
>   how a clarinet sounds.

> If you are surprised that one can know something and not be able to say it, you are perhaps thinking of a case like the first. Certainly not of one like the third.[33]

We learn the application of a family-resemblance concept such as "game" through examples, not through the apprehension of some set of necessary and sufficient conditions for being a game. When we teach the concept with examples, we expect the one learning the concept to employ those examples in a particular way (e.g., to be able to recognize other instances of games), but we do not expect him to see in those examples the common thing that we, for some reason, are unable to express. The giving of examples is not an *indirect* means of explaining, in default of a better; it *is* the explanation.[34] My knowledge of the concept of a game is completely expressed "in my describing examples of various kinds of game[s]; showing how all sorts of other games can be constructed on the analogy of these; saying that I should scarcely include this or this among games; and so on."[35] It does not require a precise definition that will once and for all cover every case (and only those cases) that fall within it.

Again, one wants to object that there *must* be something in common to all the examples that makes them "games." Otherwise, the concept of a "game" is unintelligible. But why should that be true? Why must every example of a given concept have common properties? That is a dogma, an assumption of debate. It does not reflect how we actually use language. Simply because there may be disagreement around the edges, so to speak (does *this* really count as a game?), that doesn't mean that the word is not perfectly clear in most of its applications. We attach meaning to the word even if we are not equipped with rules for every possible application of it. The fact that there is no sharp boundary simply doesn't trouble us when we use the word "game." A blurred concept can still be a concept, just as imprecise directions ("stand over there") can still be directions.

We have an overwhelming desire when doing philosophy to try to remove all doubt about how to apply a concept, and feel that any explanation is imperfect if it does not do so. Wittgenstein's goal—an exclusively negative one—is to refute that assumption by showing how words are taught and learned and used in everyday life. Once one actually looks, one breaks away from the dogma that a word can only be applied based on properties that are common to every example that falls under it. Language does not have a hidden definite sense at which our examples only vaguely point; such definiteness is simply not required, and its absence does not prevent us from being able to use words correctly in ordinary discourse.

With respect to many if not most of our concepts, we do not know the boundaries because none have been drawn. We might be able to draw such a boundary for a special purpose (e.g., in mathematics or the natural sciences). But it doesn't take a precise boundary to make the concept usable. Indeed, if someone were to draw such a boundary, he would be changing, not uncovering, the concept in question. "I could not acknowledge it as the one that I too always wanted to draw, or had drawn in my mind. For I did not want to draw one at all. His concept can then be said to be not the same as mine, but akin to it."[36] In other words, even if some Platonic philosopher communed with the forms and accordingly proposed changes to our ordinary concepts to conform with his vision, he would not be uncovering the essence that was there all along. He would not be explaining what we have always meant but imperfectly understood. He would simply be proposing a new set of concepts to replace our existing ones, which have worked perfectly well and evolved over time to fit our needs. The result would likely be, not improvement, but impoverishment. Sharp boundaries would restrict the use of the concepts within artificial bounds and block further evolution. In his quest for some illusory ideal of determinate sense, the Platonic philosopher would be proposing a set of concepts that lacks the richness and diversity and flexibility of our actual speech. As we shall see, that is precisely what so often happens in ethics and aesthetics. Prescription masquerades as description; the free-market exchange of living and vibrant language to express our desires and judgments and needs is replaced by the tyranny of a planned discourse.

THE IMPOSSIBILITY OF A PRIVATE LANGUAGE

Plato believes that unless we have objective, metaphysical anchors for our words—unless, that is, "things have some fixed being or essence of their own" to which our words can attach and which constitute the shared meaning of those words—then our words can develop only purely private meanings and "each thing has a being or essence privately for each person."[37] In other words, Plato seems to be suggesting that unless the meaning of words is given by external objects accessible to all (the forms), they must be given by internal mental objects accessible only to each individual (ideas).

Plato, of course, finds only the first horn of this dilemma acceptable. But later philosophers—notably Descartes, Locke, and Hume—grasp the second. They focus on the primacy of the mental realm as the medium of our knowledge of the world. The external world becomes a collection of ideas built up out of our sensations. Metaphysics (the theory of what exists) is displaced by Epistemology (the theory of what we can know). In the latter case, as well as the former, the Augustinian picture still holds sway. Words still find their meaning and their determinacy in objects, only now the objects are private and mental.

Wittgenstein's assault on the dogmatic assumption that sense is necessarily determinate—and his constant reminder that meaning is reflected in use—is designed to remove the props from Plato's theory of forms and any other such attempts to turn meanings into objects. It applies equally to the view that the meaning of words is given by ideas in our minds that correspond to those words. In both cases a misguided search for some fixed object that gives a precise meaning to our words leads to a static account of language that ignores the actual, often messy, use of those words in everyday speech.

The Augustinian picture, however, has a particularly powerful and insidious hold on us when we turn from words like "table," "chair," or "game," to words like "pain," "thought," and "intention." We have a tendency to look for some object to which these words correspond, but a mental object, rather a physical one. We envision our experiences in this mental realm ("I feel pain," "I have a thought in my mind") as akin to our experiences in the physical realm ("I feel the table," "I have a book in my hand"), only immaterial rather than material. This tendency leads to misconceptions that have dominated philosophy for the past five hundred years. Much of the *Investigations*, starting at section 243, is designed to eliminate these misconceptions by showing that our use of words for sensations and mental states and experiences is far more complicated (and interesting) than the Augustinian picture would indicate.

More ink has been spilled on the so-called "private language" argument than on any other aspect of Wittgenstein's philosophy. A detailed discussion of his views is beyond the needs or scope of this book, but his essential points are not difficult to grasp. Again, though, the critical reminder is that Wittgenstein is not putting forward some new theory about the mind. He is not choosing between Cartesian Dualism (the belief that the mind is a nonphysical substance that somehow interacts with the physical body in which it is, at least temporarily, entombed) and Behaviorism (the belief that mental terms refer, or are reducible, to behavior); nor is he proposing some synthesis of the two. He is instead trying to explain how a proper understanding of our actual use of words can eliminate various philosophical problems that bedevil us when we start thinking about the mind, about how it relates to the body, and how we know of the existence of other minds.

Wittgenstein makes three main observations (that meet with increasing resistance) about how we actually use such words. *First*, "an 'inner process' stands in need of outward criteria."[38] We ascribe emotions, sensations, thoughts, and feelings to others based on their behavior. We learn how to use these concepts by learning the behavior that is the criteria for their application. Without criteria, we would have no basis for applying such concepts to others and, thus, no way to learn their proper use. The outward criteria are part of the rules for the use of such words; they are part of grammar and hence at least partially constitutive of what we mean by the concept in question.

That is not to say that the word "pain" refers simply to pain-behavior (moaning, cradling one's injured arm, etc.). Pain is a sensation; it is not behavior. A person can be in pain without manifesting such behavior (he's a stoic); conversely, one can mimic pain-behavior without actually being in pain (he's a fraud). The behavioral criteria for one's being in pain are in that sense defeasible. They don't logically entail the existence of pain even though they form an important part of our concept of pain. But neither is the pain-behavior merely inductive evidence of someone's being in pain, in the way that the shape, size, and weight of a package may be inductive evidence as to its contents. We learn the proper use of the term "pain" by tying it to the instinctive pain-behavior that is regularly associated with it. The connection is made in grammar.

The natural causes and manifestations of pain (the criteria by which we judge whether or not someone is in pain) guide our proper use of the concept. They are not just symptoms that we learn from experience (in the way that we might learn that putting ice on a sore muscle will reduce the pain). That is not to say there is a firm line between criteria and symptoms, between what belongs to grammar and what to experience. This indeterminacy may be particularly true for feelings and emotions (e.g., jealousy, pride, resentment, love, understanding) that manifest themselves in a wider range of behavior depending on the character of the person in question. "The fluctuation in grammar between criteria and symptoms makes it look as if there were nothing at all but symptoms."[39] That is, it might look as if the relationship between a given feeling and behavior were a purely contingent one. But we must have rules for the use of our terms, however loose and defeasible. Otherwise, we could never learn them and apply them. Those rules—the criteria for their application—are part of the grammar of the words. But there can often be doubt as to whether, in light of particular behavior, a given person is in love, or resentful, or jealous. Certain behavioral manifestations could be decisive for me, but not for someone else who judges differently or doesn't know the person as well as I do. This lack of determinacy is an inherent and critical feature of our concepts for feelings and emotions and other mental states and hence an important feature of our lives as human beings. Concepts with fixed limits would demand a uniformity of behavior, a rigid predictability that is foreign to us. Human behavior is not uniform. That is a fact of nature, part of our form of life. Concepts dealing with human behavior are accordingly unlikely to have fixed boundaries or rigid criteria for their application.

Second, in my own case, "I do...not...identify my sensation by criteria."[40] There is a critical distinction between the use of first-person statements ("I am in pain") and third-person statements ("He is in pain"). I make the latter based on behavioral criteria. But the former I make without any criteria whatsoever. I don't need any justification for saying "I am in pain" other than my being in pain.

The straightforward fact that I need no criteria to avow my own sensations and feelings has led to an entire body of philosophy built around the assumption that I have direct knowledge of those sensations and feeling whereas I can only infer them about others based on their behavior. In my own case, on this view, I perceive the thing (be it pain or anger or love) directly, whereas for others I can only infer that they have the same thing that I have. I make a leap of faith somehow that they have what I have when I am in pain or angry or in love. I can learn what other people think and feel only through their behavior (what they say, how they look, what they do). But I have privileged access to my own mental states. This picture or assumption has led, starting with Descartes, to the view that the only indubitable form of knowledge—and hence the only possible foundation for inferences about others—is knowledge of my own thoughts, sensations, and impressions. This in turn has led to an entire series of –isms, including Dualism (the mind is a realm separate from the body), Empiricism (knowledge of the external world is based on our knowledge of sense impressions), Idealism (doubts about whether the external world even exists), and their logical end in Solipsism (doubts whether anything exists outside my own mind).

Wittgenstein contends that both the statement that "I know I am in pain," and the statement that "I don't know, but can only infer, that others are in pain" are nonsense, and they are nonsense for essentially the same reason. "Other people cannot be said to learn of my sensations *only* from my behavior—for *I* cannot be said to learn of them. I *have* them."[41] What Wittgenstein means here is that the idea that I have to perceive my own pain—on a mental analogy with seeing a table or a chair—makes no sense. I don't perceive my pain, identify it as such, and then describe it. "The verbal expression of pain replaces crying and does not describe it."[42] If I needed a criterion of identity for the sensation, then the possibility for error also exists. But that makes no sense. If someone is uncertain whether or not he is in pain, "we should think something like, he does not know what the English word 'pain' means; and we should explain it to him."[43] I am in pain or not, but this is not something I perceive (else I could be mistaken in my perception).

Our concept of pain is grounded in prelinguistic, instinctual behavior. I can express my pain verbally (by telling others about it) or nonverbally (by crying out), or I can try not to express it at all (hiding my pain). In the last case, I can be successful or not—depending on how strong the pain is and how stoic I am—and I can be successful with some people but not others (e.g., those who know me well or who are observing me closely). But this is not to say that my pain exists in a private realm to which I have privileged access. My sensations, emotions, and desires are not private in any philo-sophically interesting or problematic sense, but only in that they are *mine* and that I can conceal them. I need not always give them expres-sion. We no more perceive these alleged mental entities in our own case than we do in the case of others. Of myself, I use such words without justification, but "to use a word without a justification does not mean to use it without right."[44]

If it is wrong to suggest that "it is only from my own case that I know what the word 'pain' means," then it is equally wrong to say that I don't know if others are in pain, but merely infer that they have the same sensation that I do when I am in pain.[45] A small child falls, skins his knee, and begins to cry. We say he is in pain and comfort him. It is logically possible that he is pretending to get attention or a treat of some sort. But absent some reason to think so, there would be no basis for us to have any doubt on the question. A person who expressed such doubts would either be a monster of insensitivity or simply ignorant of the meaning of the term. "Just try—in a real case—to doubt someone else's fear or pain."[46] Absent some reason for doubt, I do know when others are in pain or angry or in love. I know quite a bit about others by observing them: how they feel, when they are happy or ashamed or hurt. "It is correct to say 'I know what you are thinking,' and wrong to say 'I know what I am thinking.' (A whole cloud of philosophy condensed into a drop of grammar.)"[47]

Third, because "my words for sensations [are] tied up with my natural expressions of sensation[,] ... my language is not a 'private' one."[48] That is to say, it is not private in the sense that the meaning of my words for sensations depend on "objects" that only I can experience directly. We have a strong inclination to say that "it is only from my own case that I know what the word 'pain' means."[49] But I don't learn the meaning of the word "pain" through a process of private ostensive definition. I don't attach a label to something that only I have and only I can perceive. As we saw above, meaning is dependent upon use and we use words according to rules. Obeying a rule is a practice, which is inherently public and shareable.

That is not to say that language must be shared. Someone can write in code in a private diary. But the code can be shared or broken. The language is not necessarily private in the sense that no one else could logically understand it because no one else has access to my immediate sensations and experiences. I don't need any criteria on which to base my statement, "I am in pain." But there *are* criteria in a man's behavior for his understanding a word and being able to use it correctly. Words acquire meaning by means of the conventions according to which we use them and these conventions cannot be irredeemably private because then no sense would attach to the distinction between performance in accordance with the conventions and performance which violates them. "Whatever is going to seem right to me is right. And that only means that here we can't talk about 'right.'"[50] Without a distinction between correct and incorrect performance the whole notion that one is using a word in accordance with certain conventions collapses and with it the notion that one has given any meaning to the word.

This is a very difficult concept because it appears that Wittgenstein is denying something that we all know to be the case: that the "word" pain refers to a sensation and, since I can feel only my own pain, not (except figuratively) someone else's, I can know what pain means only by reference to my own sensations. If I want to assign "S" to a particular sensation I can do so, perhaps by focusing my attention on that sensation and repeating the word and then reusing the word whenever the sensation reappears. And "S" will necessarily refer to something that only I have and that only I can know.

But "when one says 'He gave a name to his sensation' one forgets that a great deal of stage-setting in the language is presupposed if the mere act of naming is to make sense."[51] When we say that "S" refers to a sensation, that "shows the post where the new word is stationed."[52] "What reason have we for calling 'S' the sign for a *sensation*? For 'sensation' is a word of our common language, not of one intelligible to me alone. So the use of this word stands in need of a justification which everybody understands."[53] Well, we respond, he obviously has something. But "has" and "something" also belong to our common language. "One gets to the point where one would like just to emit an inarticulate sound.—But such a sound is an expression only as it occurs in a particular language-game, which should now be described."[54]

Wittgenstein asks us to consider that the "private thing" that we each want to insist that we have is like an object in a box: no one can look in anyone else's box and everyone says he knows what the object is only by looking in his own box. I therefore cannot know for sure whether any other person has the same thing in his box that I have in mine. But if we still use the word in the language, then the word would not be used as the name of that thing in the box. "The thing in the box has no place in the language-game at all;...it cancels out, whatever it is. That is to say: if we construe the grammar of the expression of sensation on the model of 'object and designation' the object drops out of consideration as irrelevant."[55] That doesn't mean the *pain* is irrelevant. It doesn't mean that the word "pain" does not refer to the sensation of pain. But it does mean that we can't construe our expressions about pain on the model of object and designation. "A nothing would serve just as well as a something about which nothing could be said."[56]

So what do these three points add up to? When I was in second grade, we were shown a movie about the brain. In the movie, the brain was portrayed as a sophisticated control room, with lots of data signals pouring in from the outside and a little man sitting at the desk viewing the signals and responding by pulling various levers. This homunculus (little man) was apparently intended to be the mind: the one in charge, but trapped inside the body and dependent upon it for information about the world. I wondered even at the time whether there was supposed to be another little man inside the brain of the homunculus, and so on, in an infinite regress of Russian dolls or Chinese boxes.

Wittgenstein's point is that the Augustinian picture, applied to words for feelings, emotions, sensations, and various mental states, leads us inexorably toward a homunculus theory of the mind—in which mental objects are perceived on analogy with physical objects, only somehow more directly and indubitably known: a privileged mental world that interacts only uneasily with the physical one. Such a view doesn't just push the need for explanation back a level, it is incoherent. It bears no relation to how we actually use these words, and it detracts from our appreciation of the wonderful complexity of human beings. We don't need an "explanation" here of how the mind is possible and how it interacts with the physical world. The quest for such an explanation leads to an array of theories that, however sophisticated in development, are literally nonsense and don't in any event address the amazing capacity of human beings to think and laugh and love and desire and strive; all of which are dependent in their more complex forms on man's development of language, which has vastly expanded his range of expression and hence his consciousness of himself and the world around him. (An infant can reach for and want a toy; but only a child with language can want an Xbox for Christmas.)

When I was a student of philosophy, I puzzled over the development of consciousness. It seemed to constitute a fundamental leap in evolution, a gap in nature between unthinking animals and thinking human beings. But I was in the grip of a picture of consciousness as a separate, immaterial realm and could not see how that separate realm could suddenly spring into being. There is indeed a gap between man and the animals but it lies in the amazing complexity of thoughts and feelings that man can experience and express through his development of language. Thoughts didn't preexist language, which was simply developed as an efficient means for their expression. Language and the ability to think and feel and perceive the world in ever more complex ways developed together. That is indeed a subject

of wonder and amazement; but not of explanations of the sort proffered in philosophy.

Yes, you will object, but man's development can be explained by
evolutionary biology and contemporary neuroscience. In a sense this
is true. Evolutionary biology can explain the increasing sophistication
of man's adaptations and neuroscience can explain the development
and capacities of the brain. But even if a complete such account were
offered, it would not explain the soul of man. It would not explain the
spirit of man. It would not even explain the mind of man. For these
terms, "soul," "spirit," and "mind," do not refer to the cerebral cortex,
just as "anger," "love" and "pain" do not refer to the firing of specific
neurons (which may or may not be contingently related to such emotions and sensations). Again, we cannot construe such terms on the
model of object and designation, only this time replacing physiolog-
ical objects and processes for mental ones. The language games are
distinct and one cannot be reduced to or (given the vague boundaries
of family resemblance concepts) definitively mapped on the other.
"Only of a living human being and what resembles (behaves like) a
living human being can one say: it has sensations; it sees; is blind;
hears; is deaf; is conscious or unconscious."[57] We don't say that the
brain sees or feels or hears or is conscious. We say these things of
living human beings. "The human body is the best picture of the
human soul."[58] We see there joy and sorrow, pain and pleasure,
longing and fulfillment. But the vocabulary of the soul is not
reducible to the vocabulary of either the body or the brain. If we
want an exploration of the soul we need to turn not to B. F. Skinner or
Daniel Dennett, but to Shakespeare and Proust and Henry James.

THE AUTONOMY OF GRAMMAR

Since Descartes, much of philosophy has been concerned with the
foundations of knowledge. Why are we justified in accepting the various sciences as bodies of knowledge about the world? How can we
even be sure that the external world, the world outside the mind, actually exists and truly corresponds to our impressions of it? On what
basis are we justified in concluding that other people also have minds

and internal experiences comparable to our own? A succession of philosophers either provided theories to answer these questions (to bridge the apparent gap between impressions and knowledge) or adopted more or less skeptical responses to them.

Wittgenstein seeks to clear away both the theories and the skepticism by showing that the questions themselves stem from the same deeply embedded, Augustinian conception of language. The search for indubitable foundations is a search for a single, idealized sort of justification. It is born of a failure to recognize the varying criteria for what constitutes knowledge within our many different language games, including our standard discourse about the physical world and the thoughts and feelings of other people, as well as more organized bodies of knowledge in mathematics and the natural sciences. There is no "gap" between experience and knowledge because what counts for knowledge in a particular language game is tied by grammar to what we experience. If we focus on how we actually use words, then the apparent problems simply disappear. They are shown, like the mind-body problem, to rest on a misleading picture of how words get their meaning and what counts for certainty in the language game in question.

But if we constantly fall back on our ordinary use of words as a means of dissolving philosophical problems, then the question naturally arises: what is the basis for that usage? If our various claims to knowledge all float on a series of grammatical rules governing our use of words, how can we know that those grammatical rules are themselves justified? How can we know that our grammar correctly mirrors reality?

Wittgenstein's answer here will again appear paradoxical, at least until one reorients one's thinking in accordance with it. Language cannot be justified by reality because all justification takes place within language. The rules of grammar are themselves constitutive of what we accept as justification. The aim of grammar is nothing but that of language. "Grammar does not tell us how language must be constructed in order to fulfill its purpose, in order to have such-and-such an effect on human beings. It only describes and in no way explains the use of signs."[59]

In stressing the autonomy of grammar, Wittgenstein is not denying that language allows us to make true statements about the world. He is not denying that our words refer to objects with an existence outside of language. The point is rather that language is not laid over reality in a fixed and predetermined way. The connection between language and reality is itself made in language and, *pace* Augustine, merely pointing to objects does not determine the meaning of words that refer to them. Augustine describes the learning of language "as if the child came into a strange country and did not understand the language of the country; that is, as if it already had a language, only not this one."[60] Augustine, in other words, acts as if the places for the words were already prepared, and only the particular labels were needed. In a more extreme sense, this is Plato's view: the places for our words are metaphysically predetermined; the words are simply labels applied to the forms.

But pointing to an object does not by itself fix the place of the word for that object, because "an ostensive definition can be variously interpreted in *every* case."[61] The pointing gesture itself is not unambiguous: Is the teacher pointing to the shape? The color? The number? To the object as a whole or only part of it? The pupil may or may not guess correctly. But what is it that determines whether or not he has guessed correctly? What is it that determines what is signified by a word? What else but its use, its place in the system of language. If one says, "This is sepia," pointing to an object, it is not at all clear how I am to understand this. But, if I know that "sepia" is a word for a color (if I know something of its relation to other words), then the ostensive definition will be of help to me. An ostensive definition explains the use—the meaning—of the word only when the overall role of the word in language is clear.[62]

Wittgenstein rejects the suggestion that an ostensive definition takes us outside language and makes a language-independent connection with the world. Ostensive definition uses a sample as an instrument of language.[63] It states a rule for translating from a gesture language into a word language. But it is only language that renders the act of pointing articulate, that divides and organizes the world in such a way that we can point to a part of it and communicate something with that action. The nature of the object correlated with a word is not given through the mere act of pointing and saying "This is ..." or "This is a ..." The nature of the object is given by the place of the word in the system of language, by its grammar, and an ostensive definition is but a contribution to that grammar, a contribution that is subordinate to the overall grammar of the word.

Wittgenstein accordingly rejects the Platonic notion that the rules for the use of a word follow from, are read off, the nature of the object and that we absorb these rules merely by becoming acquainted with the object. Both Wittgenstein and Plato believe that essence is expressed by grammar; that is, that the rules for the proper use of a word reflect the essence of the object (for Plato, the "form") to which the word refers. But Wittgenstein turns Plato on his head. Essence is expressed by grammar, not because our language mirrors—and is dictated by—the essential prelinguistic structure of the world, but rather because what counts as "the world" is itself given in our language. What we might be tempted to call the necessary features of our world are but a reflection of the conventions according to which we use words. "What looks as if it *had* to exist, is part of the language."64

That the objects signified by our use of words must have certain essential qualities is readily apparent, for if calling an object "a book" did not entail certain things about the nature of that object then the word "book" would be vacuous. It would convey no information. If communication is to be possible, the words for objects must be used according to certain conventions. That is not to say that the line of distinction between "essential" and "inessential" properties is a sharp one. But there must be certain distinctions upon which the use of words turns. Their place in the system of language must, to some extent, be determined.

As with "objects," the essential nature of sensations, emotions, desires, and character traits is also given by grammar, which ties those terms to certain behavioral criteria. As discussed in the last section, their essence is not revealed by introspection, any more than the essence of objects is revealed through ostensive definition. This is the point of Wittgenstein's claim that "it shows a fundamental misunderstanding, if I am inclined to study the headache I have now in order to get clear about the philosophical problem of sensation."65 So-called ontological questions, questions about the essential nature of that which exists, cannot be answered by a direct examination of things, but only through an examination of linguistic conventions, of the way we talk about things.

It is, moreover, these linguistic conventions that determine what constitutes justification within a particular language game. If two English speakers have a dispute over the color of a book, when the book is produced the dispute will be settled. It will be settled, not because the facts speak for themselves but because we have mastered the technique of speaking about the facts according to grammatical conventions. Without agreement as to those conventions it would not even be possible for us to disagree as to the facts.

These same conventions dispose of many of the classic philosophical "problems" about knowledge: our discourse about other minds is tied to behavioral criteria within grammar; so too is our discourse about objects and our sense impressions of those objects. There is no "gap" for philosophy to bridge, either in language or in experience. I don't "infer" that a chair is there from my sense impressions; I see it and I sit in it. I don't draw a cautious inference that my child is in pain when she falls and skins her knee; I comfort her. "What people accept as a justification—is shown by how they think and live."[66] That is reflected in our language, in what we call a justification or ground for a belief.

Skepticism on such matters is not just artificial; it is incoherent. "If anyone said that information about the past could not convince him that something would happen in the future, I should not understand him.... What sort of information do you call a ground for such a belief? What do you call 'conviction'?"[67] These terms—grounds, conviction, explanation—all have meaning derived from their ordinary use, and that meaning varies depending upon the language game in question. The criteria for their application in any particular instance are established in grammar, and it makes no sense to note that the criteria are present but the grounds are not. What constitutes an adequate explanation is determined within the particular language game in question. But the language game itself cannot be justified.

We cannot point to the world to justify our grammatical conventions because all justification takes place according to those grammatical conventions. "In giving explanations I already have to use language full-blown (not some sort of preparatory, provisional one)."[68] Whatever we say about the world, we are already employing a full-blown language in which that world is articulated, in which it is divided and organized. Our grammar is not dictated to us by the nature of reality; it is constitutive of what we call reality. It is in this sense that the formation of grammatical conventions, of new uses of language, new "language games," must be regarded as free and spontaneous.[69]

But language neither developed nor exists in a vacuum. It did not, like Athena, spring full grown from Zeus's head. It cannot be molded into any shape whatsoever at the will of its creator. "What has to be accepted, the given, is—so one could say—*forms of life.*"[70] Language is an intrinsic part of the complex organism that is man and that evolved with him, and the way language meshes with life is infinitely various. When Wittgenstein equates meaning with use he intends to include under the heading of use the way in which language meshes with life, the whole context in which individual acts of communication take place. Not only does our talk get its meaning from the rest of our proceedings, but the concepts we have, the distinctions we make with grammatical conventions, are a reflection of our interests and needs, of what is important to us and this, in turn, is a product of our nature and the nature of the world in which we live. Language is embedded in human life and activity and if certain general facts of nature were different (including facts about human nature) then human life and activity and with them, language, would have to be correspondingly different. (One senses this in a modest way in learning a foreign language: to the extent one speaks that language one experiences the world in a different way, from a different perspective; one's form of life has subtly shifted.)

But it must be remembered that in discussing the general framework of human experience within which language developed we are already using our language. We are not stepping outside it and comparing it with something distinct from it. Whenever we say anything about the world, that "world" is being filtered through our language. That is not to suggest that we are somehow trapped in our own language. "The great difficulty here is not to represent the matter as if there were something one *couldn't* do."[71] We can talk about the links between language and the world; about forms of life and how language would be different if certain general facts of nature were different; about the empirical question whether the languages of various human societies are sufficiently different to reflect radical divergencies in the structure of their experience and their worldview; about difficulties of translation; about how language might have developed. But in doing so we are already using a full-blown language. Language, to echo Heidegger, is always, already there.

The "autonomy of grammar" appears to be a bold philosophical theory. But I should stress, again, that Wittgenstein's point is primarily negative. By focusing on how we actually use words, by developing an overview of how words develop their meaning, he is trying to show the futility of the standard philosophical search for the foundations of knowledge. The autonomy of grammar is not intended as a philosophical thesis but rather as a constant reminder that it makes no sense to purport to justify the very grammatical conventions that give content to the concept of "justification." We cannot penetrate through language to a hidden realm, a realm reserved for philosophers, in which the true nature of virtue, beauty, and truth are revealed, and with which we can compare language (as we can compare an empirical proposition with the world in order to determine its truth or falsity). We cannot even point to ordinary physical "facts" about the world to justify our grammar because it is grammar that divides and organizes those facts and establishes any necessary connections among them. In short, our language games can receive neither an external justification nor an external condemnation. Justification comes to an end within those language games. "If I have exhausted the justifications I have reached bedrock, and my spade is turned. Then I am inclined to say: 'This is simply what I do.'"[72]

THE END OF PHILOSOPHY

I have said that Wittgenstein turns Plato on his head. This is nowhere clearer than in his conception of philosophy. For Plato, our everyday beliefs and what passes for knowledge are simply a play of shadows in the cave where we are shackled by our ignorance. The philosopher is the one who breaks those shackles and works his way out of the cave into the clear light where he can directly contemplate the forms, the sources of all true knowledge.

For the later Wittgenstein, the philosopher is one who starts in the light of everyday language and descends into a cave of darkness and confusion where he chases the shadows cast by our grammar, which he mistakes for essential truths about the metaphysical structure of the world. Wittgenstein wants to take philosophy back into the sunlight, where one can obtain a perspicuous overview (*übersicht*) of how words are actually used in a particular language game.

"A philosophical problem," according to Wittgenstein, "has the form: 'I don't know my way about.'"[73] As Augustine explained in the *Confessions*: "What, then, is time? If no one asks me, I know; if someone asks me to give an account, I don't know."[74] Augustine is in the same position as the Socratic interlocutors, who find themselves unable to give an acceptable account of virtue or courage or beauty. They don't know their way about because Socrates insists that "to give an account" must involve pointing to something fixed and immutable to which the word corresponds and which determines its use in each instance. For Plato and later philosophers, an Augustinian conception of language leads inexorably to a view that we somehow have to penetrate through phenomena to the hidden reality behind them. "A *picture* held us captive. And we could not get outside it, for it lay in our language and language seemed to repeat it to us inexorably."[75]

For Wittgenstein, by contrast, "nothing is hidden."[76] The proper focus of philosophy is not on "something that lies *beneath* the surface ... and which an analysis digs out," but on "something that already lies open to view and that becomes surveyable by a rearrangement."[77] Everything relevant to resolving a given philosophical problem lies open to view if we can but break down the blinders that prevent us from seeing it. "It is ... of the essence of our investigation that we do not seek to learn anything *new* by it. We want to *understand* something that is already in plain view."[78]

Wittgenstein returns concepts home to their actual use in human life and practice, unfolding their richness and diversity, and acknowledging their indeterminacy and autonomy. The so-called solutions to philosophical problems are shown to be so much nonsense, as are the problems themselves, because meanings are not assigned to words by anything but our use of those words. "One must always ask oneself: is the word ever actually used in this way in the language-game which is its original home?"[79] By gaining an *übersicht* of the problematic concepts, by focusing on their actual use, both philosophical problems and their purported solutions disappear.

The concept of an *übersicht* is thus central to the later Wittgenstein. But it is not a matter of finally learning the real meaning of a philosophically troublesome concept. We are already able to use the concept by virtue of our mastery of English, and to possess that ability is the principal criterion for knowing its meaning. In gaining an *übersicht* we merely untangle certain confusions that arise when, in doing philosophy, we ignore the actual context—in language games and forms of life—in which words obtain their meaning. "Philosophy is a battle against the bewitchment of our intelligence by means of language."[80]

"Our investigation is therefore a grammatical one."[81] But Wittgenstein does not share the constructive aim of modern analytic philosophy (starting with Russell and Frege), which is to obtain a systematic overview of how language functions and forges its connection with the world. Because language is so complex and only loosely laced with rules, because the way it meshes with life is "infinitely various," Wittgenstein believes any attempt to give a systematic theory of meaning is bound to oversimplify and distort. Ambiguity, vagueness, indeterminacy, metaphor, simile, the "soul" of words; all these vital aspects of language to which Wittgenstein spends so much time trying to call attention, are inevitably trampled in the rush for clear-cut rules and sharp distinctions.

Any quest for a systematic theory of meaning is thus rejected by Wittgenstein in favor of "grammatical remarks," remarks on aspects of the use of words and expressions that we tend to overlook when doing philosophy, remarks made with an eye to particular philosophical confusions and illusions that must be resolved. For Wittgenstein this therapeutic task constitutes the entire scope of philosophy. "The philosopher's treatment of a question is like the treatment of an illness."[82] Philosophy isn't anything except philosophical problems, and the philosopher's sole task is the elimination of those problems.

Obviously, there is an article of faith, a positive doctrine, underlying this negative conception of philosophy. It is that genuine philosophical problems, that is, problems calling for answers rather than dissolution, cannot arise. It is one with the belief that "every sentence in our language 'is in order as it is'"[83] and that philosophical problems only arise "when language *goes on holiday.*"[84] When we bring language home, the philosophical problem simply disappears. This is the "real discovery" of which Wittgenstein speaks, "the one that makes me capable of stopping doing philosophy when I want to.... Instead, we now demonstrate a method, by examples; and the series of examples can be broken off."[85]

Before we accept that article of faith and conclude that Western philosophy has indeed run its course, three questions present themselves. *First*, isn't Wittgenstein begging the question? Even if ordinary language is in order as it is, the whole point of philosophy is to probe beyond our naive, everyday beliefs. It is true that in doing so we don't use words in their ordinary senses, but that is precisely the point. Philosophy wants to go beyond that ordinary use in order to put to the test our everyday beliefs and the naive worldview embodied in language. Putting the point in Wittgenstein's terms, why can't words be given a use, and hence a meaning, in the "language game" of philosophy, in which one reasons about the grounds for belief, the essence of thought, and the fundamental nature of reality?

This criticism, I am convinced, is wide of the mark. As an initial matter, it would be a mistake to suggest that Wittgenstein is somehow engaged in a defense of the commonsense beliefs, or world theory, embedded in our language. Beliefs are something we express, and theories something we construct, by means of language. But language itself does not embody any beliefs and it contains no theories that can be either right or wrong, correct or incorrect. Our language contains many concepts that philosophers are wont to puzzle over (e.g., "physical objects," "causes," "minds," "thoughts," "reality"). But concepts are not theories; they are tools of language that acquire their meaning based on their use and their place in our language games and forms of life. And, as we saw in the last section, we cannot justify our language games by reference to the world because all such justification takes place within language.

There are, moreover, no "super-concepts" that somehow transcend our ordinary usage and get at "the incomparable essence" of language, thought, and reality. "If the words 'language,' 'experience,' 'world,' have a use, it must be as humble a one as that of the words 'table,' 'lamp,' 'door.'"[86] We cannot abstract those words from the context that gives them meaning and the rules that govern their use and expect them to remain intelligible. Philosophical problems trade off the standard associations of a word, while at the same time using the word in a manner that standard usage will not support. Poets can get away with that; indeed, it is an essential element of their craft. Philosophers, however, purport to be doing more than developing elaborate metaphors. They purport to be saying something true about the essence of reality. Wittgenstein's point is that the word "reality" does not have a reference beyond its use in our everyday language. "I got it from there and nowhere else."[87] By patiently focusing attention on the actual use of the word, Wittgenstein can dissolve the philosophical "problems" surrounding it by showing that they rest on misunderstandings and grammatical confusions. "How can these explanations satisfy us?—Well, your very questions were framed in this language; they had to be expressed in this language, if there was anything to ask!"[88]

Wittgenstein does not deny that we want to press against the limits of language; that we have a longing for the transcendent. He simply denies that philosophy, as traditionally conceived, can satisfy that longing. "The results of philosophy are the uncovering of one or another piece of plain nonsense and of bumps that the understanding has got by running its head up against the limits of language."[89] It seems then that we are destroying everything that is constructive and beautiful in philosophy. But "what we are destroying is nothing but houses of cards and we are clearing up the ground of language on which they stand."[90] That is not to say that the works of Plato and his successors need to be boxed up and sent to the Salvation Army; but it may mean that we need to read them in a completely different way.

This point leads directly to the *second* question posed by Wittgenstein's negative account of philosophy. What about ethics and religion? Does Wittgenstein believe that they too are a product of grammatical confusion, of language gone on holiday? Would he sweep them away along with the philosophical houses of cards?

Surprisingly, Wittgenstein has very little to say about ethics and nothing to say about religion in the *Investigations*. But it is clear enough from his other writings that he considers them language games of overwhelming importance that are largely untouched by his critique of philosophy. Indeed, one might say that much of his point in clearing away the ground of language is to make room for, and allow a proper understanding of, both ethical and religious discourse.

The only remark Wittgenstein makes about ethics in the *Investigations* comes in section 77, where he is discussing family-resemblance concepts and the fact that any attempt to draw a sharp boundary where none has previously existed literally changes the concept in question. "It is clear," he explains, "that the degree to which the sharp picture *can* resemble the blurred one depends on the latter's degree of vagueness. . . . If the colors in the original merge without a hint of any outline won't it become a hopeless task to draw a sharp picture corresponding to the blurred one? . . . Anything—and nothing—is right.— And this is the position you are in if you look for definitions corresponding to our concepts in aesthetics or ethics."91

Wittgenstein's point here is not that ethical discourse has no meaning. We learn the meaning of words such as "good" from various examples in various language games. The word has a vital use in our language that is deeply embedded in our form of life. But it is an extreme example of a family-resemblance concept whose boundary applications are easily subject to dispute. The very terms Plato is most interested in defining exactly are, in Wittgenstein's view, the least susceptible to such precision, without a distortion in our ordinary use of them. We could draw such lines—and philosophers throughout history have tried to do so—but the result is prescriptive, not descriptive. Those philosophers are changing and, in most cases, impoverishing our ethical discourse by trying to impose upon it a rigidity that it will not properly bear.

Religious belief is not mentioned at all in the *Investigations*, and is discussed only in bits and snatches of lecture notes taken by others. But here, too, Wittgenstein seems to feel that the language game of religion—which includes prayer, confession, ritual, thanksgiving, meditation, etc.—is autonomous. It can neither be justified nor proven wrong. To adapt one of his remarks about language generally, "Philosophy may in no way interfere with [religious discourse]; . . . it cannot give it any foundation either. It leaves everything as it is."92 The religious person may be able to explain why his faith is important to him and what role it plays in his life. But such explanations take place within religious discourse; they presuppose the very faith in question. That faith cannot be given an independent justification. The religious person quickly reaches bedrock and his spade is turned, and he can only say, "This is simply what I do."[93] As we shall see in the next chapter, Immanuel Kant's view of religion has important affinities with that of Wittgenstein. But Friedrich Nietzsche's announcement of the death of God—his urgent plea to excise religious discourse from modern life—may be even closer.

The *third* question Wittgenstein's conception of philosophy raises is whether the game is worth the candle. The most Wittgenstein believes we can obtain is an *übersicht* of problematic concepts, thereby eliminating certain philosophical problems. But many of the problems he discusses (the nature of language, meaning, intent), although they preoccupied twentieth-century analytic philosophy, are not of particular interest to most readers. Other problems (the nature of thought, the relationship between mind and body) may be of more general interest. But here too all Wittgenstein will allow the philosopher is to clean up the mess from sloppy thinking and eliminate the back seepage of bad philosophy into psychology and neuroscience.

The philosopher as janitor? The philosopher as plumber? Worthy tasks, perhaps, in their own way, but hardly an adequate job description for the heirs of Socrates. There is no theory construction; no positive accumulation of knowledge about the essential nature of reality, the existence of God, or the duties of man. Wittgenstein himself asks somewhat plaintively at one point, in discussing his concept of an *übersicht:* "Is this a 'Weltanschauung'?"[94] That is, is this the sort of "worldview" for which philosophers have long struggled?

I would suggest that it is. We noted at the outset that philosophy begins in a sense of wonder and generally ends in the ruins of theory. Wittgenstein was determined to preserve, and even recapture, that sense of wonder about everyday human life on earth rather than to dissipate it with false explanations and nonsensical theories. He notes that when we do philosophy, when we try to construct explanations of the traditional sort, "we fail to be struck by what, once seen, is most striking and most powerful."[95] The autonomy of our language games and forms of life can be seen as a sort of miracle, a subject of endless fascination and amazement. Gaining an *übersicht* of those practices and of the ways we are apt to misunderstand them when doing philosophy is far more conducive to wisdom than constructing illusory scaffolding to constrain and support them.

It is in this sense that Wittgenstein keeps faith with Socrates. Wittgenstein, like Socrates, seeks wisdom rather than knowledge. He directs his attention to man's institutions, his rituals, his beliefs, and, most important of all, to the language in which he establishes those institutions, conducts those rituals, and expresses these beliefs. Language constitutes a tremendous evolutionary extension of human life and activity. Man's soul developed with his language and Wittgenstein studies the soul by means of language games and the forms of life with which they are interwoven. He seeks, not a new theory, nor new knowledge, but clarity and understanding. He seeks an *übersicht* of the language games and forms of life that are the expression of the soul of man, believing that, with the attainment of such an *übersicht* will come the wisdom for which philosophers have always striven and for which, because it cannot be presented as a fixed body of doctrine, each one of us must strive anew.

PART TWO

WHAT MAY I HOPE?

W hether God exists is in some ways the most compelling, and in others the least consequential, of philosophical questions. If a higher power to which we must answer has endowed us with an immortal soul and provides the ultimate meaning of our lives, then to divine God's intent and live accordingly is our most urgent task. At the same time, the laws of nature, the demands of morality, and even the richness of our personal experiences and relationships might seem entirely unrelated to the theoretical question of God's existence. It does not disparage those who claim religion as a transformative influence in their daily lives to note that many if not most of the determinants of our behavior are nonreligious.

Still, we must each answer this question as best we can. Declining to take a position (agnosticism) is already an answer of sorts. Either God is an acknowledged presence in our lives or not. Either death is a transition from one mode of conscious, individual existence to another or death is a final annihilation and, as Thoreau put it, we are "ploughed into the soil for compost."

Religious thought typically takes one of three approaches to the question of God. First, fundamentalism posits a God with an attitude, a God who issues commandments and actively intervenes in the world. We pray to the fundamentalist God to take our side in life and to reward our obedience after death. The fundamentalist God has revealed himself and his wishes through one or more texts, such as the Hebrew Bible, the New Testament, or the Koran, which are to be taken, more or less literally, as a guide to God's favor. The greatest of the fundamentalist theologians is Thomas Aquinas (1225–1274), whose *Summa Theologica* aspires to Aristotelian thoroughness and clarity, but who also writes that the pleasures of the saved after death will be augmented by their vision of the sufferings of the damned, the better to admire God's justice.

The second approach celebrates a God who underwrites, but does not intervene in, the world. This is the God of Benedict Spinoza (1632–1677), who believes not in everyday miracles (divine events that override the laws of nature) but in the miracle of the everyday. For Spinoza, God is immanent in all things and our sense of awe and mystery in the face of nature is both the beginning and the end of religious thought. Religion for Spinoza is a matter of internal transformation, a change of perspective on the world, not an expectation of divine intervention. Kant is deeply influenced by Spinoza. He dismantles all the traditional arguments for the existence of God and disparages as childish superstition the idea of a personal God to whom we pray for favors. Nevertheless, Kant argues forcefully that God is a living presence in the universe and that only immortality can make sense of our existence as moral beings.

The third approach is atheism (or agnosticism, which amounts to nearly the same thing). The atheist finds the hypothesis of God neither helpful nor instructive, but all too often a force for ignorance and violence. A rash of recent books, by Sam Harris, Daniel Dennett, Richard Dawkins, Christopher Hitchens, and others, promotes atheism. They present compelling arguments against fundamentalist religious belief but stop there, as if the death of the fundamentalist God were an endpoint, rather than—as Nietzsche thinks—the beginning of the inquiry. Far from treating the death of God with smugness and complacency, Nietzsche believes it signals a crisis in thought that necessitates a complete revaluation of values.

In some ways, I have biased my inquiry by juxtaposing Nietzsche with Kant, rather than with Aquinas or some fundamentalist thinker for whom God can and does actively intervene in the world. I will

PART TWO: WHAT MAY I HOPE?

confess at the outset my firm belief, with Kant, that the idea of a personal God who concerns himself with the wants, needs, and foibles of every human being (not to mention every sparrow that falls) is a childish superstition (though one that, with my Catholic upbringing, it is very hard to shake). But for that very reason, Hitchens and company are the ones who bias the inquiry by setting their atheism against the straw man of fundamentalism (the philosophical equivalent, after Kant, of shooting fish in a barrel). The only God that seems to me a strong counter to atheism is the God of Spinoza and Kant. Accordingly, that is the God I present in chapter 3 and against whom I make Nietzsche do battle in chapter 4.

A common graffiti when I was in college read "'God is dead'— Nietzsche," to which others would append "'Nietzsche is dead'— God." The paradox is that, if Nietzsche is correct, then God is, too. But if God is correct, then so too must be Nietzsche. Only if both are wrong is the immortality that religion promises, and without which it is a delusion, still in play.

CHAPTER THREE
KANT AND THE LEAP OF FAITH

I have . . . found it necessary to deny knowledge, in order to make room for faith.[1]

Immanuel Kant is, or ought to be, the patron saint of all late bloomers. Had he died in early 1781, just short of his fifty-seventh birthday (an age that already exceeded the average life span of his contemporaries), he would have been, at best, a short footnote in the history of philosophy. Instead, he published his hastily composed, but much considered masterwork, *Critique of Pure Reason*, later that year, and over the remaining twenty-three years of his life, he produced book after book that revolutionized philosophy.

Kant was born on April 22, 1724, in Konigsberg, the capital of East Prussia and a small but not insignificant trading center on the Baltic Sea. (The town no longer exists, having been largely destroyed during World War II and replaced with the Russian naval base of Kalingrad.) Although his mind traveled over the entire span of human knowledge, he himself never strayed far from the town of his birth. He was the fourth of nine children to survive childhood. His father was a harness maker. Both parents were devout pietists (a movement within Lutheranism that stressed each individual's direct relationship with God and was hostile to any attempt to intellectualize faith). He received a heavily religious education, in the clutches, as he himself put it, of "pietist fanatics," before starting at the University of Konigsberg at the age of sixteen.

Unable to obtain an academic position upon graduation, he worked for years as a private tutor. At the age of thirty-one, he was finally appointed a "private docent," a position that gave him no salary but allowed him to give public lectures for which he could charge a fee. Fortunately, his lectures (on a range of subjects including mathematics, physics, and geography as well as philosophy) were extremely popular, with students arriving as much as an hour early to secure a seat. He also began to make a name for himself with his writings. After turning down several offers from other cities, he became a university professor of logic and metaphysics in 1770, at the age of forty-six.

Kant was small (5'2") and slight, with a narrow and sunken chest, but attractive features. Although he was extremely sensitive to changes in his environment and could not bear vigorous physical exercise, he was, as he explained, "healthy in a weak way." He was also extremely sociable. Elegant in dress and manner, he dined in society on a regular basis, played at cards, and went to the theater. He was so fond of good wine that he reportedly had problems on occasion finding his way back to his modest lodgings after an evening out. He was much sought after by Konigsberg society for his wit and brilliant conversation.

But Kant's behavior underwent a dramatic change in his forties. He felt the need, then, to regularize his conduct and began to live according to carefully considered "maxims," rational principles to regulate his behavior. From this time dates the story that the wives and burghers of Konigsberg could set their clocks by the regularity of his daily, solitary walk. Kant's maxims gradually squeezed out much of his social life, and he focused more and more on developing his thoughts. He went through a quiet period of almost ten years during which he wrote very little, leading up to the *Critique of Pure Reason*.

Immanuel Kant died on February 12, 1804. Inscribed on his tombstone, which can still be seen, adjacent to the reconstructed cathedral in Kalingrad, are words that summarize the great preoccupations of his life and work: "Two things fill the mind with ever new and increasing admiration and awe, the oftener and more steadily we reflect on them: the starry heavens above me and the moral law within me."[2] Kant lived in a Newtonian universe of rigid, mechanical causation in space and time. Yet he also believed in the ability of humans to act freely in accordance with the precepts of a binding moral law. He based his belief in God on that moral freedom. Kant thus found himself with a need to limit the realm of the natural sciences (the realm of knowledge) in order to make room for faith. At the same time, he was hostile to organized religion insofar as it was dogmatic and sought to impede the free exercise of reason and the development of the natural sciences. Thus, while he set limits on knowledge to make room for faith, he also, with equal if not greater vigor, set limits to faith to make room for knowledge. In this, he was a true child of the Enlightenment.

Kant himself said that the *Critique of Pure Reason* was attempting to affect a Copernican revolution in thought. By this he meant that traditional metaphysics treated the mind as merely a stationary mirror of reality, which revolved around it; whereas he treated the mind as an active, moving force. But the analogy is misleading. Copernicus replaced a worldview in which Earth was the center of the universe, with one in which Earth was but a speck of dust whirled about a random star in a random corner of a random galaxy. Kant, by contrast, restored man to the center of his universe by focusing upon the shaping power of his own reason in creating that universe as it is known to him. He believed that the structure of that universe is provided by the categories of our understanding, which offer necessary truths about the world in space and time, and provide a solid foundation for the natural sciences. At the same time, Kant traced the boundaries of human reason, from the inside so to speak, in such a way as to leave open at least the possibility of a realm outside those boundaries, a realm in which God, freedom, and immortality—while not objects of knowledge—could remain as objects of belief.

A better analogy for Kant's work might be to the nebular hypothesis, for which Kant shares credit with the subsequent work of Pierre-Simon Laplace. According to that theory, Earth's solar system was formed from a gaseous cloud (solar nebula) that rotated, slowly at first but with increasing speed as it gradually collapsed and flattened through the force of gravity to form stars and planets. In Kant's view, the categories of our own understanding impose a necessary order and structure on the world, such as to make it an object of possible experience and possible knowledge. Our reason is the shaping force through which we know the world, and to which the world insofar as it is an object of knowledge must conform. That theory, which has flattened and collapsed the boundaries of our known world, has also led to the increased speed of modern intellectual life, in which man's free-form recasting of his experience has often threatened to spin out of control.

RATIONALISM AND EMPIRICISM

Kant's writings are among the most fascinating in all of philosophy, but they are not for the faint of heart. His thinking is always intricate, his prose is often labored, and his basic doctrines seem at crucial points absurd. But the same might be said of Einstein, and as we will see there are some interesting parallels between the two thinkers, despite their completely different approaches to understanding the underlying nature of reality. Carefully considered and understood in context, Kant's work is deeply compelling and in one form or another has shaped our modern consciousness.

As he explains in the preface to the first edition of the *Critique of Pure Reason*, "the chief question [for the philosopher] is always simply this: what and how much can the understanding and reason know apart from all experience?"[3] Kant, in his capacity as a philosopher, is not interested in what we can learn *from* experience. That is the realm of the scientist. Kant wants to know what we can know "*a priori*," that is, apart from and prior to experience.

That may seem an odd question. We are deeply steeped in an empiricist tradition in which all knowledge is thought to derive from experience. But Kant believes that experience itself—to be intelligible to us—has a necessary form and structure and that the philosopher, by exploring that form and structure, can thereby chart the boundaries of *possible* experience. In the process, the philosopher gains certain knowledge; knowledge that must be universally true of all experience because it is a condition of experience. In this way, the philosopher can simultaneously refute the claims of the skeptics—who refuse to acknowledge even the possibility of objective knowledge—and the metaphysicians, who would go beyond the boundaries of possible knowledge.

Does that sound familiar? It might well, since Wittgenstein has a similar agenda in the *Tractatus*. But Kant's own agenda must be understood in his own historical context, which includes the competing schools of philosophy (rationalism and empiricism) that he combats and the Newtonian physics for which he attempts to provide a solid foundation. Understood in that context, we end up finding Kant much closer to the later Wittgenstein in his appreciation of man's autonomy as a thinker and creator of his world.

Kant's mature philosophy is formed in immediate reaction to two other thinkers. The first, Gottfried Leibniz (1696–1716), is a proponent of rationalism. Leibniz believes that we can ascertain necessary truths about reality through the exercise of reason alone. Correspondingly, he denigrates the world of commonsense experience as one of mere appearance. Reality is known only through the direct perception of certain innate ideas that are part of our birthright as rational beings. Leibniz argues that space and time have no objective reality; they are merely relations between what we perceive as physical objects and events. We have knowledge of reality independent of space and time, and hence independent of the material world, because we have knowledge of our own core being, the "I" that thinks and reasons. For Leibniz, this reality consists of "monads," irreducibly simple, eternal centers of force and thought that are arranged and harmonized by God. Even though we humans appear to interact in the world of mere appearance, the monads themselves do not interact. They float in isolation, beguiled by appearances, but with access through reason to a parallel, more genuine reality. (Now you know where the idea for *The Matrix* came from.) It is the philosopher's job to adopt the perspective of God and to understand the laws and principles (mathematical, logical, and moral) according to which he has ordered reality.

The second philosopher against whom Kant reacts is David Hume (1711–1776), who is at the opposite extreme from Leibniz. For Hume, there is no such thing as objective knowledge. All beliefs come from sense experience and hence are dependant upon the subjective perceptions of the observer. Reason cannot operate without ideas, which are themselves acquired through the senses. Thus, all individual beliefs must be warranted by subjective sense impressions. Necessity is to be found only in the relations of ideas, not in the world. In this sense, all knowledge is *a posteriori* (after experience) rather than *a priori* (prior to experience). These views lead Hume to a radical skepticism. The physical world is only a construct of my individual sense impressions. We have no knowledge that objects exist independent of our observations of them. Nor do we have knowledge that the law of cause and effect—which is only a by-product of the association of ideas—will hold true in future experience. Even the "I," which is the possessor of all my thoughts and experiences, is only a construct. We have no direct knowledge of an immaterial self that persists through time.

Kant is leery of the claims of Leibniz. But it is Hume who he says has awoken him from a "dogmatic slumber." Kant considers it a scandal that philosophy is unable even to acknowledge the claims to genuine knowledge provided by Newtonian physics. Kant accordingly wants to provide a solid foundation for such knowledge and refute Hume's skeptical arguments. At the same time, he wants to banish the flights of pure fancy indulged in by Leibniz and other rationalists.

EMPIRICAL REALISM

Kant's solution to the dilemma posed by Hume and Leibniz lies in his recognition that neither experience nor reason alone provides knowledge. Both are needed and both make a critical contribution. "Without sensibility," he explains, "no object would be given to us, without understanding no object would be thought."[4] In the first point, he agrees with Hume that experience is critical to give content to our concepts. But the second point is much more subtle: what Kant suggests is that there is no such thing as unfiltered experience. Experience is intelligible to us only because our understanding acts upon it and orders it by way of concepts.

Here, we need to introduce some Kantian terminology. Kant is very much focused on mental faculties. The key ones are sensibility and understanding. Sensibility operates upon what Kant calls intuitions (what Hume calls sensations). Understanding operates upon concepts (what Hume calls ideas). Both are necessary, Kant tells us, for any sort of knowledge. "Thoughts without content are empty, intuitions without concepts are blind."[5] Concepts must be tied to intuitions in order to have any genuine content. But intuitions must be brought under concepts in order to be intelligible. The organization of intuitions into concepts is not a result of experience, as Hume thinks, but a necessary precondition of experience.

This is not to say that we don't make empirical judgments based, as Hume believes, on abstractions from sense impressions. But Kant believes that all such judgments have certain formal characteristics that correspond to the categories of our understanding. We impose these characteristics upon experience in making it an object of possible knowledge. Because the characteristics are the necessary conditions of knowledge, we can know them *a priori*. Those characteristics, however, have a subjective rather than objective source. They are essential to our experience not because they inhere in the objects of our understanding, but because they are inseparable from our understanding itself. If experience *has to be* a certain way in order for it to be intelligible to us, then those critical features of experience are something that we impose upon it, rather than derive from it. "We can know *a priori* of things only what we ourselves put into them."[6] There is a necessary order and structure to experience, but only because our understanding plays an active role in shaping that experience in order to make it intelligible to ourselves.

So what are these necessary features of experience? Kant argues that for experience to be intelligible, for it to be an object of possible knowledge, there must be an "I" that has the experience and an "it" that is experienced. More specifically, experience requires an "I" persisting through time, and it requires objects external to our consciousness that exist in space and time and that follow regular rules of causation and reciprocal interaction. This seems like a big jump, so let's take it one step at a time.

We'll start with space and time. Leibniz views space and time as simply abstractions from relations between objects and events, with no independent reality. For Kant, space and time are not abstractions *from* our perceptions, they are the necessary *forms* of all our perceptions. We can imagine space empty of objects, but we cannot imagine the nonexistence of space. Similarly, we can imagine time empty of events, but we cannot imagine any perception or experience that would not take place in time. In this, Kant is closer to Newton, who views space and time as absolutes: space is a limitless empty box in which the universe is placed; time is a cosmic clock ticking uniformly from and for all eternity. But Kant adds a dramatic twist to Newton. Newton's view, Kant thinks, involves the absurdity of two eternal and infinite self-subsistent nonentities that are there without anything real being there merely in order to receive everything real into themselves. Things exist in space. Events occur in time. Space cannot itself be a thing nor time an event. Kant accordingly concludes that space and time are neither objects of perception nor empirical concepts derived from experience. They are a necessary condition of objects and events as they appear to us. They are necessary features of our own sensibility.

This will seem bizarre, and it is, but bear with me, because modern physics is in some ways closer to Kant than to either Newton or Leibniz on this question. Much of the reason that Kant feels that time and space are features of our own sensibility (pure forms of perception rather than either objects perceived or relations between objects perceived) is that, without time and space, experience itself would be impossible because we would not be able to form a conception of objects distinct from our experience of them, which means we would not be able to form a conception of a self persisting through time that has these experiences. This is an intricate and absolutely brilliant point that still has philosophers marveling to this day.

Hume takes the intelligibility of sense impressions (intuitions) for granted. He assumes we can construct ideas of objects, on the one hand, and the self, on the other, from that raw, unfiltered data. But what Kant shows, and shows convincingly, is that Hume has it backward. The unity of consciousness "*precedes* all experience, and… makes experience itself possible."[7] My experience consists of the flow through time of my intuitions and thoughts (which together he refers to as representations). But they must all be "my" representations to allow me to impose an order upon them that makes them intelligible. "It must be possible for the 'I think' to accompany all my representations.... All the manifold of intuition has, therefore, a necessary relation to the 'I think' in the same subject in which this manifold is found."[8] Kant calls this, rather obscurely, the "unity of pure apperception," but the idea is quite simple: there must be a subject persisting through time that has all these representations. I don't develop the idea of that subject by combining various representations. Rather, the subject makes any such combination possible, by persisting through time and unifying the various representations. "We are conscious *a priori* of the complete identity of the self in respect of all representations which can ever belong to our knowledge, as being a necessary condition of the possibility of all representations."[9]

But, and here is the critical step, to support this concept of "self" it is also necessary to have the concept of something independent of the self. I have no perception of the "I" that has these experiences. How, then, am I able to think this "I" that cannot be intuited? Kant's insight is that the self can be understood and comprehended only in contrast to the external objects of experience. Experience must allow for a distinction between what is experienced and my experience of it. My experience must be understood as only one path through an objective world that exists independent of my experience. I must have experience of *something* distinct from myself, and persisting through time, about which I can make objective judgments. This is necessary if the degree of self-consciousness (these are all *my* representations) required for consciousness (the bringing of intuitions under concepts) is to be possible.

In some ways, what Kant is arguing can be seen as an early analogue of Wittgenstein's private language argument. Private intuitions (upon which Hume constructs all knowledge) are unintelligible standing alone; they must be brought under concepts that are public and shared and, as such, objects of potential knowledge. Hume, like Wittgenstein's private linguist, thinks that subjective intuition alone gives content to our concepts and hence that those concepts are themselves subjective. But for Kant, objective concepts are a precondition of any sort of intelligible experience. As Kant explains, "inner experience is itself possible only mediately, and only through outer experience."[10] Hume's "appearances might, indeed, constitute intuition without thought, but not knowledge; and consequently would be for us as good as nothing."[11] Or, as Wittgenstein more provocatively argues, "a nothing would serve just as well as a something about which nothing could be said."[12]

Thus, no intelligible experience is possible without such an objective ordering of objects in space and time. Continuity in consciousness—which is necessary to bring intuitions under concepts—presupposes continuity in the objects of perception. It follows, Kant thinks, that Hume is talking nonsense when he suggests that we have no knowledge of the existence of an external world separate from our intuitions. In fact, our intuitions are themselves intelligible only in the context of our knowledge of an external world. We have certain knowledge of the persistence of objects in space and through time because such knowledge is a precondition of intelligible experience. Moreover, Kant thinks, because space and time are necessary as the pure forms of perception, we can have necessary knowledge of certain axioms about space and time. We know that time is one dimensional, that it flows in one direction (the arrow of time), and we know that different moments in time are successive not simultaneous. We also know, thanks to Euclid, the geometry of space. Like Plato, Kant places critical reliance on geometry as a paradigm of *a priori* knowledge. But for Kant, the *a priori* geometry of space is explicable only as a necessary feature of our own sensibility that we impose upon experience.

Kant also believes that the external world must obey certain physical laws in order to be an object of knowledge and we can therefore know those laws *a priori* as well. Specifically, substance must persist through time with its "quantum in nature...neither increased nor diminished,"[13] and it must be subject to the laws of cause and effect and reciprocal interaction. Again, this is a big jump. But Kant's central argument seems sound. In order to develop the concept of an external world, the framework of space and time must provide a matrix for identifying objects as persisting through time. We need a stable backdrop against which change through time can be determined. That means that when objects change they must do so according to laws that we can comprehend. We will not be able to reidentify and relocate objects through time if substance simply disappears, if events happen without causes, and if objects do not stand in relation to, and react with, one another in space. We require an abiding, law-governed and unified world existing in space and time as the object of our experience in order for us to have any intelligible experience at all. We require, in short, Newton's billiard-ball universe, in which, if you knew the position and velocity of all particles in space at time A, you could predict with certainty their positions at any time B.

We will discuss some of the problems with this specifically Newtonian vision in our post-Einsteinian universe. But it is worth taking a moment first to marvel at Kant's accomplishment. He answers Hume's skepticism in convincing fashion and puts in its place an "empirical realism" that validates our standard conceptions of an external world persisting in space and time. By refocusing philosophy on the conditions of possible knowledge, he shows how certain *a priori* claims can be established and, in the process, changes man from a mere spectator into active participant in the process of imposing a conceptual order on the world. He provides an apparently solid foundation for the physical sciences. Yet, at the same time, he charts the outer bounds of such knowledge. And, in so doing, he lays the foundation for a devastating critique of speculative metaphysics, to which we will turn in the next section.

THE ILLUSIONS OF METAPHYSICS

The flipside of Kant's empirical realism is what he calls transcendental idealism. The choice of terms is unfortunate because it seems as if Kant is proposing an affirmative metaphysical doctrine. But the thrust of his transcendental idealism is supposed to be purely negative and cautionary. Beyond their empirical reach, our concepts have no meaningful application. We can know the conditions, and hence the limits, of possible experience, but we can never transcend those limits. That is, we cannot take our *a priori* concepts, abstract them from experience, and purport to form judgments about some ultimate, underlying reality. "The pure concepts of understanding can never admit of transcendental but always only of empirical employment."[14]

It follows, Kant thinks, that we can have no knowledge of things as they are in themselves. We know objects as they appear to us, as

they are shaped by the combined forces of our sensibility and understanding. Those objects are empirically real. They are not just constructs out of our sense perceptions because their objective reality is
necessary to a determination of our own existence through time. In
that sense, standard idealism is refuted. But we can still know them
only as objects of possible experience. They must be given to us in
perception. In that sense they are "transcendentally ideal." We have
no idea what they are in themselves, apart from our experience of
them. Indeed, the whole notion of an "object" has only empirical content and hence no legitimate application outside of experience. Thus,
the contrasting notion of things-in-themselves, or "noumena," as
Kant sometimes calls them, is a purely negative one. Noumena is "not
the concept of an object" but a "problem unavoidably bound up with
the limitation of our sensibility."[15] This problem tells us that we have
reached the limits of possible knowledge and ventured into a realm of
pure speculation.

Such ventures are inevitable and even admirable, but nonetheless
doomed to failure. "Human reason," Kant explains, "has this peculiar
fate that . . . it is burdened by questions which . . . it is not able to ignore,
but which, as transcending all its powers, it is also not able to
answer."[16] We feel that we can break free of everyday experience and
apply our reason to the reality that underlies experience. But pure
reason, untethered from experience, unconditioned by intuition, leads
only to fallacy and illusion.

> The light dove, cleaving the air in her free flight, and feeling its
> resistance, might imagine that its flight would be still easier in
> empty space. It was thus that Plato left the world of the senses, as
> setting too narrow limits to the understanding, and ventured out
> beyond it on the wings of the ideas, in the empty space of the pure
> understanding. He did not observe that with all his efforts he made
> no advance—meeting no resistance that might, as it were, serve as a
> support upon which he could take a stand, to which he could apply
> his powers, and so set his understanding in motion.[17]

Kant develops a typology of metaphysical illusions in a section
called the Transcendental Dialectic. The term "dialectic" is a direct
reference to Plato, who contends that the true nature of the forms can

be understood through a process of conceptual analysis abstracted from experience. Kant takes the *a priori* concepts derived from his analysis of possible experience and shows how, when applied beyond possible experience, they necessarily lead us astray. His true target in this section, however, is not Plato, but Leibniz.

Accordingly, Kant begins with the Leibnizian notion of a "monad," conceived of as a thinking substance that is absolutely simple in nature, that persists through time, and that would continue to exist even in the absence of a material world. You will recall that Kant considers the "unity of pure apperception" to be critical to any concept of experience. "I think" must be capable of accompanying all my representations. But this "I" that thinks is a purely formal concept, a requirement that a temporally extended series of experiences have sufficient unity and connectedness to constitute a single, subjective path through an objective world. The unity of apperception is not the perception of unity. The "I" is not itself a possible object of intuition.

Thus, the logical simplicity of my thought of my self does nothing to guarantee that that self is a simple substance (or indeed any kind of substance). The reason the thought is simple is that it is utterly abstract. It is given no content by means of intuition. It is merely the thought of that which thinks my thoughts. Similarly, the fact that this "I" is always the subject does not mean that the "I" is a persistent something. Nor is there any basis for concluding that this "I" would continue to exist in the absence of material things (including my own body). At the same time, there is no basis for concluding the opposite: that the "I" is not a simple substance, that it does not persist through time, and that it could not exist in the absence of material things. Kant rejects both Dualism and Materialism. Neither has any legitimate claim to knowledge. Both theories try to go beyond the legitimate application of our concepts to experience and hence, from the standpoint of reason, are purely speculative.

Kant draws a similar boundary for cosmological speculation. Here, he develops a series of "antinomies" in which he shows that once we go beyond the limits of Newtonian physics both a proposition and its apparent contradiction can lay an equal claim to validity, which is to say that neither is an object of knowledge. Kant focuses primarily on the world in space and time. He presents us with pairs of propositions such as: The world has a beginning in time; the world has no beginning in time. The world is limited as regards space; the world has no limits in space. Everything in space and time is composed of irreducible simples; everything in space and time is subject to infinite dissection.

Kant develops "proofs" for each of these propositions that consist largely in showing that the alternative is incoherent. For example: The world cannot have a limit in time because then it is always legitimate to ask what happened before that beginning; yet the world cannot be unlimited in time because it would then have no beginning leading to the present moment. The proofs themselves are far from convincing, but that is really part of the powerful point that Kant is making. Beyond the limits of possible experience *in* space and time, our standard concepts begin to break down, and it is difficult to make coherent and persuasive claims to knowledge. We are engaged largely in speculation. The proper role for the philosopher, then, is to keep away from both positions (finite and infinite). That is not to say that scientists cannot continue to expand our knowledge of space and time and the ultimate constituents of matter (though Kant himself is thoroughly embedded in Newtonian physics as a complete blueprint for possible scientific knowledge). But insofar as they make progress, scientists do so by giving experiential content to the expanding application of our concepts. Most philosophers, by contrast, attempt to divorce our concepts from the experience that gives them meaning and apply them outside the bounds of sense. Only illusion can result from such a practice.

Kant's third category in the typology of metaphysical illusion deals with the standard proofs for the existence of God. He exposes those proofs as thoroughly inadequate. God is not an object of theoretical knowledge, and yet Kant finds ample, alternative grounds for faith that depend precisely upon the limitations of our knowledge. Before we turn to Kant's leap of faith, however, it is worth exploring a bit further how the platform from which Kant takes that leap (his peculiar combination of empirical realism and transcendental realism) survives in a post-Newtonian universe.

KANT AFTER EINSTEIN AFTER WITTGENSTEIN

Most thinkers of Kant's day believe that Isaac Newton has solved all the basic problems of physics. Details remain to be filled in, but the central laws of the universe have been revealed and are subject to mathematical formulation. All events are strictly determined within the absolute grid of space and time. The planets follow a fixed course in the heavens based on the effects of gravity. The smallest elements of matter obey similar laws in their interactions. The universe is, in effect, a huge, three-dimensional billiard table, and if we know the position, size, and velocity of every particle at a given point in time, we can calculate the exact position of all those particles both back in time and into the future. Things get a bit fuzzy at the margins (the exact nature of the basic constituents of matter; how gravity is able to act on objects at a distance; what it means for space and time to be infinite, empty receptacles), but the essential principles are in place and are not going to change.

Kant finds these principles both exhilarating and debilitating— exhilarating, because their very simplicity and elegance render the universe comprehensible to man; debilitating, because the mechanistic nature of this universe leaves no room for human freedom or divine intervention. Kant's solution, as already noted, is to distinguish the sphere of science from the sphere of religion and morality. He does so by arguing that some of Newton's most fundamental principles—strict causation, the Euclidean grid of space, the mathematical sequence of time, the conservation of matter—do not apply to things as they are in themselves but rather are imposed on the world of experience by the action of our sensibility and understanding.

Despite the implausibility of this position, we have seen that Kant has some compelling arguments in its favor. But what happens to those arguments in a world of quarks, general relativity, alternative geometries, quantum mechanics, and string theory? Should Kant simply be dismissed as a quaint artifact of solely historical interest? No. Kant actually adapts to modern science in very interesting ways.

Take general relativity. Einstein showed, contra Newton, that space and time are not absolutes. They depend on the viewer's frame of reference, and measurements of time can be radically different for different observers, even though spacetime—in which time is conceived as a fourth dimension inextricably connected with the three dimensions of space—is invariable from every frame of reference. If anything, general relativity seems to fit more closely with the Kantian view that space and time are forms of our sensibility that we impose upon experience. In general relativity, space and time do not have existences independent of one another. They are not empty containers for objects and events but form a fabric of spacetime with its own shaping force imposed upon the objects of perception.

Alternative geometries can also be accommodated by Kant. Kant thinks Euclidean geometry is the *a priori* geometry of space. But non-Euclidean geometries, in which lines with a common perpendicular can converge or run away from one another, had not yet been discovered. The elliptic geometry of general relativity (in which spacetime is bent by the gravitational force of matter) can still fit, albeit less comfortably, within Kant's model of *a priori* knowledge.

But Kant seems wholly out of place in the subatomic world of quantum mechanics, in which the laws of causation (which Kant thinks are an *a priori* feature of experiential reality) break down altogether. Einstein himself launched quantum mechanics with his discovery that light simultaneously behaves like particles and waves. This insight led in turn to the realization that the behavior of subatomic "particles" is not strictly deterministic. Quantum reality obeys statistical laws, but not laws of rigid cause and effect. Heisenberg's "uncertainty principle" established that it is not possible to measure both the position and the velocity of a particle at the same time since the very act of measuring one changes the other. But this "uncertainty" is not just a limitation on our ability to know both position and velocity; it is a fundamental feature of quantum reality, in which it makes no sense to talk about a particle having an actual position until it is measured.

Einstein rejected the implications of quantum mechanics, famously opining that "God does not play dice with the universe."[18] He accordingly spent the last decades of his life searching for a "unified theory" that would reconcile general relativity (which works on vast scales), classical mechanics (which works very well on our everyday, human scale), and quantum mechanics (which works on a very small scale) in a single overarching system of equations that did not depend on probability and chance. He did not succeed, and in fact Einstein (the rebel *par excellence* who did more than anyone else to break with classical physics and usher in the modern age) was increasingly viewed by the young turks as a reactionary conservative.

But Einstein may turn out to have been right after all and so, in a curious way, may Kant. Certainly, the modern proponents of superstring theory believe that it is possible to unify all the known natural forces in a single set of equations by replacing pointlike particles with one-dimensional, extended objects known as strings. In the process, however, they have to posit (because otherwise their equations don't work) at least nine dimensions of space and one of time. Moreover, space turns out not to be empty after all, but is itself teeming with quantum irregularity (think of it as random wrinkles), which led to the formation of the stars, planets, and galaxies. The arrow of time turns out to be simply a function of gradually increasing entropy, as the universe steadily degenerates from the highly ordered state at its inception. And in string theory both space and time turn out not to be continuous, but rather to have a discontinuous, atomic structure.

More fundamentally, as Brian Greene, a leading string theorist, explains, string theory works on a scale at which the usual concepts of space and time may simply not apply. Space and time may only be "approximate, collective conceptions."[19] The unified spacetime of experience may be an "illusion" that "emerges from the collective behavior of strings."[20] This sounds very much like Kant's assertion that space and time are mere appearances that we impose upon experience. They are not fundamental features of reality, even though they have an "all-embracing position in experiential reality."[21] As Greene puts it, space and time are "silent, ever-present markers delineating the outermost boundaries of human experience."[22]

It is tempting, then, to view string theory as consistent with Kant's fundamental distinction between appearances (as shaped by our sensibility and understanding) and things in themselves (an underlying, unknowable reality). But that would be a mistake. String theory certainly runs counter to our everyday experience, as does quantum mechanics and even general relativity. But insofar as those theories are legitimate (and the legitimacy of string theory is still very much in dispute), they have an experimental and hence experiential content that keeps them on the "appearances" side of Kant's great divide. String theory doesn't uncover what Kant called "things in themselves" any more than classical mechanics did.

So when Brian Greene notes that "the overarching lesson that has emerged from scientific inquiry over the last century is that human experience is often a misleading guide to the true nature of reality,"[23] he is not making a Kantian point about phenomena and noumena. He is making a scientific point, which is that our intuitive sense of space and time and even of causation turn out not to be very accurate when investigating very small or very large events. That is a point that Kant could embrace, though not without significant adjustments to his *a priori* categories. Kant himself, as a fervent admirer of the Enlightenment, would never purport to impose limits on scientific inquiry. He simply supposes that there are fixed boundaries to possible human knowledge created by our own sensibility and understanding. What modern science indicates is that those boundaries may be much more fluid than he imagines. But Kant's essential point remains: through our concepts and the form of our judgments, we impose a certain order on the world and when we push those concepts beyond their application in experience they begin to break down. Not even string theory can give a coherent explanation of a time before time or of a condition before the universe was born.

So understood, Kant's fundamental insight into the shaping power of the human understanding is closer to Wittgenstein's than we might at first have supposed. Such a statement will appall Kant scholars as an anachronism. But I am primarily interested in the platform for Kant's leap of faith, and that platform in its essentials survives the buffeting of modern science and even the collapse of Newton's invisible cosmic scaffolding. To see why that is so, it is helpful to emphasize four significant common features between Kant and Wittgenstein.

First, both Kant and Wittgenstein agree that we impose order on the world through the formation of our concepts and judgments. Those concepts and judgments have an experiential content but they are not determined by experience; in part, at least, they are constitutive of what we call experience. Wittgenstein emphasizes the social nature of our concepts; he starts from the third-person plural (our common speech) and works backward. Kant focuses on the features of our understanding; he starts with the first-person singular (the "I" that thinks) and works outward. Remarkably, though, they end in a very similar place. Man is not a mere spectator but an active agent in the formation of the concepts and judgments that constitute our knowledge of the world.

Second, although both recognize our active role in the formation of these concepts and judgments, both also recognize that certain regularities are necessary to our ability to wield them. Kant thinks these regularities are unalterable features of experience (space, time, causation, the conservation of matter). Wittgenstein, by contrast, urges a much looser conception that is more appropriate to contemporary science. None of the features of our form of representation are immune to revision. But those features are grounded in our forms of life and certain regularities in nature. If nature were not in some degree governed by rules, we could not have the concepts and form the judgments that we do. That doesn't give us a rigid foundation for Newtonian physics, but it does supply a stable backdrop against which such theories can be formulated and tested and revised over time.

Third, both Kant and Wittgenstein want to put an end to the pretensions of traditional metaphysics by showing why such statements are only so much nonsense. Kant explains that metaphysics arises from the use of concepts beyond the sphere of experience that gives those concepts content. Wittgenstein calls the problem "language on holiday."[24] Although Kant's diagnosis of the origins and nature of metaphysical illusion is far more systematic than Wittgenstein's, their essential point is the same. Wittgenstein sees metaphysics as misleading shadows cast by our grammar; Kant sees it as the confusion of subjective necessity (the categories we impose upon experience) with transcendental reality. Kant's analogy about Plato's dove in frictionless space, quoted above, finds a compelling parallel in Wittgenstein's remark: "We have got on to slippery ice where there is no friction and so in a certain sense the conditions are ideal, but also, just because of that, we are unable to walk. We want to walk: so we need friction. Back to the rough ground!"[25]

Finally, both Kant and Wittgenstein believe that moral and religious discourse is fundamentally different from our everyday talk about objects and events in space and time. Both believe that even if all scientific questions could be answered, the question of the meaning of life would remain. Only Kant, however, makes a systematic attempt to answer the questions "What may I hope?" and "What ought I to do?" and he finds their answers to be intimately related.[26]

GOD, FREEDOM, AND IMMORTALITY

In a strictly Newtonian universe, there is little room for God (except perhaps as the original winder of the cosmic clock) and no room at all for personal freedom. All actions and events are strictly determined in space and time. Kant, however, by limiting the sphere in which scientific knowledge has sway, by showing that we ourselves impose these mechanistic categories on experience, creates an opening for belief.

This recognition of the limits of pure reason, Kant thinks, has "the inestimable benefit that all objections to morality and religion will be for ever silenced, and this in Socratic fashion, namely, by the clearest proof of the ignorance of the objectors."[27] But, although a proof of ignorance may silence objectors, it is hardly an auspicious beginning for believers. Kant tries to provide such a beginning in his distinction between pure and practical reason.

Pure reason may deduce *a priori* judgments about experience; but when it attempts to extend those judgments beyond all possible experience, it reaches a dead end. That includes judgments about God, conceived of as a perfect being and the author of all that exists. In the *Transcendental Dialectic*, Kant catalogues and methodically dismantles the traditional arguments for the existence of God, which he says are of three and only three types.

Ontological arguments contend that God must exist because the very concept of God is that of a perfect being and God could not be perfect unless he existed. What Kant shows is that existence adds nothing to the concept of an object. A concept is defined by its predicates, but existence is not itself a predicate. We make no addition to the concept of an object when we further declare that the object exists. The concept is complete and an object fitting that concept either exists or does not; just as existence does not change the concept, so too non-existence does not reduce its supposed perfection. Put another way, there is no contradiction in denying the existence of a perfect being. "If its existence is rejected, we reject the thing itself with all its predicates; and no question of contradiction can then arise."[28] We must go outside the concept to ascribe existence to the object. "When...I think a being as the supreme reality, without any defect, the question still remains whether it exists or not."[29] Thus, the mere concept of God is no guarantee of the existence of God.

Cosmological arguments argue that there must be a noncontingent ground upon which all contingent being depends. If anything contingent exists, there must be a being whose existence is necessary. The same argument can be put in terms of causation: insofar as there are causal connections in the world, there must be a first cause that started the sequence. Something must have set the cosmic clock in motion. Kant's response to this line of argument parallels his response to the antinomies, discussed above. Concepts such as necessity and causality have meaning and criteria only for their application in the sensible world. The cosmological argument attempts to employ these concepts beyond the bounds of their legitimacy. "The concept of necessity is only to be found in our reason, as a formal condition of thought; it does not allow of being hypostatized as a material condition of existence."[30] Since we can have no experience of the unconditioned, we have no justification for concluding that a contingent series terminates in something that is absolutely necessary.

Arguments from design, or what Kant calls physical-theological proofs, attempt to argue by analogy to human artifacts that the intricate perfection of the universe could not possibly have arisen simply by accident but requires a divine clockmaker.

> This world presents to us so immeasurable a stage of variety, order, purposiveness, and beauty, as displayed alike in its infinite extent and in the unlimited divisibility of its parts, that even with such knowledge as our weak understanding can acquire of it, we are brought face to face with so many marvels immeasurably great, that all speech loses its force, all numbers their power to measure, our thoughts themselves all definiteness, and that our judgment of the whole resolves itself into an amazement which is speechless, and only the more eloquent on that account.[31]

Notwithstanding the emotional appeal of the argument, which Kant says "always deserves to be mentioned with respect," Kant finds it inadequate as a proof.[32] We cannot break outside "the solid ground of nature and experience."[33] We must instead rely upon scientific explanations within the realm of experience to account for the order and diversity of nature. Everything in experience is conditioned; thus, nothing gives us knowledge of the unconditioned. Knowledge concerning the ultimate design of nature and the things-in-themselves that underlie our experience is denied to us.

In short, none of the traditional arguments for the existence of God can compel assent. But Kant finds the argument from design a powerful inducement to belief because it satisfies his wonder at the "starry heavens above." An even more powerful inducement is to be found in the "moral law within." Here, Kant focuses not on "what exists," but on "what ought to exist" as the guarantee of the highest possible good. Once we understand the moral law, Kant thinks, we must postulate "a moral being, as the original source of creation," and the highest fulfillment of that law.[34] It is fruitless to employ reason in theology in any purely speculative manner. So Kant proposes a theology based not on ideas, but on ideals, ideals which have "practical power (as regulative principles), and form the basis of the possible perfection of certain actions."[35]

Kant begins with the question of how morality is even possible in a world of strict cause and effect. If all my actions are determined, then I have no freedom of choice. In that case, no moral judgment could attach to my actions because I could not do otherwise. Yet, Kant thinks, we all have direct knowledge of our own freedom to act in accordance with the moral law. "Ought," he famously remarks, "implies can." Moral laws are necessarily laws of freedom, laws that we can choose to follow in accordance with our sense of duty. Insofar as we believe in the moral law, therefore, we believe in the possibility of freedom. "We do not understand [this freedom], but we know it as the condition of the moral law which we do know."[36]

The central focus of Kant's ethical theory, therefore, is on the good will, that is, the will that acts in accordance with the moral law and for the sake of the moral law alone. "To have moral worth an action must be done from duty."[37] There can be no admixture of the personal. Compassion, affection, a desire to help—none of these feelings are relevant to the morality of the action. Nor is the consequence of one's action: whether it actually helps anyone or adds to the sum total of the world's happiness. The only thing that matters is the good will, by which Kant means that the action is done solely out of a desire to conform to one's moral obligation. This is a very austere ethics. We must be "beneficent not from inclination but from duty."[38] We must not only conform our actions to the moral law, but we must act solely "for the sake of the law."[39]

This very austerity is critical to Kant's notion of moral freedom. By the "moral law," Kant means a law that is binding on all rational beings solely as rational beings. The morality of an action cannot depend upon the unique perspective of the actor: his wants, desires, needs. It depends, rather, on the objective point of view of a free, moral agent who transcends his personal circumstances and acts solely according to the mandate of reason. "Only a rational being has the capacity of acting according to the conception of laws, i.e., according to principles."[40]

But how can reason alone determine the proper course of action? Here, Kant's genius and originality are again in full display. Kant believes we can determine the formal (*a priori*) conditions of morality that are binding on all rational beings, in much the same way that we were able to determine the formal (*a priori*) conditions of experience. But whereas the latter resulted in *a priori* judgments as to the conditions for any possible experience, the former results in *a priori* imperatives that any moral action must satisfy.

Kant draws a fundamental distinction between hypothetical and categorical imperatives. A hypothetical imperative has an "if/then" quality: if I want to have friends, I should be kind and loyal. The action is good to some purpose in promoting my happiness. Hypothetical imperatives are practical maxims, guides to the good life. A categorical imperative, by contrast, is absolute: I must act in accordance with the moral law regardless of my own wants and desires. "The categorical imperative would be one which presented an action as of itself objectively necessary, without regard to any other end."[41]

Kant formulates the categorical imperative in various ways. The most famous is that you must "act only according to that maxim by which you can at the same time will that it should become a universal law."[42] In other words, you must be able to say of any given action that every moral being in comparable circumstances should act in the same way. If you lie to evade an inconvenient obligation, then you must accept that others should lie in similar circumstances. If, by contrast, you recognize that evading obligations by lying should not be a universal law— since our trust in one another would break down—then you recognize that you should not do so either. You cannot make a personal exception: by taking any given action you in effect bring it under a maxim that commands the action for all persons in similar circumstances.

This imperative is only a "formal" condition for any valid moral law, and yet it has tremendous practical force. Indeed, it comes very close to the Christian precept to treat others as you would have them treat you. A related formulation offered by Kant is that you must "act so that you treat humanity, whether in your own person or in that of another, always as an end and never as a means only."[43] In other words, every individual has an intrinsic worth and value that precludes simply using that person for your own ends. The key to morality is to recognize the inherent moral worth of others as rational beings and treat them as equal in value to oneself. "Every rational being exists as an end in himself and not merely as a means to be arbitrarily used by this or that will."[44]

I will not discuss Kant's ethical theory in any detail here, though I will note that philosophers are still strongly influenced by his account of the formal conditions that any ethics must satisfy. The more important point for our purpose is that by making the moral law a command binding on all rational beings, Kant can divorce moral action from all the normal determinants of behavior (desires, needs, ambitions). Accordingly, our apprehension of the moral law is itself an indication of our possible freedom. "Independence from the determining causes of the world of sense (an independence which reason must always ascribe to itself) is freedom."[45] Only when our actions are determined by the moral law—by the dictates of practical reason rather than the dictates of self-interest—do we escape the tyranny of the laws of nature. "A free will and a will under moral laws are identical."[46]

This idea—that freedom lies not in doing what you want to do but in doing what is absolutely required—is paradoxical in at least two respects. First, we generally conceive of freedom as an absence of external constraints. We are free precisely when we are able to realize our own desires, not when we are commanded to set aside those desires. Kant redefines freedom as an ability to transcend our parochial concerns and choose to act solely from a sense of duty. But that leads to the second and more fundamental paradox. Kant must acknowledge that the possibility of escaping the tyranny of the laws of nature, i.e., of acting outside the chain of Newtonian causation, is not strictly intelligible to us.[47] Freedom, as conceived here, is a transcendent idea. And Kant spent most of his great work explaining why the application of concepts beyond the empirical world leads only to metaphysical illusion.

This is Kant's great leap beyond the bounds of sense. The dictates of practical reason (what we ought to do) lead us to recognize a transcendental freedom that we experience but cannot fully comprehend. Speculative reason can never resolve this paradox; practical reason can, but only in action according to the moral law. Through our apprehension of the moral law, we *know* the possibility of freedom. We must accordingly view ourselves from two different standpoints: as belonging to the world of the senses subject to the laws of nature; and as belonging to a world of freedom subject to moral laws founded on practical reason.

Through our freedom, then, through our ability to act in accordance with the moral law, we have a window onto the "thing-in-itself" that underlies the world. I exist not only as a being in the world bound by the laws of nature but also as an autonomous will bound by the moral law, the law of practical reason. I am simultaneously determined and free. I am one thing conceived in contrasting ways. The precise conclusion that we could not reach using pure reason alone (that the "I think" which can accompany all my representations is a "thinking substance" that somehow stands outside the constraints of space and time) is the conclusion that practical reason demands. That "self" is a member of a moral realm to which the categories of the understanding do not apply.

So what exactly does that mean, and how does it relate to the existence of God? It would be easy enough to recast Kant's insight in Wittgensteinian terms. We could simply note that scientific discourse in terms of cause and effect and moral discourse in terms of reasons for action are each autonomous, independent of one another, and of equal validity. There is no contradiction between simultaneously discussing a given event in scientific terms (including the firing of neurons in the brain) and in moral terms (including action against self-interest in accordance with one's duty). Neither form of discourse has priority over the other; each has its own grammar and its own criteria for its application.

In this instance, however, such recasting would not just be anachronistic. It would miss the fundamental point. Wittgenstein demystifies our various language games; everything is laid on the surface, so to speak. Kant wants us to focus on the miracle of a moral law that is binding on all rational beings and that demands that we transcend our individual self-interest. Such a law can exist—it can have a legitimate claim upon us—only if it takes us outside the world of surface appearances in space and time. We each feel the claim of this moral law, Kant believes. It is a fundamental fact of our existence. Through this moral law, therefore, we are connected to a transcendental realm, even if we cannot comprehend it with reason alone.

Kant grounds his belief in God and immortality upon this connection. Speculative reason could not prove either the existence of God or the immortality of the soul. But neither could it disprove them. Hence, we are free to believe, and our apprehension of the moral law gives us a reason to believe. Indeed, it makes such belief "morally necessary"[48] because our concept of the highest good can be realized only if God exists and the soul is immortal. If the highest good cannot be realized "then the moral law which commands that it be furthered must be fantastic, directed to empty imaginary ends, and consequently inherently false."[49] Yet we know, to a moral certainty, that the moral law is valid and binding upon us.

Kant here lapses into two rather unconvincing subarguments. First, the ideal of the moral law is that of a pure will that acts solely from duty in accordance with the dictates of practical reason. It is morally required that we strive for this state of holiness, but it is impossible to realize such perfection in the empirical world. Accordingly, we must postulate immortality to allow for the "endless progress"[50] of the soul and the ultimate realization of the highest good. Second, the good will acts solely from duty, not from a desire for happiness, and there is no guarantee in the empirical world that morality will bear any relationship to happiness. Yet there is "a natural and necessary connection between the consciousness of morality and the expectation of proportionate happiness as its consequence."[51] Accordingly, we must postulate "a cause adequate to this effect,"[52] that is, a Supreme, all-powerful, and beneficent creator.

As I said, neither of these arguments, baldly stated, seems very compelling. But the central thrust of Kant's moral theology is compelling indeed. In a sense, God underwrites our freedom as moral agents. In a deeper sense, morality underwrites our belief in God. We must believe we are free in order to act in accordance with the moral law. The possibility of such freedom is not fully comprehensible, but the reality of that freedom is known to us directly and through it our existence as autonomous moral agents standing outside the realm of mere appearances. We have a window on ultimate reality conceived of as a realm in which the moral law holds sway, however imperfectly realized it may be on this earth. This in turn leads to a belief in a moral being as the author of the world and in the possibility of a Kingdom of Ends in which morality reaches its perfection. So conceived, God is the guarantor of the highest possible good and bids us to live a life that transcends our private, merely selfish concerns. God is an object of both veneration and hope, and our highest aspiration is to live in "harmony with this will."[53]

RELIGION WITHIN THE LIMITS OF REASON ALONE

Socrates argues that a pious action is loved by the gods because it is pious; it is not pious because the gods love it. Kant makes a similar point. We do not derive our morality from our belief in God; rather, it is our direct encounter with the moral law that leads to our belief in God. It follows, Kant thinks, that our only religious duty is "good life-conduct"[54] and that "anything which the human being supposes that he can do to become well-pleasing to God is mere religious delusion and counterfeit service of God." In his book *Religion Within the Limits of Reason Alone*, Kant accordingly rejects the hierarchy of the established church, the traditional rituals of worship, the superstitious belief in miracles and the efficacy of prayer, the primacy of Christianity, and the divinity of the Bible.

This book is a marvel and shows Kant's courage in following the path of reason as he conceived it. After it was published, Kant was forbidden to write further on religious topics by Frederick Wilhelm II, and did not do so again until the death of that monarch. Kant was fortunate not to have been stripped of his academic position and his pension; his widespread fame protected him from that fate, but he certainly tempted it with an attack on the "sorcery" and "fetishism" of standard religious worship that would seem more appropriate to a French revolutionary than to the quiet scholar of Konigsberg.

The thrust of Kant's argument is that religion, properly understood, can require no duties other than the duties of morality that we owe to our fellow man. He is accordingly dismissive of all doctrine that is not focused on promoting the moral law. A doctrine such as the Trinity, he explains, "has no practical relevance at all."[55] It is thoroughly unintelligible to us, and whether there are said to be three or ten persons in God can make no difference to our rules of conduct. The same is true for any scriptural teachings that we can know only by "revealed faith." Such faith "is not in itself *meritorious,* and lack of such faith, and even doubt opposed to it, in itself involves no *guilt.* The only thing that matters in religion is deeds."[56] Thus, the Bible (or the Koran or any other avowedly religious text) can be considered a vehicle of religion only insofar as it promotes the moral precepts of reason by propagating them publicly and strengthening them within men's souls.

Kant strongly objects to the hierarchy of priests, with their focus on church rituals and doctrinal revelations. Instead of helping the members of the church realize their moral obligations, they become "the exclusive chosen interpreters of a holy Scripture."[57] As a result, rules of faith and observances, rather than principles of morality, make up the essence of the church. Kant calls this *fetish-service,* an attempt to win divine favor through the equivalent of bribery and flattery. It is a delusion to think that through religious acts of cult— such as the profession of statutory articles of faith or the observance of ecclesiastical practices—we can achieve anything in the way of justification before God. Such actions are morally indifferent—they can be performed by the most wicked human being just as well as by the best. Attempts to conjure up God's support through formulas of invocation, through professions of a servile faith, through ecclesiastical observances and the like are a kind of "sorcery" that "borders very closely on paganism."[58]

Kant also wholly rejects the influence of spiritual beings or divine forces or miracles as inimical to scientific inquiry and the free exercise of reason. To want to perceive heavenly influences in daily life is a kind of "madness" and "a self-deception detrimental to religion."[59] He accordingly rejects prayer as well, whether conceived as "an inner ritual service of God" or as "the declaring of a wish" to God.[60] It is "an absurd and at the same time impudent delusion to have a try at whether, through the insistent intrusiveness of our prayer, God might not be diverted from the plan of his wisdom (to our present advantage)."[61]

What Kant advocates is a pure and natural religion governed by one *universal* rule: do your duty from no other incentive except the unmediated appreciation of duty itself. In other words, love God (the embodiment of all duties) above all else. Kant contends that this universal religion of reason is the supreme and indispensable condition of each and every religious faith. "In what really deserves to be called religion, there can be no division into sects (for since religion is one, universal and necessary, it cannot vary)."[62] The one and true religion contains nothing but moral laws that are unconditionally binding on each of us.

Kant does not reject churches and sects altogether. They can serve a useful function in promoting and propagating the good and in awakening and sustaining our attention to the true service of God. Nor does he wish to disparage the uses and ordinances of one sect as contrasted with another. But he distinguishes sharply between the statutory teachings that compose *ecclesiastical* faith and the moral teachings that compose pure *religious* faith. The former are all "accidentality and arbitrariness."[63] The latter are universal and necessary. A division into sects can never occur in matters of pure religious belief. It is always to be found where ecclesiastical faith is mistakenly treated as essential rather than merely contingent.

In Kant's view, a pure religious faith is within the grasp of every human being. The concept of God arises naturally from reflection upon the sacred nature of morality. Kant echoes Plato's *Meno*—in which the slave boy was shown to have the truths of geometry innately accessible to him—when he argues that "this faith can be elicited from every human being, upon questioning, in its entirety, without any of it having ever been taught to him."[64]

What, then, does it mean for Kant to believe in God? Everything and nothing. Nothing, because such belief arises from our moral duties; it does not give rise to those duties or alter them in any respect. Everything, because then hope can arise that we will someday be rewarded for adhering to those duties. Nothing, because the commands of practical reason would be exactly the same even if God did not exist. Everything, because immortality and the Kingdom of Ends are thereby guaranteed. Nothing, because God is not an active force in the world; we can have no intuition of God (and could not trust it as other than a delusion if we did). Everything, because life and the empirical world are thereby given a purpose.

This last point becomes particularly important to Kant in his later years. He grows increasingly dissatisfied with Newton's mechanical view of the universe. In his *Critique of Judgement*, written when he was sixty-six, Kant is inclined to view the world in teleological terms, that is, in terms of purposes and goals. He famously remarks that there could never be a Newton to explain a single blade of grass.[65] Life is not reducible to the blind interaction of mechanical forces. Organisms are self-generating and self-organizing. The whole is not explained by the parts; rather, the parts are explained in terms of their function within the whole. Kant suggests that it is helpful to view all of nature *as if* it were itself an organism in which each individual object and creature plays a role in the overall design, somewhat the way the parts of a single animal (heart, lungs, legs) play a role and have a function in the life of that animal. Viewing nature in teleological terms, Kant argues, is a useful "regulative idea" because it assumes purposiveness and order. Ever the careful empiricist, Kant does not suggest that we have any theoretical basis for concluding that all of nature is like an organism in this sense. Nor does he suggest that God actively intervenes in the world of our experience in any direct manner. But he argues that we should nonetheless presuppose something intelligible in our scientific inquiries that allows us to comprehend nature and bring it under laws.

Kant thus circles back to the argument from design, which he has always found compelling if not theoretically conclusive. In the process, he goes some way toward bridging his own divide between appearances and things-in-themselves. For if all of nature is seen as the product of a divine understanding, the distinction between the natural and the divine begins to disappear. So too does the paradox of an empirically determined being acting freely in accordance with the moral law.

In this regard, Kant once again anticipates Einstein. Like Kant, Einstein places morality at the center of all human endeavors. "Our inner balance and even our existence depend on it. Only morality in our actions can give beauty and dignity to life."[66] Like Kant, Einstein also traces the natural progression from scientific ideas to religious ones. He is dismissive of the idea of "a personal God" actively intervening in human affairs or influencing the course of events in response to prayers and ritual observances. Yet he feels that behind all the discernible laws and connections of nature "there remains something subtle, intangible and inexplicable," something "whose beauty and sublimity reaches us only indirectly."[67] Einstein feels "veneration for this force beyond anything that we can comprehend" and "utter humility toward the unattainable secrets of the harmony of the cosmos."[68] This, he declares, "is my religion."[69] It is Kant's religion as well.

CHAPTER FOUR

NIETZSCHE AND THE DEATH OF GOD

A new pride my ego taught me, and this I teach men: no longer to bury one's head in the sand of heavenly things, but to bear it freely, an earthly head, which creates a meaning for the earth.[1]

riedrich Wilhelm Nietzsche was born on October 15, 1844, in the small village of Röcken, near Leipzig. The red (symbol of the military) and the black (symbol of the clergy) combined at his birth, as in the Stendhal novel he so admired, and shaped him through his opposition to each. He was named for the king of Prussia, Friedrich Wilhelm IV, whose birthday he shared. The king was a strong proponent of German unification and military power. Nietzsche was to rail frequently against the stupidity and brutality of German nationalism.

His father and grandfather and two of his uncles were Protestant pastors. Nietzsche himself was raised in the expectation that he would become a clergyman. Instead, he became one of the two greatest scourges of established religion in history. The other, Martin Luther, tacked his ninety-five theses on the chapel door in Wittenberg, less than seventy miles from Röcken, in October 1517.

Nietzsche lived happily in the vicarage for his first four years. He was slow to speak, but showed an extraordinary sensitivity to music that would blossom into a keen appreciation and a remarkable gift for improvisation at the piano.

Nietzsche's father died in 1849, succumbing to nervous seizures and what was diagnosed as "softening of the brain." His younger brother Joseph followed just a few months later. Nietzsche and his sister, Elizabeth, along with their mother, soon moved to Naumberg, where they lived with his grandmother and two aunts.

In some ways, Nietzsche was a typical, active boy of the period. He enjoyed sledding, skating, swimming, horseback riding, and regular walks. But by the age of thirteen he began to suffer from blinding headaches, a harbinger of ill health to come.

Nietzsche obtained a scholarship to attend the nearby Pforta school, one of the premier preparatory schools in Germany. His regime for the next six years started with a 5 AM wake-up (earlier if he wanted unimpeded access to one of the few wash basins), followed by ten hours of alternating classes and study halls. He received a thorough grounding in the classics, as well as studying Hebrew, French, and Italian.

At sixteen, Nietzsche was an ardent Christian, undergoing confirmation and even writing an oratorio. He was an equally ardent aesthete, forming a cultural society with two close friends, with monthly meetings at which each member would read (or perform) his own works. The three friends pooled their money to purchase the score of Richard Wagner's recently premiered *Tristan and Isolde*, and played it through repeatedly during the school holidays.

After Pforta, Nietzsche attended the University at Bonn, where he dutifully began studying theology. That lasted for one semester before he switched to classical philology. In a valiant but ultimately vain effort to fit in with his fellow students, Nietzsche briefly joined a fraternity, drank beer in taverns, and even fought a ritual duel—based on an argument about literature—that left him with a permanent scar across his nose (at that time a necessary badge of courage).

After a year at Bonn, Nietzsche transferred to Leipzig, which had a stronger program in the classics. He briefly joined the artillery, during Prussia's conflict with Austria. But he cracked his sternum and tore the muscles in his chest while jumping an unruly horse, which ended his military career. He also contracted syphilis in one of the brothels in town.[2] At that time, there was no cure for syphilis and it lay in Nietzsche, as it would in Osvald Alving, from Ibsen's *Ghosts*, a ticking time bomb, waiting to claim his sanity and his life.

Nietzsche quickly established himself as a brilliant student—so brilliant, in fact, that in January of 1869 he was appointed to a chair of classical philology at Basel at the extraordinary age of twenty-four, before he had even written his dissertation or sat for his doctoral exams. At Basel, he was befriended by Jacob Burkhardt, the great historian of the Italian Renaissance. Even more significantly, he became a regular visitor at Richard Wagner's house in nearby Tribschen. Nietzsche fell deeply under the sway of the megalomaniacal composer, and his subsequent break with Wagner was one of the traumatic events in his life, as well as a vital step in his own intellectual development.

When the Franco-Prussian War began in 1870, Nietzsche volunteered as a medical assistant, caring for the wounded. He contracted diphtheria and dysentery and returned with his health shattered. He continued his heavy teaching load, however, and wrote his first book, *The Birth of Tragedy out of the Spirit of Music*. It was a stunningly original, groundbreaking book, as well as a willful act of academic suicide. In it, Nietzsche attacked the established view of Greek culture as serene, rational, beauty-loving, and filled with light (a view he associated with Apollo, the god of light and art). Nietzsche argued that darker forces—wild, chaotic, irrational, and orgiastic—were even more fundamental to Greek life and that tragedy evolved out of a bacchanal honoring Dionysus, the god of wine. The great tragedies of Aeschylus and Sophocles, Nietzsche contended, involved a delicate balance, in which the Dionysian passions were not denied or ignored but shaped into an Apollonian vision that affirmed and rendered beautiful even the most horrific aspects of life. He also argued that the demise of tragedy (in the time of Euripides, whose overly didactic and discursive dramas he detested) was due to the influence of Socrates in emphasizing reason above all and attempting to extirpate the role of the irrational in human life.

The classical philologists of Nietzsche's day might have forgiven his novel thesis had it been stated in suitably dry, heavily footnoted academic prose. But Nietzsche's writing was condensed, lyric, and highly polemical. Even worse, he appended to his book a series of sections arguing that Richard Wagner's mythologized music dramas constituted the rebirth of Greek tragedy in modern times.

Nietzsche seems to have lamented only in passing the destruction of his academic reputation. He chafed under the constraints and demands of his professorship in classical philology. At one point, he vainly tried to obtain a chair in philosophy but was considered unqualified. The successful applicant had written a dissertation on the use of prepositions in Aristotle's *Metaphysics*.

Nietzsche ultimately resigned from the university in 1879 on grounds of ill health. He was suffering by then from severe migraines, eye pain, acute sensitivity to light, and bouts of vomiting, probably caused by ulcers. These ills were made even worse by the medical quacks of the day. Nietzsche, always extremely nearsighted, went through periods of almost complete blindness.

With his modest pension, Nietzsche became a wanderer on the face of the earth, a man of no fixed abode seeking clear skies and healthful air. He had friends whom he occasionally visited. He even made a couple hasty proposals of marriage, which were just as hastily rejected, probably to his relief. His one serious, if brief, attachment was to Lou Salome, a beautiful, brilliant, and unstable young Russian woman, who was later to become the lover of the poet Rainer Marie Rilke and a confidant of Freud.

Nietzsche dreamed of disciples. He longed to found a commune of "like minded" free spirits of which he would be the center, essentially a re-creation of the literary society of his youth. But solitude was his essential lot and indeed the essential condition in which his books were forged. He was a man without wife or children, without a job or a home, without a country, and without a church. He was, perhaps, as thoroughly alone as it is possible to be.

Nietzsche walked in the mountains, in the woods, and along the shores of lakes. He always carried a little notebook with him to record his thoughts and an umbrella to shade his hypersensitive eyes. He spent many summers in the small village of Sils Maria in Switzerland, renting a back room in the home of a grocer. (The house is now a museum, and the little room is movingly preserved.) He spent his winters in Italy trying to find enough sunshine and warmth to enable him to work.

The itinerant Nietzsche provides a pathetic but deeply affecting spectacle. (Nietzsche himself hated pity, which he considered a means for the weak, by inciting such feelings, to obtain power over the strong.) His health was in shambles, he was rarely free from pain, and never free from loneliness. Yet he mustered the courage and strength to write book after book that shook the foundations of Western culture. The books are highly polemical, sometimes even hysterical, in tone. But no one has struggled harder or more profoundly with the essential question that he confronts: how can life have value in a godless world?

In his final published book, *Ecce Homo* (Behold, the Man!), Nietzsche was already falling victim to the megalomania that is a harbinger of advanced syphilis. Yet even his grandest boasts have a profound ring of truth. "One day my name will be associated with the memory of something tremendous—a crisis on earth, the most profound collision of conscience, a decision that was conjured up *against* everything that had been believed, demanded, hallowed so far."[3]

Nietzsche suffered a complete mental collapse in Turin in 1889. He survived, but in body only for eleven more years. His sister, an anti-Semitic proto-Nazi, with only a limited understanding of her brother's work, set up a Nietzsche archive, where his posthumous papers were edited and the philosopher himself was occasionally displayed to distinguished visitors. He died on August 25, 1900.

THE DEATH OF GOD

In 1882, Nietzsche announces the death of God as "the most fateful act" of the past two thousand years.[4] It is an event of earth-shaking importance, he explains, which is just "beginning to cast its first shadows over Europe."[5] It is also the central fact around which all his writings revolve.

By "the death of God," Nietzsche does not of course mean that God once existed but no longer does. He means that "the belief in the Christian god has become unbelievable."[6] God has died *to us* because belief in him is no longer tenable. Our churches are but "the tombs and sepulchers of God,"[7] and the only respectable intellectual stance is now an "unconditional and honest atheism."[8]

This is not a smug and comfortable atheism, however. It is profoundly disturbing. "For the few at least, whose eyes—the *suspicion* in whose eyes is strong and subtle enough for this spectacle, some sun seems to have set and some ancient and profound trust has been turned into doubt; to them our old world must appear daily more like evening, more mistrustful, stranger, 'older.'"[9] The death of God leaves a feeling of disorientation and desolation. "Is there still any up or down? Are we not straying as through an infinite nothing? Do we not feel the breath of empty space?...Is not night continually closing in on us?"[10] With the death of God, the earth has been unchained from the sun. Man has been separated from all the absolutes that gave value, meaning, and structure to his existence.

And yet, at the same time, the death of God brings "a new and scarcely describable kind of light, happiness, relief, exhilaration, encouragement, dawn."[11] It is possible, Nietzsche believes, for man himself to give value, meaning, and structure to his existence. It is possible for "an individual to posit his own ideal and to derive from it his own law, joys, and rights."[12] For philosophers, then, and creators of value, the horizon suddenly appears clear. "At long last our ships may venture out again, venture out to face any danger; all the daring of the lover of knowledge is permitted again; the sea, *our* sea, lies open again; perhaps there has never yet been such an 'open sea.'"[13]

These two themes—the death of God and the creation of value by man—alternate throughout Nietzsche's later writings. He traces the nihilistic consequences of a philosophy that rejects all absolutes. He smashes the idols of the past, including Christian morality. He mercilessly and with great psychological acumen exposes their all-too-human origins. Yet at the same time he tries to effect a revaluation of existing values that celebrates their human origins and creates a meaning for the earth.

Given the centrality of Nietzsche's atheism, one would expect powerful arguments to support it. But Nietzsche offers none. "What have I to do with refutations!" he asks.[14] "I do not by any means know atheism as a result" of arguments.[15] Rather, "it is a matter of course with me, from instinct. I am too inquisitive, too *questionable*, too exuberant to stand for any gross answer. God is a gross answer, an indelicacy against us thinkers—at bottom merely a gross prohibition for us: you shall not think!" In the end, he says, the "discipline for truth" simply "forbids itself the *lie* in faith in God."[16]

Yet, scattered throughout Nietzsche's writings are sufficient hints of his reasons for disbelieving in God, for refusing to take any leap of faith of the sort that finally tempted Kant. You will recall that Kant painstakingly deconstructs all the standard proofs of God's existence. He probes their weaknesses. He exposes their false steps. He convincingly concludes that such arguments cannot provide any foundation for religion. Instead, God becomes for Kant a postulate, a sort of working hypothesis that makes sense of the moral law and the apparent purposiveness and order in nature.

Nietzsche ridicules this last turn in Kant's thought. Kant, he says, shows those who want to believe, who need to believe, "a secret path by which they may, on their own initiative and with all scientific respectability, from now on follow their 'heart's desire.'"[17] He does so by turning the "thing in itself"—the unknown and inherently unknowable—into God. The result is an "ever thinner and paler"[18] concept of God, "the last smoke of evaporating reality."[19]

For Nietzsche, the Kantian God is an unjustified abstraction with no real explanatory power. "God" as promoted by Kant is simply a label we give to the lack of an explanation. In the end, he says, these "votaries of the unknown and mysterious as such...now worship the *question mark itself* as God."[20] They set up a contrast between an apparent, but known, world and a "true," but unknown, world and then worship the latter at the expense of the former. Yet "the criteria which have been bestowed on the 'true being' of things are the criteria of not-being, of *naught*; the 'true world' has been constructed out of contradiction to the actual world."[21] Our own "will to truth," Nietzsche stresses, should forbid our going beyond "what is thinkable for man, visible for man, feelable by man."[22] "The 'apparent' world is the only one: the 'true' world is merely added by a lie."[23]

Also important in Nietzsche's thinking is Darwin's *The Origin of Species*, published in 1859. Kant has a fondness for teleological arguments, even though he exposes them as inconclusive. He thinks that the inherent order and purposiveness in nature allows us to presuppose some intelligible driving force in our scientific inquiries. It is in this purposiveness, Kant thinks, that the "true" world manifests itself in the apparent one. (These twin themes of "manifestation" and "purposiveness" are appropriated by G. W. F. Hegel [1770–1831], whose teleological description of the world spirit unfolding itself in history dominated European philosophy in the first half of the nineteenth century.) Life, Kant thinks, is not reducible to the blind interaction of mechanical forces and hence there can never be a Newton to explain a single blade of grass.

Yet Darwin becomes that new Newton. Darwin shows how the blind interaction of chance forces can lead to highly complex and sophisticated organisms and a dizzying array of diversity in life on earth. Darwin makes it clear that we no longer need to look at the world in teleological terms, following a course laid down by God. Evolution is the product of random mutations and a constant struggle for existence. There is no preconceived plan, no design. There is no purposiveness in human existence. Nietzsche calls this *"our conclusive transitoriness"*:[24] "formerly one sought the feeling of the grandeur of man by pointing to his divine *origin*: this has now become a forbidden way, for at its portal stands the ape, together with other gruesome beasts, grinning knowingly as if to say: no further in this direction!"[25]

Nietzsche has his quarrels with Darwin, chiefly because (as discussed below) Nietzsche thinks the essence of life is a will to power and self-overcoming rather than to mere survival and perpetuation of the species. But Nietzsche recognizes acutely that Darwin, by explaining evolution in terms of chance and purely natural forces, has dealt a savage blow to religion. The explosion of scientific knowledge in the late nineteenth century is crowding out the space that religion has previously occupied, by eliminating some of the very question marks upon which religion relies. Most important, man is sundered from any sense of a divine purpose or destiny. After Darwin, we can "find no God—either in history or in nature or behind nature."[26]

In the end, however, Nietzsche charges neither Darwin (science) nor Kant (philosophy) with the death of God, but rather Christianity itself. In part, this is Nietzsche's love of provocative paradox. Yet he has penetrating reasons for his accusation.

Nietzsche argues that the very emphasis on truth and moral seriousness that we have learned from Christianity has made it impossible to take Christianity itself seriously anymore. "You see what it was that really triumphed over the Christian god: Christian morality itself, the concept of truthfulness that was understood ever more rigorously, the father confessor's refinement of the Christian conscience, translated and sublimated into a scientific conscience, into intellectual cleanliness at any price."[27] Religion is a form of discourse that can no longer be taken seriously according to the very standards of truth and integrity established by Christian morality. This is particularly true of (though not limited to) the particular set of beliefs that constitute Christianity.

> A god who begets children on a mortal woman; a sage who calls upon us no longer to work, no longer to sit in judgment, but to heed the signs of the imminent end of the world; a justice which accepts an innocent man as a substitute sacrifice; someone who bids his disciples drink his blood; prayers for miraculous interventions; sin perpetrated against a god atoned for by a god; fear of a Beyond to which death is the gateway; the figure of the Cross as a symbol in an age which no longer knows the meaning and shame of the Cross—how gruesomely all this is wafted to us, as if out of the grave of a primeval past! *Can one believe that things of this sort are still believed in?*[28]

Nietzsche finds it simply contemptible that the great majority of people are willing to accept such beliefs. Many noble and gifted people, he acknowledges, belong to this great majority. "But what is goodheartedness, refinement, or genius to me, when the person who has these virtues tolerates slack feelings in his faith and judgments and when he does not account *the desire for certainty* as his inmost craving and deepest distress—as that which separates the higher human beings from the lower."[29]

Nietzsche demands "*integrity* in matters of the spirit," and "that one makes of every Yes and No a matter of conscience."[30] He refuses to take what he considers a leap into foolishness and incoherence. In the Christian view, we must become as little children to enter the kingdom of heaven. "But we have no wish whatever to enter into the kingdom of heaven: we have become men—*so we want the earth.*"[31]

Ultimately, it is in the denial or denigration of "the earth," "the apparent world," that Nietzsche finds the most decisive objection to religion. The concept of "God," he explains, was invented as "a counterconcept of life," and the "concept of the 'beyond,' the 'true world' invented in order to devaluate the only world there is—in order to retain no goal, no reason, no task for our earthly reality!"[32] "'God' represents a turning away from life, a critique of life, even a contempt for it."[33] Nietzsche himself condemns the "weariness that wants to reach the ultimate with one leap, with one fatal leap, a poor ignorant weariness that does not want to want any more: this created all gods and afterworlds."[34] In some of his most powerful lines, he writes:

> You know it well: your cowardly devil within you, who would like to fold his hands and rest his hands in his lap and be more comfortable—this cowardly devil urges you, "There *is* a God." With this, however, you belong to the light-shunning kind who cannot rest where there is light; now you must daily bury your head deeper in night and haze.[35]

With wry intent, Nietzsche thus reverses the ontological argument, which finds in the perfection of the concept of God the necessity that God exists. Nietzsche finds the very concept of "God" objectionable and untenable because inherent in it is a negation of life and the world. He experiences what has been revered as God, not as "godlike," but "as miserable, as absurd, as harmful, not merely as an error but as a *crime against life*."[36] "God's only excuse," he finally maintains, "is that he does not exist."[37]

THE GENEALOGY OF MORALS

Nietzsche's ultimate target, however, is broader than the Christian God. He also takes aim at Christian morality. "Those who have abandoned God," he notes, "cling that much more firmly to the faith in morality."[38] He is determined to undermine that faith because he believes that Christian morality is even more inimical to life than belief in God. Furthermore, he wants to slam shut the "backdoor" through which Kant reintroduced God.[39]

Even after rejecting all the traditional proofs of God's existence, Kant concludes that the only way to make sense of the moral law is to posit a divine sanction and a divine reward for moral behavior. He finds the categorical nature of the moral law—and the fact that we consider it binding upon ourselves—to be otherwise inexplicable. The moral law establishes an ideal which—because it cannot be realized in this world—demands recognition of another world, a kingdom of ends, in which it will be realized.

Nietzsche attacks Kant's "backdoor philosophy" by attacking the categorical imperative. Kant's basic formulation of that imperative is to act always so that you could will your action to be a universal law. Kant purports to derive this imperative from the concept of virtue itself, as a formal condition that any moral law must satisfy. Unless a moral injunction is universal in the sense of binding on all persons in similar circumstances then it isn't a *moral* (i.e., categorical) injunction at all; it is simply a hypothetical imperative (of the form: if you want *x*, you must do *y*).

Nietzsche, however, finds this formal conception of morality (or "virtue," to use the broader term he favored) highly impoverished. Kant reduces morality to a kind of penal code, upon the basic principles of which, he thinks, all can agree. But questions of virtue are not limited to whether, and under what circumstances, one may lie or steal or murder. For Nietzsche, every decision one takes—what career one follows, how one spends one's time, who/if one marries, who one's friends are, even what one eats—is a moral decision because it both shapes and expresses one's character. Such decisions cannot be made universal laws because they are unique to the individual in question. "Every action that has ever been done was done in an altogether unique and irretrievable way"; "all regulations about actions relate only to their coarse exterior (even the most inward and subtle regulations of all moralities so far)."[40]

For Nietzsche, Kant's universal law is far too crude a measure of morality. Everyone has "*his own* virtue, *his own* categorical imperative."[41] Our virtue is "*our* most necessary self-expression,"[42] and "to experience one's own judgment as a universal law ... betrays that you have not yet discovered yourself nor created for yourself an ideal of your own, your very own—for that could never be somebody else's and much less that of all, all!"[43] A purely formal principle such as the categorical imperative does not even begin to account for the subtleties of morality. Even the tenets of a penal code—which necessarily overlook subtleties of circumstance in order to establish binding and readily understood rules—cannot be explained by reason alone or derived from a formal principle such as the categorical imperative. Their origins lie instead in altogether human concepts of retribution and revenge.

The same is true, Nietzsche believes, for Christian morality. It cannot be derived from purely rational principles. Nor, if God is indeed dead to us, can it be derived from divine revelation. Therefore, one must search out its human origins. Kant, like most philosophers, merely accepts the Christian morality of his day as a given and then seeks to provide a rational foundation for it. But if moral values are not given by God or derived from reason, then the values themselves are open to question and evaluation.

"There are no moral phenomena at all," Nietzsche explains, "but only a moral interpretation of phenomena."[44] We humans provide that moral interpretation. Indeed, that we do so, and how we do so, is a vital part of who we are as humans. The fact that we create our own moral values does not mean that they are arbitrary. Our moral values are, to use Wittgenstein's terminology, deeply embedded in our forms of life. But the fact that they are created, not given to us, does mean that they are subject to reinterpretation and criticism. There is no guarantor of moral value. Nothing is underwritten.

For this reason, Nietzsche finds it critical to focus on the origins, the genealogy, of our moral values. That is not because he succumbs to the fallacy that the end product is determined and limited (much less refuted) by its origins. But by understanding the process by which our current values were created and evolved we come to grips with their contingent, historical nature. Institutions—particularly moral and religious institutions—strive for a sense of inevitability, a feeling that they are fixed and determined and not the product of any historical accidents. Genealogy exposes that myth. It exposes Christian morality as human, indeed as all-too-human, in its origins and hence as subject to question, as subject to change. Genealogy, as a method of historical criticism, replaces the absolute and the given with the contingent and the questionable.

In the case of Christian morality in particular, Nietzsche believes that genealogy exposes the "fetters of false values and delusive words" that stifle rather than promote genuine virtue.[45] It shows "how much hypocrisy, comfortableness," "how many lies" are "hidden under the best honored type of...contemporary morality."[46] In our age, when a show of piety is absolutely required of a politician, Nietzsche's denunciation of hypocrisy has a special resonance. "Where has the last feeling of decency and self-respect gone when even our states-men, an otherwise quite unembarrassed type of man, anti-Christians through and through in their deeds, still call themselves Christians today and attend communion?"[47]

Nietzsche does not, interestingly enough, disparage the truly religious person. "Genuine, original Christianity"—which he considers "not a faith, but a doing"—will be possible at all times.[48] But "the religious person," he claims, "is an exception in every religion."[49] The moral value judgments of the Christian church were developed for the many, not the few. "Under what conditions did man devise these value judgments good and evil? *and what value do they themselves possess?* Have they hitherto hindered or furthered human prosperity? Are they a sign of distress, of impoverishment, of the degeneration of life? Or is there revealed in them, on the contrary, the plenitude, force, and will of life, its courage, certainty, future?"[50] These are the questions he sets out to answer in *On the Genealogy of Morals.*

Nietzsche begins by noting that Christianity reversed an existing table of values. In the classical world, particularly that of Homer, the "good" was established by reference to powerful, aristocratic characters who dominated the world around them. They were kings and warriors who showed "that enthusiastic impulsiveness in anger, love, reverence, gratitude, and revenge by which noble souls have at all times recognized one another."[51] This "aristocratic value-equation (good = noble = pow-erful = beautiful = happy = beloved of God)" celebrated "a powerful physicality, a flourishing, abundant, even overflowing health, together with that which serves to preserve it: war, adventure, hunting, dancing, war games, and in general all that involves vigorous, free, joyful activity."[52] The "bad" was then defined in contrast to the "good" as what is "base," "ignoble," common, plebian, low. The base person was one who was insignificant, without strength or even a proper regard for himself.

Christianity, however, effected a remarkable inversion of these aristocratic values. Christianity celebrated meekness and humility and the opposite of worldly success: "the wretched alone are the good; the poor, impotent, lowly alone are the good; the suffering, deprived, sick, ugly alone are pious, alone are blessed by God, blessedness is for them alone—and you, the powerful and noble, are on the contrary the evil, the cruel, the lustful, the insatiable, the godless to all eternity; and you shall be in all eternity the unblessed, accursed, and damned!"[53]

Accordingly, the Christian "good" became opposed not to "bad" (in the sense of base) but to "evil" (in the sense of violent, cruel, and dominating). "How different these words 'bad' and 'evil' are," Nietzsche notes, "although they are both apparently the opposite of the same concept 'good.' But it is *not* the same concept 'good.'"[54] The one who is "evil" in the new table of values is "*precisely* the 'good man' of the other morality, precisely the noble, powerful man, the ruler, but dyed in another color, interpreted in another fashion, seen in another way by the venomous eye of *ressentiment*."[55]

The concept of *ressentiment* is critical to Nietzsche's analysis. The weak unsurprisingly resented the oppression and dominance of the strong. They longed to overthrow that strength or at least turn it to their own advantage. Christian morality was imposed by the many against the few, by the weak against the strong for the protection of the weak. This process occurred not in open revolt, but through more devious and subtle means. Christianity introduced concepts of guilt and sin in order to cabin the vigorous, free, joyful activity of the strong. Christian morality accordingly took its stand precisely against life, against fullness, against strength. It constituted a major revaluation of values, what Nietzsche calls "*the slave revolt in morality*." "The slave revolt in morality begins when *ressentiment* itself becomes creative and gives birth to values."[56]

These two opposing tables of values, "good and bad," "good and evil," have struggled against one another on earth for two thousand years, and the latter has largely prevailed. Nietzsche does not, despite his rhetoric, consider this altogether a bad thing. For he thinks *ressentiment* itself has made man deeper, more complex, more thoughtful, and above all more interesting. "Human history would be altogether too stupid a thing without the spirit that the impotent have introduced into it."[57]

The noble man is all on the surface, living in trust and openness with himself. His spirit does not inquire; it does not burrow. But when the instincts of the noble man are not given a natural expression, they *turn inward*—"this is what I call the *internalization* of man: thus it was that man first developed what was later called his 'soul.'"[58] Under the guidance of Christianity, man first developed a conscience, which Nietzsche insists is not "the voice of God in man" but rather "the instinct of cruelty that turns back after it can no longer discharge itself externally."[59] Such internalized cruelty, he says, is "one of the most ancient and basic substrata of culture that simply cannot be imagined away."[60]

In this discussion of conscience and the internalization of cruelty, Nietzsche anticipates Freud, and particularly his book *Civilization and Its Discontents*, which was not published until 1930. Freud's thesis is that the growth of civilization required man to deny expression to many of his most basic instincts, which accordingly turned inward and found their expression in various neuroses and mental conflicts. Nietzsche offers a similar analysis in 1887: "I regard the bad conscience as the serious illness that man was bound to contract under the stress of the most fundamental change he ever experienced—that change which occurred when he found himself finally enclosed within the walls of society and of peace."[61]

Christianity was the main agent of (or at least the main intellectual framework for) this change. All men became of equal value in the eyes of God. Superiority became suspect; dominance became evil. Poverty and impotence were celebrated. Christianity was thus the great leveler, a harbinger of the "herd mentality" that Nietzsche condemns in democracy and socialism.

Why, we must ask, is Nietzsche so hostile to this development? We naturally (and I believe rightly) consider a strong sense of the value and dignity of each human being to be a bedrock of any legitimate morality. Nietzsche, though, does not. He thinks that the great mass of men is a "sum of zeroes,"[62] and that the history of mankind is justified only by its highest exemplars. Man, he thinks, is something that needs to be overcome, in a Darwinian sense, on the path to a truly superior being who will naturally dominate and freely express his power. We will discuss this conception of the "superman" below and whether it is as repulsive as Nietzsche at his most polemical makes it seem. (In fact, though he occasionally cites Napoleon and Caesar Borgia, his main exemplars of the "highest men" are artists and philosophers—creators of value, not political tyrants.)

For the moment, though, it is worth exploring what aspects of Christian morality (aside from its emphasis on the intrinsic value of each human being) Nietzsche finds so objectionable. The first is its emphasis on revenge, punishment, and retribution. These concepts are a direct outgrowth of "the *ressentiment* of natures that are denied the true reaction, that of deeds, and compensate themselves with an imaginary revenge."[63] "'Judge not,' they say, but they consign to hell everything that stands in their way."[64] Such hypocrisy Nietzsche does not attribute to Christ, but rather to the Christian church which distorted and adapted his teaching to its own ends of exercising power and control over conscience. "What could possibly be more unevangelical," he asks, "than 'retribution,' 'punishment,' 'sitting in judgment'!"[65]

He finds the notion of reward for the faithful equally objectionable, since it constitutes a barter and exchange of just the sort that Kant insists undermines morality. "The principle of 'Christian love': in the end it wants to be *paid* well."[66] A pretense of unselfishness for the most selfish of reasons promotes hypocrisy, not virtue. We should love our virtue "as a mother her child," and "when has a mother ever wished to be paid for her love? Your virtue is what is dearest to you."[67]

Most objectionable of all, however, is Christianity's forcible sundering of man from his animal past, its "declaration of war against the old instincts upon which his strength, joy, and terribleness had rested hitherto."[68] Christianity, with its notions of "sin," "guilt," and "immaculate conception," has taught man to despise the very first instincts of life. It has taught men "to experience the presupposition of life, sexuality, as something unclean"; it has condemned the strong sense of self that is necessary for an accumulation of forces and hence of growth; and it has instead celebrated typical signs of decline and contradiction of the instincts—"the 'selfless,' the loss of a center of gravity, 'depersonalization' and 'neighbor love' (*addiction* to the neighbor)"—as the highest value.[69]

The Christian church, Nietzsche argues, attacks and tries to extirpate the passions instead of sublimating them and channeling them. "An attack on the roots of passion means an attack on the roots of life." The practice of the church is, accordingly, "inimical to life."[70] That is why it leads to so much hypocrisy and repression and resentment and desire for revenge. "They did not know how to love their god except by crucifying man."[71] Nietzsche draws a sharp contrast between Christianity and Greek mythology, in which the gods were reflections of man's overflowing power and spirit: "the *Greek gods*, those reflections of noble and autocratic men, in whom *the animal* in man felt deified and did *not* lacerate itself, did *not* rage against itself!"[72] Christianity, by contrast, "is the hatred of the *spirit*, of pride, courage, freedom, liberty of the spirit; Christian[ity] is the hatred of the *senses*, of joy in the senses, of joy itself."[73]

Nietzsche accordingly wants to break with Christian morality and take his stand *beyond* good and evil. He does so by rejecting the entire notion that morality is given to us as something fixed and immutable, to which we must conform. "*There are altogether no moral facts*. Moral judgments agree with religious ones in believing in realities which are no realities."[74] This is not to say that there are no moral values. But we must recognize that those values have a human, not a divine, origin. As such they are open to revision and revaluation. By clearing the decks of Christianity and Christian morality, Nietzsche believes that a rebirth, a re-envisioning of man becomes possible. "Atheism and a kind of *second innocence* belong together."[75]

OVERCOMING NIHILISM

Before we can attain this second innocence, however, we must confront and overcome the loss of all value that the death of God seems to entail. We have left behind not just the Christian God and Christian morality. We have abandoned any fixed point of reference in our lives. We have abandoned the entire task of religion and philosophy as we have known them for two thousand years—which is to reveal truth, to worship the absolute, and to uncover and revere the tablets of good and evil according to which our earthly lives must be governed. "Man has lost the faith in his own value when no infinitely valuable whole works through him; i.e., he conceived such a whole in order *to be able to believe in his own value.*"[76]

Western philosophy starting with Plato repeatedly attempts to adopt the perspective of God, to pass beyond the world of mere appearances and gaze serenely upon fixed, immutable, and eternal truth. For those not philosophically inclined, Christianity—which Nietzsche called Platonism for the people—serves a similar role, shrouded in ritual and mystery. We cannot easily abandon such a quest. It is embedded in our psyche. "Even we seekers after knowledge today, we godless anti-metaphysicians still take our fire, too, from the flame lit by a faith that is thousands of years old, that Christian faith which was also the faith of Plato, that God is the truth, that truth is divine."[77]

But that flame has gone out. We have lost our faith not just in God, but in the divine perspective that we have accepted as a warrant for truth. Nietzsche here is making a very Wittgensteinian point, which is that our concepts, including the concept of "truth" itself, are thoroughly human creations. Our language is how we map the world. But alternative maps are possible. There is no fixed perspective. "One should not understand this compulsion to construct concepts, species, forms, purposes, laws ('a world of identical cases') as if they enabled us to fix the *real world*; but as a compulsion to arrange a world for ourselves in which our existence is made possible."[78]

The history of philosophy and religion, Nietzsche tells us, is the history of the deification and mummification of such concepts. Our so-called truths are simply worn-out metaphors; ways of ordering the world that we ourselves have invented. "All that philosophers have handled for thousands of years have been concept-mummies; nothing real escaped their grasp alive. When these honorable idolators of concepts worship something, they kill it and stuff it."[79] Just as he called Christianity the Platonism of the people, Nietzsche calls grammar the "metaphysics of the people."[80] "I am afraid we are not rid of God," he warns, "because we still have faith in grammar."[81]

If there is no fundamental connection between word and thing, if our grammar is autonomous, as Wittgenstein has put it, then there is nothing left of the divine. The philosopher is no longer "carrying the deity in his bosom" and acting as "the mouthpiece of imperatives from the beyond."[82] Our values do not exist anywhere in themselves. Truth, beauty, goodness—we ourselves created them as values and imposed them on the world.

We are awakening then as from a dream. We can no longer believe in absolute values against which the world of appearances is to be judged. We cannot even believe in the moral significance of existence. Everything built upon our faith in the divine flame must collapse. With the death of God, not just religion, but morality and philosophy as we have known them have also come to an end. *"Dead are all gods."*[83]

For the minister's son, who grew up in a highly pious world, the death of God is a crisis of the highest order. Even from our more secular vantage point, we can appreciate the loss of any sense of purpose and meaning that it entails. The "true world" may have been unattainable and indemonstrable, but the very thought of it was "a consolation, an obligation, an imperative."[84] From it we derived all our highest values. "Now that the shabby origin of these values is becoming clear, the universe seems to have lost value, seems 'meaningless.'"[85] Without God, existence itself is a thoughtless accident. It has no goal or end, and we are forced to recognize man's "smallness and accidental occurrence in the flux of becoming and passing away."[86] "Becoming aims at *nothing* and achieves *nothing.*"[87]

That is indeed a bleak prospect, particularly since we have conditioned ourselves to find value only in the unconditioned. Things of the highest value, we feel certain, "cannot be derived from this transitory, seductive, deceptive, paltry world, from this turmoil of delusion and lust. Rather from the lap of Being, the intransitory, the hidden god, the 'thing-in-itself'—there must be their basis, and nowhere else."[88] When that other world is taken from us, we plunge to the opposite extreme of nihilism, the belief that nothing has value. *"Complete nihilism* is the necessary consequence of the ideals entertained hitherto."[89]

We are now paying for having been Christians for two thousand years. We have lost God but we still gauge everything from a Christian perspective. We measure the value of the world "according to categories *that refer to a purely fictitious world.*"[90] No wonder, then, that our world is found wanting. "A world we can revere, that is adequate to our drive to worship—that continually proves itself—by providing guidance in the particular and the general: this is the Christian viewpoint in which we have all grown up."[91] Once belief in God and a transcendent moral order became untenable, we lost the center of gravity by virtue of which we lived. "One interpretation has collapsed; but because it was considered *the* interpretation it now seems as if there were no meaning at all in existence, as if everything were in vain."[92]

> The Sea of Faith
> Was once, too, at the full, and round earth's shore
> Lay like the folds of a bright girdle furled.
> But now I only hear
> Its melancholy, long, withdrawing roar,
> Retreating, to the breath
> Of the night-wind, down the vast edges drear
> And naked shingles of the world.[93]

Nietzsche hopes that this loss of value is "only a *transitional stage*," but acknowledges that it may require centuries before the full depth of the question whether existence has any meaning at all can be sounded.[94] Meanwhile, we are likely to look for new gods, new authorities that "can *speak unconditionally* and *command* goals and tasks," such as social or political movements, or charismatic leaders, or even "*history* with an immanent spirit and a goal within," anything so that one does not have to take on the responsibility, the risk "of positing a goal *for oneself*."[95] All these tendencies to lose oneself in something "greater," something "outside oneself,"[96] which Nietzsche considers throwbacks to the Christian value ideal and themselves signs of nihilism, must be rooted out and pulled up.

Nietzsche accordingly views philosophy's first, and most urgent, task to be a revaluation of all existing values. By that he means that any lingering remnants of a Platonic/Christian worldview, as well as the nihilism that is its inevitable outcome, must be ruthlessly exposed and rejected. Nothing is to be treated as sacrosanct or accepted as given or fixed or immutable. "Whoever must be a creator in good and evil, verily, he must first be an annihilator and break values."[97] Only "naturalistic values," values that give a new meaning to human life, can take their place. "Lead back to the earth the virtue that flew away, as I do—back to the body, back to life, that it may give the earth a meaning, a human meaning."[98] We must examine and weigh our values in accordance with our deepest needs and our highest (but still human) aspirations. He calls such a revaluation "my formula for an act of supreme self-examination on the part of humanity."[99]

Ultimately, the only way to overcome nihilism is to embrace the loss of any fixed point of reference. Bereft of all certainties, man must rely upon his own will to create goals and values for himself that will give meaning to his life. He must learn to will, to want, and to love. "Through esteeming alone is there value: and without esteeming, the nut of existence would be hollow."[100] Nietzsche rejects the "monstrous insipidity" of the poseur who "places existence itself upon his scales and finds it wanting."[101] Man must say yes to his own life. Man must celebrate the "will's joy in begetting and becoming" without reference to ends and goals imposed on us from any higher authority than our own will and desire.[102]

But, Nietzsche asks, are we "strong enough for such freedom"?[103] In most cases, he answers no. This is where his idea of the man of the future or the *ubermensch* enters. He is not a man who wants to dominate over others socially or politically. He is simply a "spirit who has become free,"[104] a man who has simultaneously liberated himself and his will both from the deep-seated remnants of religious values and from "the great nausea, the will to nothingness, nihilism,"[105] thereby redeeming the world and restoring hope to man: "this Antichrist and antinihilist; this victor over God and nothingness—*he must come one day*."[106] In fact, he has already come, and his name, of course, is Friedrich Nietzsche.

THE PHILOSOPHER OF THE FUTURE

Nietzsche presents himself as the archetype of the new philosopher, one who shuns any systematic attempt to shore up and provide foundations for our everyday beliefs. The will to such a system he considers "a subtle corruption, a disease of the character," if not a form of willful stupidity.[107] It treats our existing concepts and values as if they should be fixed in stone rather than exposed as contingent, human creations, subject to revaluation and revision.

Philosophy, according to Nietzsche, must instead be a process of creative destruction, in which nothing is held sacred. In this respect, Nietzsche has leap-frogged Wittgenstein and left him far behind. Wittgenstein also shuns systematic philosophy and thinks that it is not philosophy's job to provide a foundation for our existing concepts and values, as reflected in ordinary language. But neither does he consider it philosophy's job to challenge or revise those concepts and values. At most, philosophy can clear away conceptual confusion. Otherwise, it "leaves everything as it is."

Wittgenstein thus fails to confront the radical implications of his own thought, implications that Nietzsche has already embraced a hundred years earlier. If our grammar is truly autonomous, if our concepts and values are man-made—a function of our evolving language and not rooted in any fixed, predetermined structure in the universe—then we are free to create new ways of speech and with them new values.

> What dawns on philosophers last of all: they must no longer accept concepts as a gift, nor merely purify and polish them, but first *make* and *create* them, present them and make them convincing. Hitherto one has generally trusted one's concepts as if they were a wonderful dowry from some sort of wonderland: but they are, after all, the inheritance from our most remote, most foolish as well as most intelligent ancestors. This piety toward what we find in us is perhaps part of the moral element in knowledge. What is needed above all is an absolute skepticism toward all inherited concepts (of the kind that one philosopher *perhaps* possessed—Plato, of course—for he taught the reverse).[108]

What Nietzsche understands, long before Wittgenstein, is that our concepts create our world. "It is enough to create new names and estimations and probabilities in order to create in the long run new 'things.'"[109] By changing those concepts the philosopher can create a new truth and with it, a new world for man to inhabit. "Philosophy is this tyrannical drive itself, the most spiritual will to power, to the 'creation of the world,' to the *causa prima*."[110] Most important, through revising our concepts of "good" and "evil" and "virtue" and "value," the philosopher "creates man's goal and gives the earth its meaning and its future. That anything at all is good and evil—that is his creation."[111] The philosopher need not, as Wittgenstein does, simply accept the old usages. He can forge a new language for a new table of values. "New ways I go, a new speech comes to me; weary I grow, like all creators, of the old tongues. My spirit no longer wants to walk on worn soles."[112]

In Nietzsche's view, then, the philosopher is a creative artist seeking "to bestow on life and action the greatest possible profundity and significance."[113] He does so by proposing, in effect, a new mythology according to which man should live. That entails a simultaneous destruction of the old mythology. The philosopher of the future is thus a creator as well as a destroyer. Indeed, he cautions, "we can destroy only as creators."[114] We can ultimately root out old values and outmoded truths only by replacing them with new values and new truths, which will in turn be replaced by others. The true philosophers *are commanders and legislators: they say, 'thus it shall be!'"* They "determine the Whither and For What of man, and in so doing have at their disposal the preliminary labor of all philosophical laborers, all who have overcome the past."[115]

This notion of overcoming the past is absolutely critical to Nietzsche's thought. In any endeavor, "the old boundary markers and the old pieties"[116] must eventually be overthrown. "The good men are in all ages those who dig the old thoughts, digging deep and getting them to bear fruit—the farmers of the spirit. But eventually all land is exploited, and the ploughshare of evil must come again and again."[117] This process of development, exhaustion, revolution, and a new beginning in accordance with a new paradigm occurs again and again, in the arts, in philosophy, and even in the sciences, as Thomas Kuhn documents in *The Structure of Scientific Revolutions*.

Nietzsche portrays this process in his parable "On the Three Metamorphoses," which is the first speech of Zarathustra, the prophet and hero of Nietzsche's wholly secular re-envisioning of the Gospels. "Of three metamorphoses of the spirit I tell you: how the spirit becomes a camel; and the camel, a lion; and the lion, finally, a child."[118] The camel represents the "strong reverent spirit that would bear much."[119] The camel wholly absorbs the existing values and the tradition that they represent and whose culmination they are. In philosophy, he masters the writings of his most important predecessors and contemporaries and strives to deepen and extend their insights. In music or art or literature he masters the language and styles of the tradition in which he finds himself. In science, he absorbs the paradigm of his time and works to solve the problems created by that paradigm. The difficult and most difficult are what his strength demands. "Like the camel that, burdened, speeds into the desert, thus the spirit speeds into its desert."[120]

Here, the second metamorphosis occurs, where the spirit becomes a lion who would conquer his freedom. He revolts against the constraints of tradition. He rejects the "thou shalts" that block his way and declares instead "I will." He thus becomes a rebel and a destroyer of existing values and existing paradigms, which he no longer considers adequate to his needs. He now finds "illusion and caprice even in the most sacred."[121] The lion creates a new freedom for himself and assumes a right to new values.

But to create new values and a new paradigm, "that even the lion cannot do."[122] For that the child is required, for the child is innocence and forgetting, a new beginning and a sacred "Yes." Having both absorbed and freed himself from the tradition in which he operates, the creator must find a new affirmation within himself and forge a new paradigm in accordance with his deepest needs. "The spirit now wills his own will, and he who had been lost to the world now conquers his own world."[123]

This beautiful parable is at the core of Nietzsche's thought. He considers art and philosophy (and to a lesser extent science) to be man's highest activities because they engage the human spirit in imposing order on, and infusing value into, the world. Out of such activities something develops "for whose sake it is worth while to live on earth; for example, virtue, art, music, dance, reason, spirituality—something transfiguring, subtle, mad, and divine."[124] What Nietzsche is willing to face is that these aesthetic and moral values to which we cling so ardently are themselves fragile and transitory. There is no ultimate wisdom, ultimate goodness, or ultimate power, before which we can stop to rest. Art and philosophy are an endless process of creation, destruction, and recreation, but no less beautiful for that.

Will and wave.—How greedily this wave approaches, as if it were after something! How it crawls with terrifying haste into the inmost nooks of this labyrinthine cliff! It seems . . . that something of value, high value, must be hidden there.—And now it comes back, a little more slowly but still quite white with excitement; is it disappointed? Has it found what it looked for? Does it pretend to be disappointed?—But already another wave is approaching, still more greedily and savagely than the first, and its soul, too, seems to be full of secrets and the lust to dig up treasures. Thus live waves—thus live we who will—more I shall not say.[125]

BECOME WHO YOU ARE!

In Saul Bellow's wonderful novel *Henderson the Rain King*, the protagonist Gene Henderson is a man at war with himself and his world. He is overwhelmed by the moral and personal demands of parents, wives (current and ex), children, farm, music, and drink, to name just a few. He is a man who has "struggled without rest," but deep inside him is a small voice that says, "I want, I want, I want." Just what he wants, Henderson does not know and he flees to Africa to try to find out. Henderson speeds into his own desert, quite literally, where he encounters a tribe and participates in a ritual that calls for him, in a show of tremendous strength, to carry a huge wooden idol—one of the gods of the tribe—and results in his becoming the Rain King. In that role, he joins with the chief in a series of bizarre yet deeply moving sessions—one could only call them lessons—with a lion, in which they accustom the lion to their presence and learn to run and to roar in union with him. "Be the beast!" the chief instructs him. "You will recover humanity later, but for the moment be it utterly."[126] Henderson learns to roar in order to purge himself of the accumulated dross of his life. He learns to roar in order to prevent the death of his soul.

When he decides to return home, which requires him to escape from the tribe and its demands, Henderson reports that "the sleep is burst, and I've come to myself."[127] On the plane he encounters a young, recently orphaned boy going to live with relatives in Nevada. The plane stops in Newfoundland to refuel, and Henderson wraps the boy in a blanket and takes him outside and "over the frozen ground of almost eternal winter, drawing breaths so deep they shook me, pure happiness, while the cold smote me from all sides."[128] With the child held tightly to his chest, Henderson begins to run laps around the plane. "I guess I felt it was my turn now to move, and so went running—leaping, leaping, pounding, and tingling over the pure white lining of the gray Arctic silence."[129]

Bellow's fable is constructed deliberately around Nietzsche's parable of the three metamorphoses of the spirit. (The exactness of the parallels could not be accidental.) Gene Henderson goes through each stage, the camel, the lion, and the child, in order to come to himself and to wake as from a dream. He throws off secondhand thoughts and secondhand values and reconstructs his life around his own aspirations and desires. In the process, he obtains innocence and forgetting, a new beginning and a sacred "Yes."

This is Nietzsche's ultimate injunction: "Become who you are!"[130] This injunction stands in stark contrast to the Socratic "Know Thyself!" For Nietzsche the "self" is not a fixed entity that we discover through rational inquiry. Becoming who you are requires an act of creative reconstruction, akin to writing a novel or developing a philosophy. Each individual must "posit his own ideal and...derive from it his own law, joys, and rights."[131] He must rescue himself, as Gene Henderson does, simultaneously from the commands of others and a lack of satisfaction with himself. If you are lost to yourself, you are no good to anyone else. Indeed, whoever is, like Henderson at the beginning of the novel, "dissatisfied with himself is continually ready for revenge, and we others will be his victims."[132]

Socrates demands that we give an account of our lives in terms of the reasons for our moral beliefs. Nietzsche asks a very different, if still related, question: "How does your individual life receive the highest value and the deepest significance? How is it least wasted?"[133] His answer is not that you must learn to justify the moral beliefs of the day, which he considers to be rife with hypocrisy and *ressentiment.* Indeed, he cautions us to "stop brooding about the 'moral value of our actions'!"[134] Rather, we must become the masters of our own virtues. In other words, we ourselves must overcome the values of our time by positing our own goals and our own values. "That my life has no aim is evident even from the accidental nature of its origin; that *I can posit an aim for myself* is another matter."[135]

We must learn, as Henderson does, to throw off "secondhand thought, secondhand learning, secondhand action," and organize the chaos within ourselves.[136] That is not a process of rational deliberation or justification. It has more in common with art than with philosophy as traditionally conceived. Nietzsche calls it "giving style" to one's character. "It is practiced by those who survey all the strengths and weaknesses of their nature and then fit them into an artistic plan until every one of them appears as art and reason and even weaknesses delight the eye."[137] Passions are not extirpated or suppressed. They are shaped and channeled in accordance with an overall plan. "In the end, when the work is finished, it becomes evident how the constraint of a single taste governed and formed everything large and small. Whether this taste was good or bad is less important than one might suppose, if only it was a single taste!"[138]

What exactly does this mean in concrete terms? How does one even begin to go about "giving style to one's character," which seems a wholly artificial goal? Henderson discusses this very point in his "lion" stage:

> I accepted the discipline of being like a lion. Yes, I thought, I believed I could change; I was willing to overcome my old self; yes, to do that a man had to adopt some new standard; he must even force himself into a part; maybe he must deceive himself a while, until it begins to take; his own hand paints again on that much-painted veil. I would never make a lion, I knew that; but I might pick up a small gain here and there in the attempt.[139]

The point is to posit an ideal and to work at it, slowly, carefully, courageously over time. As Henderson explains, "what Homo sapiens imagines, he may slowly convert himself to."[140]

But how do we choose this ideal about which we are to organize our lives? That is actually less important, Nietzsche tells us, than the fact that we choose. What is essential is that we re-create ourselves in accordance with our highest aspirations and deepest needs, which we will discover only after the three metamorphoses of the spirit: a long discipline, a fierce rebellion, and a new beginning. Your true self, he tells us, lies immeasurably high above you and when you start toward it you will have little idea of the end. "To become what one is, one must not have the faintest notion *what* one is."[141]

The pursuit of such an ideal is "a question for the single one," not the party or the state or the church. "I live in my own light," says Zarathustra. "I drink back into myself the flames that break out of me."[142] Most men, Nietzsche concludes, are incapable of such discipline and longing. Only the strongest natures will "enjoy their finest gaiety in such constraint and perfection under a law of their own."[143] Others cannot command themselves and thus covet someone who commands them—"a god, prince, class, physician, father confessor, dogma, or party conscience."[144] He dismisses such men as a "sum of zeroes," promoters of a "herd instinct."[145] Nietzsche's view of human value is fundamentally aristocratic. He expresses contempt for mediocrity and mere contentment, and a virulent opposition to all leveling tendencies, in which he indiscriminately includes democracy, socialism, and Christianity.

One need not share that contempt, however, to share his admiration for the "spirit who has become free."[146] Life is valuing and professing. If all our values and professions are derived from others, then in what sense have we had any life of our own? For Nietzsche, the only way for an individual to give meaning to his existence is by achieving power over his pros and his cons and learning to shape them in accordance with his own highest aim.[147] He accordingly celebrates the artists and philosophers who have transformed themselves and in the process created new values and a new meaning for life.

Failure, of course, is the most likely outcome of such aspirations. But, he tells us, "I know no better aim for life than to be broken on something great and impossible."[148] "The secret for harvesting from existence the greatest fruitfulness and the greatest enjoyment is—to *live dangerously!* Build your cities on the slopes of Vesuvius! Send your ships into uncharted seas!"[149] Life itself can be an experiment for the seeker after knowledge.[150] Only thus can a man "'live resolutely' in wholeness and fullness."[151]

Nietzsche cites the pre-Socratic Greeks as "the best turned out, most beautiful, most envied type of humanity to date."[152] The Greeks were not searching for a reality hidden behind appearances. They stopped "courageously at the surface, the fold, the skin." They knew how "to adore appearance, to believe in forms, tones, words, in the whole Olympus of appearance." Those Greeks, he tells us, "were superficial—*out of profun-*

dity."[153] Even their mythology was focused on a heightening of appearance, not its denial, on a celebration of life, not its suppression.[154]

Perhaps even more important, the Greeks acknowledged the terrors of life (its violence, its brutality, its arbitrary and transitory nature) along with its joys. They embraced the latter without shutting their eyes to the former. Hence, the glories of Greek tragedy and the Homeric epics, for which Nietzsche never lost his love. For Nietzsche, it is critical for man to avoid false consciousness about his world, to recognize it for what it is, and to make of it what one can. "Have you ever said Yes to a single joy? O my friends, then you said Yes too to *all* woe. All things are entangled, ensnared, enamored; if ever you wanted one thing twice, if ever you said, 'You please me, happiness! Abide, moment!' then you wanted *all* back."[155]

The puzzling notion of the eternal recurrence (stripped of any metaphysical overtones) is Nietzsche's formula for living. We must live "as if" each moment were to recur again eternally. We must choose as if we were choosing for eternity. It is a wry twist on Kant's moral law, which asks whether you can will your action to be a universal law for mankind. Nietzsche asks whether you can will this action for yourself "once more and innumerable times more."[156] As we look back on our lives, we must be able to say: I would have nothing different because anything different would lead to a different present and I embrace and accept my present. I accept the pains, the humiliations, the losses because they brought me to this point and made me what I am. I say yes to my life and to what I am and in doing so I accept my entire past and would live it again, unchanged. "My formula for greatness in a human being is *amor fati*: that one wants nothing to be different, not forward, not backward, not in all eternity. Not merely bear what is necessary, still less conceal it—all idealism is mendaciousness in the face of what is necessary—but *love* it."[157]

It is a hard doctrine and a selfish one, since it weighs all joy and suffering on a single, wholly personal scale. Yet it is also a noble and selfless doctrine, which pours all one's energy into the pursuit of ideals that, however transitory, make life worthwhile. Nietzsche himself acknowledges that it is not a road for all. "This is *my* way; where is yours?—thus I answered those who asked me 'the way.' For *the* way—that does not exist."[158]

It is worth inquiring, then, how Nietzsche's formula for greatness applies to his own life, particularly in light of the long humiliation with which it ended. At the time of his breakdown, his Turin landlady, responding to unusual sounds from above, peered through the keyhole to find the good professor—who had proclaimed: "I would believe only in a god who could dance"[159]—dancing naked in his room in a Dionysian frenzy, his mind completely gone. He spent his next ten years in a largely vegetative state, just as he had spent his prior ten years as a lonely and impoverished wanderer climbing the highest peaks of Western thought.

Yet Nietzsche I think would have embraced it all, his madness along with his loneliness, in exchange for creating his own peak for future thinkers to climb. His uncompromising analysis of the death of God, his penetrating psychological insights, his impassioned belief in values as free creations of a free spirit out of his deepest being: these views have fundamentally and irrevocably altered our conception of man and his place in the world. How could he be deemed lonely who was on such intimate terms of passionate discourse with Plato and Kant and Aristotle and, now, with Wittgenstein and Heidegger?

The madness of Nietzsche may even be a fitting modern counterpart to the death of Socrates. Alexander Nehamas, in *Nietzsche: Life as Literature*, argues that Nietzsche is trying to be a Plato to his own Socrates. Plato created Socrates as an archetype of the human spirit and his death was an essential part of that mythology. Nietzsche re-created himself in his writings as a new archetype, the philosopher of the future, who views life as an experiment and who is ultimately "broken on something great and impossible."[160] We cannot mourn or disavow his end or the pain that he suffered in his life, or even the pathetic spectacle of the portly, bespectacled professor who believed he was the reincarnation of the god Dionysus. All accounts are more than squared in the greatness of his writings, the clarity of his vision, and the nobility of his quest. "But by my love and hope I beseech you: do not throw away the hero in your soul! Hold holy your highest hope!"[161] Thus spoke Zarathustra. Thus spoke Friedrich Nietzsche.

PART THREE
WHAT OUGHT I TO DO?

W e can dismiss academic philosophy as mere logic chopping. We can ignore the hard question of God (taking refuge either in agnosticism or in reflexive belief). But we can never escape the daily reality of moral choice. We act in a world full of people. Our actions affect others for better or for worse. We may spend little or no time thinking expressly about what we owe to one another. But, as Socrates showed, we all have an intuitive sense of right and wrong conduct, of the line between selfishness and care, and of the varying obligations that those closest to us, and those farthest from us, place upon our emotional and material resources. These intuitions are a powerful force in our lives, even (or perhaps especially) when we flout them.

Our ethical intuitions, however, are remarkably untidy. They compete with one another, and we have no clear way to choose between them. They also break down at the margins, leaving us with assertions matching assertions. Is abortion always (ever) wrong? May I sacrifice one person to save many more? Can infidelity be justified? How much should I give to charity? Should I tell a "white lie" to spare someone's feelings?

Philosophers, who detest untidiness, have long sought a precise method for resolving such questions. Their efforts can be divided, very roughly, into two categories. Consequentialism determines moral worth based entirely on the results of our actions. The most important such theory, Utilitarianism, was developed by Jeremy Bentham (1748–1832) and found its greatest expression in the writings of John Stuart Mill (1806–1873). Utilitarianism argues that an action is moral only insofar as it promotes the greatest happiness for the greatest number.

Deontological theories, by contrast, are duty based. They focus entirely on the rightness or wrongness of the action itself, regardless of its consequences. For the deontologist, an action is moral only insofar as it accords with a principle that clearly and precisely states our duty. Kant's categorical imperative, discussed briefly in chapter 3, is the most compelling exposition of a deontological theory.

The problems with both types of theories are well known. Deontological theories are too rigid and tend toward a moral absolutism that ignores the practical effect of our actions. Consequentialist theories are too loose and tend toward a wholesale pragmatism that ignores rights and obligations. Neither in fact provides us with a decisional calculus that eases the burden of human choice. The key tenets of Utilitarianism (promote the greatest happiness of the greatest number) and Kantianism (act as if your conduct would become the universal law) are too abstract to resolve the concrete dilemmas of daily life.

The more fundamental problem with all such theories, however, is that they impoverish and distort our moral discourse by focusing on a limited subset of moral choices (such as whether to lie or cheat or steal) and then imposing a single metric for making such choices. Our ethical intuitions are untidy precisely because the circumstances in which they can be applied are so varied. Moreover, the rightness of a given action can depend not just on the particular circumstances but also on the dispositions and emotions of the actor and those affected by the action. Being a moral human being in a messy world is a much more nuanced affair and the range of actions that reflect moral choice is much broader than either the consequentialists or the deontologists acknowledge.

What Nietzsche shows so convincingly is that our every action is a moral one. Whom we marry or spend time with, how we earn our living, how we interact with our children, what hobbies we pursue, how easily we get angry, how deeply we love others: all of these choices, attitudes, and dispositions are a reflection of our moral being. Moreover, it is *our* moral being that is in question, not someone else's. The right choice for me may be the wrong choice for another. It is fruitless to ask, in the abstract, how to determine whether any given action is moral or otherwise. For Nietzsche, it is far more important to ask what sort of person I am and what sort of person I want to become. Those are also the questions that Aristotle and Heidegger seek to answer, each in very different ways.

CHAPTER FIVE
ARISTOTLE AND PUBLIC VIRTUE

Virtue is up to us, and likewise also vice.[1]

In canto IV of *The Inferno*, Dante the pilgrim arrives in limbo, where the virtuous pagans are condemned to an eternity apart from God. While technically in the first circle of hell, the virtuous pagans are subjected to none of the torments imposed on the sinners Dante will visit in the lower circles. Indeed, the setting is very like the Elysian fields of Greek mythology, a "meadow of fresh verdure," where people with "looks of great authority" and "gentle voices" converse softly together. But these virtuous pagans experience the absence of God and hence a "sorrow without torments." As Virgil, Dante's guide and mentor, explains, "We have no hope and yet we live in longing."

From an "open space, bright and high," Dante sees the great poets and heroes of ancient Greece and Rome. When he raises his eyes "a little higher," he sees "the master of those who know sitting amid a philosophic family, all of them regarding him and all showing him honour."[2] The "master of those who know" is Aristotle, who is elsewhere referred to simply as "the Philosopher." Even Socrates and Plato pay him homage.

By Dante's day, Aristotle's name had become synonymous with

philosophy, with vast erudition, with indefatigable industry, and with a serene wisdom that contemplated the entire expanse of human knowledge and found it good. Perhaps most important was his ardent faith in the ability of reason to comprehend the universe and man's place in it. Aristotle, whose works (unlike most of Plato's) had been translated into Latin, exercised a tremendous influence on early Catholic thinkers, particularly Thomas Aquinas, who sought to reconcile reason with religion or, more precisely (since Aquinas saw no conflict between the two), to employ reason in the service of religion. He thereby indirectly instilled in Catholic thought the very will to truth and to intellectual integrity that, in Nietzsche's view, ultimately made belief in Christianity itself impossible. There is a deep irony then, one not appreciated by Dante, in Aristotle's placement at the gaping mouth of the Christian hell, holding forth to a rapt audience on the power of human reason to satisfy human longing.

Aristotle was born in 384 BCE in northern Greece. His father was a physician to the king of Macedon. In 367, at the age of seventeen, Aristotle moved to Athens, where he studied at the Academy under Plato and quickly became his most important pupil. But when Plato died in 347, someone else was chosen to succeed him. Shortly thereafter, at the age of thirty-seven, Aristotle left Athens, though it is unclear whether he did so because of disappointed hopes or because his Macedonian ties made it increasingly unsafe for him in Athens.

Thus began an extended and productive period of travels, accompanied by a circle of friends and disciples who helped with his research. In 343, Philip II of Macedon made Aristotle tutor to his son, Alexander, the future world conqueror. Although the arrangement lasted two years and is delightful to contemplate, there is no discernible indication that either of these towering figures had any effect on the other. In 335, Aristotle returned to Athens and set up his own school in the Lyceum (a gymnasium and public space just outside the walls), where he taught and wrote extensively.

Despite his long residence, Aristotle never became an Athenian citizen. When Alexander died in 323 BCE, and anti-Macedonian feelings were at their apex, Aristotle left Athens a second time, suggesting that he wanted to spare the city, which had already killed Socrates, from sinning twice against philosophy. Aristotle retired to Chalcis on the island of Euboea, where he died less than a year later, in 322, at the age of sixty-two.

Aristotle was indeed the "master of those who know." He wrote on every conceivable topic in mathematics, mechanics, the natural sciences (including physics, astronomy, zoology, and biology, among others), psychology, medicine, poetics, rhetoric, law, economics, politics, and all aspects of philosophy, including logic, metaphysics, epistemology, and ethics. Of his known writings, barely a third survive. We have no examples of his popular dialogues and other polished writings, much praised in their day for the elegance of their style. Instead, the books that remain to us are largely compilations of lecture notes, rough in style, uneven in development, and more like detailed outlines than finished treatises.

The loss of the popular works in particular seems a tragedy, and certainly no one could but lament our inability to compare Aristotle's finished writings with those of Plato. Yet the works that remain to us have a beauty of their own. In Plato, matter and manner blend perfectly as faultless prose ascends to the poetry of the forms. In Aristotle, matter and manner are equally well-matched. In his surviving writings we can experience the thinker at work, his tentative gropings, his careful repetitions, his gradual deepening of the subject matter. There is nothing finished or complete in Aristotle's work; it is a constant invitation to further thought. That very quality helps make the *Nicomachean Ethics* the wisest, most considered book ever written on the subject of the good life for man and the ability of human reason to realize that good life.

The Republic may be the greatest jewel of Western thought. It shines undiminished through the centuries, yet it is firmly ensconced in its setting in ancient Greece. The *Nicomachean Ethics*, by contrast, is a thoroughly modern work. It preceded them by more than two thousand years, but it is post-Wittgenstein and post-Nietzsche. The centuries are indeed as nothing to Aristotle. He is already waiting at the end of the path along which Wittgenstein and Nietzsche struggle so painfully. In Dante's limbo, they would sit at his feet with the rest.

DETERMINING THE GOOD LIFE FOR MAN

Aristotle focuses the *Nicomachean Ethics* on a single question: what is the good life for man? Socrates and Plato of course ask the same question. But Socrates disclaims any knowledge on the subject and finds that those he questions are also unable to give a proper account. Plato develops his theory of forms precisely to place his own account beyond the reach of Socratic questioning and uncertainty. Unfortunately, he also places it beyond the reach of human understanding.

Aristotle, as in so many places, strikes a middle ground. He does so in the simplest and most commonsense way imaginable. First, he politely but firmly (because "piety requires us to honour truth above our friends")[3] rejects Plato's suggestion that there must be some form of the good that is present in all instances. He notes that the word "good" is meant in different, if related, ways in different contexts and concludes "that there could not be any common good that is one and universal, for if there were it could not have been meant in all the ways of attributing being but only in one."[4] Plato insists that there *must* be such a universal concept; Aristotle looks at actual usage and concludes that there is none. Words such as "good" and "justice," he points out, are "meant in more than one sense, but since their ambiguity is between meanings that are close together, it escapes notice, and is not, as in the case of things far apart, so obvious."[5] The good, in other words, is what Wittgenstein would call a "family-resemblance concept," and nothing but confusion results from assimilating it to a single form.

For related reasons, and just as Wittgenstein rejects his own early addiction to the determinacy of sense, Aristotle rejects the Socratic insistence on a precise definition of the good for man that will enable some sort of mathematical demonstration of the proper course of conduct in each instance. Ethics, he explains, is not an exact science and we must seek only as much precision as is appropriate to the subject matter. Here, we are dealing with action, character, and feeling: all matters that are open to discussion and potential disagreement, not demonstration. "One ought to be content, when speaking about such things and reasoning from such things, to point out the truth roughly and in outline, ... for it belongs to an educated person to look for just so much precision in each kind of discourse as the nature of the thing one is concerned with admits."[6] To demand demonstrations in ethics makes no more sense than to accept probable conclusions from a mathematician.

Aristotle frequently starts his discussion of a given issue with what people ordinarily say on the subject. He quotes from poets, he cites other writers, and he reports on common beliefs. Such received opinions, he notes, are well worth considering and provide a natural starting point for any deeper inquiry. Aristotle suggests that if we are able to sort through the difficulties raised by common views without departing from them too much, we shall have dealt with the issues "in an adequate way."[7] He tests received views with real world examples, he sorts through apparent or real contradictions, and he arrives at what appears to be the best-considered outcome. But that is often just a first sketch that is amplified after similar treatments of related issues, so that his stated views become ever deeper and ever more contextual.

Plato of course is deeply suspicious of common views and thinks the philosopher has to transcend them and then, based on his knowledge, radically transform human life. Aristotle is far more cautious and empirical and his goals are correspondingly more modest. He seeks to make human life marginally more rational and thoughtful and hence to bring the good life closer to us. Plato takes a foundational approach to ethics. He wants to base ethical judgments on absolute bedrock knowledge of the forms. With such knowledge in hand, received views can simply be swept aside except insofar as they happen to correspond with the deeper knowledge provided by philosophy. Aristotle, by contrast, starts *in media res*, as he notes good plays and epic poems do. He accepts our common discourse about ethics, and seeks to understand it and to improve the rationality of the practice from within.

Yet Aristotle does not slavishly follow received wisdom. "Such things have some trustworthiness," he explains, "but the truth in matters of action is discerned from deeds and from life, since they are the determining thing in these matters. So we ought to examine the things that have been said by applying them to deeds and to life, and if they are in harmony with the deeds one ought to accept them, while if they are out of tune one ought to consider them just words."[8] This is an absolutely critical point for Aristotle. The purpose of his study of ethics is practical, not theoretical. Its end "is not knowing but action."[9] Medicine is valid only insofar as it promotes health. Military strategy is valid only insofar as it promotes battlefield success. So, too, ethics must promote the good life for man. In this context, mere abstract knowledge, knowledge that does not inform our lives and our behavior, is of no use to us. "We are investigating not in order that we might know what virtue is, but in order that we might become good, since otherwise there would be no benefit from it."[10]

Plato thinks that "to know the good is to do the good," and that one does wrong only out of ignorance. That is in keeping with his view that the forms stand beyond all the messy complications and contradictions of everyday life and provide a completely harmonious and impregnable account of the good. A philosopher attaining such understanding cannot but harmonize his soul and his actions with the form of the good. Aristotle is again both less exalted and more pragmatic, recognizing on the one hand that our knowledge of the good is inherently tenuous and sketchy and on the other hand that human weakness and frailty can give way in the face of various temptations and fears. His goal accordingly is the formation of a stable character that puts practical judgment into action, not only recognizing the good as best we can, but also choosing the good in each instance. Most people, he cautions,

> take refuge in theory and think they are being philosophers and will become good in this way, behaving somewhat like patients who listen attentively to their doctors, but do none of the things they are ordered to do. As the latter will not be made well in body by such a course of treatment, the former will not be made well in soul by such a course of philosophy.[11]

It is legitimate to ask whether what Aristotle is doing is properly called philosophy, or whether the *Nicomachean Ethics* is simply a precursor of advice books that tell us how to win friends and live rich and fulfilling lives. This question is not frivolous, for Western philosophy has been in an identity crisis since its inception. The dominant tradition from Plato through Kant to at least the early Wittgenstein seeks a vantage point "outside" the practice in question (be it ethical, scientific, political, or linguistic) in order either to place the practice on a firm foundation or reform it from the bottom up. Striving for this divine or at least superhuman perspective is what defines the philosopher's mission. But an alternative tradition, from Aristotle through Nietzsche and the later Wittgenstein, sees our practices as more free-floating and autonomous. The practices themselves neither require nor admit external justification.

So what, then, does the philosopher do in this alternative tradition, besides throw brickbats at the dominant tradition? For Wittgenstein, not much of anything—the philosopher simply describes a practice in light of certain philosophical confusions that he is seeking to dissolve and otherwise leaves everything as it is. As a personal matter, Wittgenstein thinks ethics is immensely important, but he does not think that philosophy has anything interesting to tell us about it. That is why Wittgenstein advises his disciples to give up philosophy and do something productive instead.

But Aristotle and Nietzsche, following Socrates, are still concerned with how best to live our lives. As Aristotle explains, "virtue is up to us, and likewise also vice."[12] We have to make choices in our lives, and the sum of those choices is who we are or, rather, who we have become. Thinking hard and unblinkingly about those choices is ultimately what both Nietzsche and Aristotle mean by philosophy.

Aristotle and Nietzsche accordingly go beyond Wittgenstein where ethics is concerned. They believe that the philosopher has a legitimate role to play in critiquing the inconsistencies (and, for Nietzsche, the many hypocrisies) of ethical discourse from within and working changes in our conception of human life and its possibilities. For Nietzsche, this transformation—outlined in his parable of the three metamorphoses of the spirit—is radical, as is his critique of the ethical discourse of his day. For Aristotle, the transformation is more ameliorative and less dramatic but no less important.

An apparent reason for this difference is that Aristotle has faith in the power of reason to evaluate choices, whereas Nietzsche dismisses ethical reasoning as rationalization; his criteria for ethical choice tend to be aesthetic. Accordingly, Aristotle appears to operate within limits circumscribed by reason whereas Nietzsche celebrates the irrational and the frenzy of creativity. But, as we will see, this distinction is less genuine than we might at first think, for even Aristotle, properly translated, is concerned with "the beautiful" in human action and human character, not with rationally developed rules for conduct.

The deeper reason for the difference is that Aristotle believes that human nature is malleable only within certain limits, whereas Nietzsche views human choice as altogether untethered. Alasdair MacIntyre, in his brilliant book, *After Virtue*, seizes on this difference in contending that Aristotle and Nietzsche represent fundamentally different approaches to ethical theory.[13] He argues that Aristotle's focus on human nature as the source of ethical judgments provides an answer to Nietzsche's "emotivism." By "emotivism," MacIntyre means the view that moral judgments are nothing more than assertions of personal preference. Such judgments are not grounded in religion or reason or any other objective source. Nietzsche dismisses moral discourse as so much hypocritical prattling because moral judgments, properly considered, are just masks to conceal the will to power of individuals and groups. By contrast, MacIntyre argues, Aristotle provides an account of ethics that is grounded in a fixed conception of human nature and he derives objective ethical judgments from his close consideration of that nature. By offering an account of essential human purposes, value judgments can become factual statements about how best to realize those purposes.

I do not think this is a completely accurate account of either man's views, but there is an important point here. Aristotle is not trying to ground ethics in a fixed conception of human nature. He is not trying to provide any foundation whatsoever for ethics. But he does recognize that our basic ethical judgments are intertwined with our judgments about human nature. We should think of Aristotle's discussion of human nature as similar to Wittgenstein's references to forms of life. Our language games are constitutive of our forms of life but the forms of life also shape the language games. There is a chicken-and-egg problem that makes it impossible to ground one in the other. Wittgenstein's point is not to reduce one to the other, but simply to note that to imagine a different language game is to imagine a different form of life; we can do that within limits, but some language games (e.g., that of the primitive builders that opens the *Investigations*) are so foreign to us that the form of life they entail seems to us nonhuman and hence not something that we can envision adopting.

So, too, in ethics: for Aristotle, our choices are both constitutive and reflective of our human nature. Our nature is shaped by our actions and our actions are a reflection of our nature. We cannot "ground" one upon the other, but neither can we divorce the two and focus solely on freedom of choice without regard to the apparent constraints of our own humanity.

To put the same basic point in a different way, Aristotle operates on the assumption that we have enough of a moral vocabulary in common to make his particular inquiry productive. We are inclined to agree in discussing ethics on many if not most of our judgments, and that common core of agreement can then be further developed and enhanced. Aristotle starts from our basic ethical views, including our views about human nature, and seeks to explore and refine those views and test them in the crucible of practical experience. This is a circular, but nonetheless highly illuminating, undertaking. Nietzsche, by contrast, believes that the vocabulary of morality has become so debased and shot through with hypocrisy and disguised will to power that it is not worth salvaging. He does not want to refine it. He simply wants to change the subject. As a result, there is in Nietzsche not enough recognition of our common humanity—in the good sense of that term, rather than in the all-too-human sense he so disdainfully dismisses. But that does not mean that we have a stark, either/or choice between Aristotle and Nietzsche. Their similarities are greater and more important than their differences.

The ethics with which Aristotle is grappling is a purely human ethics, based on human character, human reason, and human choices. It has no transcendental or religious component. Thinking hard and unblinkingly about our life choices does not mean adopting some perspective that is abstracted from the particularities of our individual existence or developing some sort of decisional calculus that does the work for us. It involves no divine commands and depends upon no system of rewards and punishments in an eternal life. Aristotle is concerned with the here and now of human life. "It is clear," he says, "that one ought to examine virtue of a human sort, since we were looking for the human good and a human happiness, and by human excellence we mean the kind that belongs not to the body but to the soul, and we assert that happiness is an activity of the soul."[14]

The reference to "the soul" does not change this human emphasis or interject a note of religion. For Aristotle, the soul is not something separate from the body but rather a certain sort of activity and potentiality of the body.[15] One might call it the animation of the body. "That is why," he explains, "we can dismiss as unnecessary the question whether the soul and the body are one: it is as though we were to ask whether the wax and its shape are one, or generally the matter of a thing and that of which it is the matter."[16] In Aristotle's view, "the soul is inseparable from its body,"[17] a view echoed in Wittgenstein's remark that "the human body is the best picture of the human soul."[18]

There is a potential exception to this position that we will discuss below. In discussing the life of contemplation, Aristotle says that the rational part of the soul is not part of the body and thus can survive separately from it. He suggests that humans engaging in contemplation are fostering the divine in themselves and living a life akin to the gods. To what extent Aristotle intends that remark as metaphorical (rather than metaphysical) is unclear. I read it in the former light. More important, however, this interjection of the "divine" has no effect whatsoever on the rest of the *Nicomachean Ethics*, which is purely human and immanent in its focus. Aristotle is the first true humanist, and it is altogether fitting that the rediscovery of his works sparked the Renaissance.

LIVING AND FARING WELL

Aristotle notes that all animate objects seem to have a natural development and that we judge their particular excellence (or virtue) by reference to that development. Oak trees that are tall and sturdy are excellent examples of their species, just as horses that are fast and strong are excellent examples of theirs. They are flourishing, and what is good for oak trees and horses is what tends to promote that flourishing. Aristotle similarly believes that there is an ideal development or particular excellence of human nature that will result in human flourishing. There must be an overall good for man, just as there is a good for oak trees and horses.

Despite the teleological terminology, one could see the basic point as highly Darwinian. Natural selection has resulted in living things that are able to cope with their environments and the best examples of each species are those that flourish the most and hence are best adapted to survive. Aristotle, however, is not anticipating Darwin. He is personifying nature. But nature does not have purposes; humans have purposes and those depend upon context. One owner might want a horse that is fast and sleek for running races, another might want a horse that is strong and slow for hauling loads, while a third might want a horse that is steady and has great endurance for going into battle. There is no one "good" horse; rather, there are a variety of excellent types of horses, and a jockey, a carter, and a dragoon will each appraise them differently.

If anything, one would think it even more difficult to uncover "the good" for man, who is more varied and sets himself a wider range of "purposes" than we set for horses. Some men pursue pleasure, some honor, some riches, some love, and some knowledge. The list could be expanded, and most in fact pursue a mixture of these goods. Aristotle is fully aware of that fact. In each of these cases, however, he thinks the "good" pursued is an intermediate good. It is valued both in itself and for something in addition. "If," he explains, "there is some end of the things we do that we want on account of itself, and the rest on account of this one, and we do not choose everything on account of something else (for in that way the choices would go beyond all bounds, so that desire would be empty and pointless), it is clear that this would be the good, and in fact the highest good."[19]

Aristotle uses an umbrella term—*eudaimonia*—to specify this highest good. The word is commonly translated as "happiness," and that translation works up to a point. If pressed, we will readily say that we want pleasure or riches or honor because those things, we think, will make us happy. It makes little sense (outside a religious context) to press further and ask to what end we want to be happy, "since we choose this always on account of itself and never on account of anything else, while we choose honor and pleasure and intelligence and every virtue indeed on account of themselves (for even if nothing resulted from them we would choose each of them), but we choose them also for the sake of happiness, supposing that we will be happy by these means. But no one chooses happiness for the sake of these things, nor for the sake of anything else at all."[20]

Happiness thus seems to qualify as "something complete and self-sufficient" and "the end of actions," for which Aristotle is searching.[21] But there are two related problems with this translation. First, the term *happiness* tends to focus on feelings and emotions. In our usage, even a simpleton could be considered happy if he has a warm feeling in the pit of his stomach and a smile on his face. But Aristotle would never admit that a simpleton is *eudaimon*. The *eudaimon* life is certainly accompanied by pleasant feelings, but *eudaimonia* itself is a more active, engaged concept that embraces all the virtues of which men are capable, including most especially intelligence. A second, related problem is that when the word *happiness* is used to translate *eudaimonia*, the passage quoted in the previous paragraph seems false: we do not choose "every virtue... supposing that we will be happy by these means." We choose some virtues (e.g., courage in a dangerous situation, truthfulness when the truth is not to our advantage, justice in declining more than our fair share) *despite* the threat those virtues seem to pose to our happiness, narrowly construed.

Aristotle himself paraphrases *eudaimonia* as "living and faring well."[22] It constitutes success in the activity of being a complete human being and living a full and rich life. As J. O. Urmson notes, *eudaimonia* is the sort of life that parents want for their children.[23] Parents, of course, often say: "I don't care what he/she does, as long as he/she is happy." But that is hypocrisy. Parents want their children to flourish, to succeed in life, to experience all the best aspects of being human. They want their children to have a complete and full life. For Aristotle, living and faring well encompasses what we would call happiness, but it is much more than that. A close, but quite awkward translation, is "human flourishing," particularly since that conveys the naturalistic sense that Aristotle seeks of flourishing at being human, or realizing our full potential as human beings. But it is probably best to stick with Aristotle's own paraphrase, "living and faring well."

Is it correct, then, that all humans seek to live and fare well and that all intermediate goods (pleasure, wealth, virtue, honor) are sought for the sake of living and faring well? Yes, but only in the empty and circular sense that living and faring well just is, for the moment, the umbrella term that Aristotle introduces to impose order on the array of "intermediate" goods that men seek. Living and faring well is a bucket into which all those various goods are placed pending further discussion, and Aristotle expressly recognizes it as such when he introduces the term. As soon as he gives it a more specific content, i.e., to specify a particular mix of goods as the components of living and faring well, it will no longer be true that all men seek that particular mix; we will have moved from the descriptive to the prescriptive, from a general organizing principle to a specific recipe for the good life.

Despite its initial circularity, the centrality of Aristotle's notion of living and faring well is critical in two respects. First, it is a recognition of the complexity of human nature and the variety of ends sought by men. Unlike Plato and most later moralists, Aristotle is not interested in reducing human life to a single component or developing it along a single dimension. He is not reductionist. He recognizes the messy complexity of human life and our varied desires and values, and he does not believe that reducing or ignoring that complexity is a reflection of wisdom.[24] A full human life is not just contemplating the forms, or following the categorical imperative, or promoting the greatest good for the greatest number. For Aristotle, ethics is a matter of living and faring well as a full and complete human being.

Second, the initial circularity is itself critical to Aristotle's methodology, and we see it repeatedly in the *Ethics*. Aristotle introduces a term such as *eudaimonia* in the most general way imaginable in order to capture a broad agreement in our judgments. He then, through successive discussions, refines our understanding of those judgments by giving more and more specific content to the term. He does this with other key terms such as the good, the beautiful, virtue, character, habit, choice, and practical wisdom. That is why the best commentary on the *Ethics* may simply be a glossary of the most important words in the book.[25] Grappling with the way in which Aristotle gradually and steadily deepens (and changes) our understanding of these terms is the surest way to follow his argument.

Aristotle accordingly begins his account of living and faring well with a description of some of its commonly agreed-upon components, while recognizing that men will vary in their views on the relative weighting to be given to each. These include virtue and honor and intelligence, but also health and pleasure, and even good looks, reasonable wealth, and longevity. This is a highly pragmatic account.

As noted, Aristotle is not interested in purifying our conception of living and faring well or shutting his eyes to the importance of the many nonmoral goods that constitute such a life. A complete human life has need of "goods of the body, and of goods that are external and from fortune, in order that [it] not be impeded on account of them." Aristotle says that those who insist that the good man has no need of such things, and that even "someone who is being tortured, or someone who falls into great misfortunes," is still living and faring well as long as "he is a good person are either intentionally or unintentionally talking nonsense."[26]

That said, Aristotle immediately sets aside health, wealth, beauty, and other such external goods. They are "conditions that need to be present" for living and faring well, or things that "naturally assist" such a life, but the subject matter of ethics is the active response of the soul to external conditions.[27] This is a critical point for Aristotle. Living and faring well is "something that happens, and not something that is present like some possession."[28] The proper work of a man is to make the best possible use of his faculties in response to the conditions of life. This in turn requires the careful exercise of reason to guide and develop those faculties so that "each thing is accomplished well as a result of the virtue appropriate to it."[29] Virtue or excellence consists in the proper exercise of these faculties in accordance with reason.

In some ways, Aristotle is circling back to the teleological terminology with which he started. He suggests that the ability to reason is what separates man from all other creatures and thus the peculiar excellence of man must involve the full exercise of that faculty. But the teleological terminology (and resulting personification of nature) is not essential to the argument. Aristotle is simply stressing that humans are able to enlist reason to help them realize their ends. The proper exercise of that capacity is accordingly critical to a full and rich human life; failure to exercise it would lead to "a life suitable to beasts."[30]

The exact role of reason in living and faring well will become clearer as we discuss the individual virtues of character. But it is important to note first that Aristotle is not suggesting that reason alone either determines what is good or provides any incentive to be good. Aristotle is not propounding a formal ethics, as Kant does, in which reason determines the universal character of obligations that are recognized as binding on all rational beings. For Aristotle, practical reason plays a role only within our existing ethical practices. He notes that "we deliberate not about ends but about the things that are related to the ends."[31] Taken at face value, this remark may seem obviously wrong: we often deliberate not only about how to pursue our goals but also what goals to pursue. But I think Aristotle is making several related points specific to ethics. First, we don't deliberate about whether to be virtuous. That is a matter of upbringing and character. If those fail us, reason will not bridge the gap. Second, we don't deliberate about our final end: that just is "living and faring well." Finally, we don't deliberate even about the intermediate goods that make up living and faring well. Virtue, honor, intelligence, and even pleasure are all self-evident goods and all key ingredients of living and faring well. They have value both in their own right and for their contribution to the good life.

What we do deliberate about is how best to act in, and react to, certain situations. This practical deliberation is related to the issue of character discussed in the next section. We also deliberate about certain life choices, about where and how to focus our energies. Virtue is a fixed ingredient in the good life, but the mix of other goods is a matter more of personal choice. Aristotle is disdainful of a man who focuses on a life of physical pleasure (food, drink, and sex) and believes that such a man fails to realize his full human potential, living a life more suitable for beasts. But he is no ascetic and certainly recognizes that such pleasures are legitimate components of a good life, as long as they are pursued consistently with the virtues of character. The good life, he acknowledges, interweaves pleasure into living and faring well.

THE MAN OF EXCELLENT CHARACTER

The prior section raises an obvious question: why should we consider virtue to be necessary to living and faring well? Wealth, pleasure, honor, even intelligence all seem critical components of the good life. But couldn't a bad person enjoy all those goods? Indeed, in *The Republic*, Thrasymachus argues that the bad man is more likely to enjoy them because he would not be impeded in his pursuit by any scruples about virtue.

In considering this question, we have to remember two things. First, Aristotle is taking our standard ethical judgments for granted. He is not trying to provide foundations or arguments for those judgments that will compel acquiescence by a confirmed skeptic like Thrasymachus. He is writing for those who already care about virtue and want a better understanding of its nature. He is writing for those who assume that virtue is a critical component of a good life. Second, Aristotle is not using the word virtue (*arête*) in a narrowly moral sense, but rather in the sense that we might speak of the virtues of a good horse or a talented pianist. The word is often translated as "excellence," and it connotes whatever makes something an outstanding example of its kind. In applying the term to human beings, Aristotle is concerned with excellence of character, in the broad sense of that term, rather than with particular moral obligations. The Christian notion of morality—insofar as it is focused on charity and sexual abstinence—is very far from Aristotle.

For Aristotle, the virtues are ideals of character and behavior that are beautiful (noble) in and of themselves. Thus, the man of excellent character will disdain to lie, cheat, and steal not because some moral theory tells him it is wrong to do so, but because those are base and ignoble actions. In this sense, a person without virtue could not be *eudaimon* because he would be a miserable specimen of a human being.

The connection, again, with Nietzsche is self-evident. The good (noble) is contrasted with the bad (ignoble) and is chosen "for the sake of the beautiful, since this is the end that belongs to virtue."[32] Even apparently "unselfish" acts—acts of great courage or friendship—are performed to realize an ideal of character and excellence. There is no hypocrisy in such actions, no disguised will to power masquerading as altruism. One performs them because it is a beautiful and fitting thing to do so. The will to power (or to excellence) is right on the surface.

It would be a mistake, however, to focus exclusively on virtuous actions. Virtue for Aristotle—more so than for Nietzsche—has as much to do with disposition, practical intelligence, and feelings as with actions. Virtue is an active state of the soul that makes it disposed to act properly, to perceive the proper action in a given set of circumstances, and to accompany that action with the proper set of feelings. If any of these accompaniments are lacking, the exact same action could not be considered a product of virtue. "While the actions are called just or temperate whenever they are the sorts of things that a just or temperate person would do, the one who does them is not just or temperate unless he also does them in the way that just and temperate people do them."[33]

Aristotle notes that "it belongs to virtue...to be pleased and pained at what one ought and as one ought."[34] A man who feels excessive fear but still stands his ground is not, in Aristotle's view, as courageous as a man with steadier feelings. Similarly, a man who must struggle to master his temptation to drink too much is less temperate than the man who has no desire to drink excessively. This inversion may seem odd to us. After all, is not courage precisely the overcoming of fear and temperance the overcoming of temptation? The man who is not afraid or not tempted does not seem to require either courage or temperance. We are inclined to think (prompted by modern psychology) that we cannot help our feelings, but that virtue lies in what we do *despite* those feelings.

Aristotle would strongly disagree. He believes that with proper education and good habits one's feelings become aligned with and reinforce one's actions. One becomes naturally disposed toward virtuous actions and feels no internal tension that must be overcome. "By refraining from pleasures we become temperate, and once having become temperate we are most capable of refraining from them; and it is similar in the case of courage, for by habituating ourselves to disdain frightening things, and by enduring them, we become courageous, and having become courageous we shall be most capable of enduring frightening things."[35]

It is important to remember that Aristotle is concerned with excellence of character as a key component of living and faring well. The Garden of Gethsemane—the anguished night of the soul—is a foreign concept. Excellence of character for Aristotle is a settled disposition, a stable equilibrium of the soul that naturally perceives and embraces what is fine and beautiful. "What is most conducive to virtue of character," he explains, "is to enjoy what one ought and hate what one ought."[36]

We learn to enjoy what we ought and to hate what we ought through training and habit. That is, "we become just by doing things that are just, temperate by doing things that are temperate, and courageous by doing things that are courageous."[37] That may seem circular, but it makes perfect sense. "We do take on the virtues by first being at work in them, just as also in other things, namely the arts."[38] We learn to play the piano by playing, simply and painfully at first, but with increasing facility and subtlety as time goes on. Aristotle thinks learning virtue is more complicated than learning an art—since disposition, feelings, intelligence, and actions must all be aligned (though one could argue the same for the piano)—but the process is essentially the same. Moreover, just as with the piano, some people will take to the training more readily than others. They will accept the ethical standards of their day, strive to master and apply them, and become increasingly sensitive to the nuances of situations, behavior, and feelings. Behaving, feeling, and thinking in the proper way will become more and more "second nature" to them.

Thus, "excellence of character comes into being as a consequence of habit," and so, too, its opposite.[39] "By acting in our dealings with people some of us become just, others unjust, and by acting in frightening situations and getting habituated to be afraid or to be confident, some of us become courageous and others become cowards."[40] Over time, we become fixed in our characters and change is increasingly difficult. "It makes no small difference, then, to be habituated in this way or in that straight from childhood, but an enormous difference, or rather all the difference."[41] Just as virtue can become a settled disposition of the soul, so too can baseness become fixed in our nature.

Excellence of character is a stable equilibrium of the soul acquired by habit and sound training. The soul of the good man is balanced between excess and deficiency, for "virtues are of such a nature as to be destroyed by deficiency and by excess."[42] This is Aristotle's famous doctrine of the mean: "virtue is concerned with feelings and actions, in which excess and deficiency go astray, while the mean is praised and gets them right, and both of these belong to virtue."[43] His point is not that we must always act with moderation or be moderate in our feelings.[44] Some circumstances (e.g., a threat to one's family) may call for bold action and extreme anger. Other circumstances (e.g., a minor, unintentional slight) will properly be brushed aside with no action taken and no feelings of anger. Being moderately angry in both circumstances would not be the mark of an excellent character. A man of excellent character will feel and react appropriately to the circumstances. He will neither be impassive in the one instance nor overly touchy in the other.

The "mean condition" Aristotle identifies with virtue "is a mean condition between two vices, one resulting from excess and the other from deficiency, and is also a mean in the sense that the vices of the one sort fall short and those of the other sort go beyond what is appropriate both in feelings and in actions, while virtue both discovers and chooses the mean."[45] Courage is a mean condition between cowardice and foolhardiness. Temperance is a mean condition between dissipation and insensibility. Having an even temper is a mean condition between irascibility and impassivity. Generosity is a mean condition between stinginess and wastefulness. Again, this is not to say that the man of courage will be only "moderately courageous." Rather, he will be courageous in all circumstances, some of which will place him at extreme peril, others of which may expose him to very little peril. His feelings and actions will be calibrated accordingly. Similarly, the temperate man may enjoy food, drink, and sex in appropriate circumstances, but he will not live a life of dissipation or the life of an anchorite. He will disdain the pleasures of the dissipated person but will at the same time appreciate "pleasant things that are not impediments to health and good condition, and are not contrary to what is beautiful, and not beyond his resources."[46]

As Aristotle explains, "there is no excess or deficiency of temperance or courage, because the mean is in a certain way an extreme."[47] The mean is like a bull's-eye struck by an expert archer. It is a mark of true excellence, not of an average condition. At the same time, there is no mean condition of cowardice or foolhardiness or of dissipation or insensibility because "however one does them one is in the wrong."[48] The same is true of certain feelings, "such as joy at others' misfortunes, shamelessness, and envy."[49] There are no "right conditions" under which such feelings should arise. Whichever way one moves from the bull's-eye, one has missed the target. Aristotle's doctrine of the mean recognizes that "it is possible to go wrong in many ways," but "there is only one way to get something right."[50] Irascibility may manifest itself as "getting angry at people one ought not to get angry at," or "in circumstances in which one ought not," or "more than one ought," or "more quickly, and for a longer time."[51] Impassivity will likewise manifest itself as a failure to get angry at people with whom one should be angry, in circumstances where anger is warranted, or if anger is aroused it may not be sufficient to the occasion or too slow to manifest itself or be dissipated too quickly. Only the man of excellent character strikes exactly the right balance in each case.

Calibrating that balance is far from easy in the midst of constant wrong signals from those who lack the virtues in question. The people at each extreme will justify themselves by accusing the person at the mean of being at the other extreme. Thus, "the coward calls the courageous person rash while the rash person calls him a coward, and analogously in the other cases."[52]

The virtuous man himself will have to make use of the extremes in calibrating his own character and feelings. In determining how to improve one's character, Aristotle tells us, "one ought to consider what we ourselves are carried away toward."[53] If we have a tendency to timidity we ought to affect boldness. If we are too rash, we should err toward circumspection in our actions. Similarly, if we have a tendency toward stinginess we should force ourselves even to be excessively generous, and vice versa. "We ought then to drag ourselves over toward the opposite side, for by pulling far away from going wrong we will come to the mean, the very thing that people do who straighten warped pieces of lumber."[54] In all such cases we must guard against what seems to us the most comfortable and pleasant action, since pleasure can warp judgment until through habit pleasure is aligned with virtue. "In everything the pleasant or pleasure is most to be guarded against; for we do not judge it impartially."[55]

There is then "some boundary" marking the mean condition between an excess and deficiency and the virtuous man adjusts his aim toward that target, tightening or loosening his grip as needed. Virtue is an active condition that makes one apt at hitting that target because both disposition and feelings are aligned with it by habit and training. "But while speaking this way is truthful," Aristotle candidly acknowledges, "there is nothing clear in it."[56] A key ingredient has to be added to the mix, and that is practical judgment or practical reason or practical wisdom or prudence (which is how the word *phronesis* is variously translated). Practical judgment is the means by which one determines the right and proper response to a given set of circumstances. It is the third critical element—along with proper disposition and right feelings—that makes an action virtuous and a character excellent.

Practical judgment for Aristotle plays a critical role in virtue but is not itself virtue, as it was for Socrates. Socrates thought that virtue and knowledge were synonymous, whereas Aristotle thinks that virtue requires knowledge. In other words, Socrates "erred in thinking that all virtues are forms of wise judgment, but he asserted beautifully that there is no virtue without wise judgment."[57] Wise judgment is no guarantee of virtue, since weakness of will may prevent one from following it. But virtue is impossible without wise judgment since otherwise choice will be unguided and miss the mark. "Choice will not be right without practical judgment or without virtue, since the latter makes one bring the end into action, and the former makes one enact the things related to the end."[58] We need both to know how to realize the good and to possess the proper dispositions and feelings to apply that knowledge.

Aristotle, however, does not believe, as Kant does, that ethics can be reduced to rules derived from reason alone. "Virtue is not just an active condition in accord with right reason, but one that *involves* right reason, and practical judgment is right reason concerning such matters."[59] The difference is critical. Ethics requires practical judgment to choose wisely, but the exercise of that judgment is context dependent. There are too many nuances to be reduced to rules. Practical judgment is a considered art, not a rational process of deduction. The activity is imbued with intelligence the way that Glenn Gould's playing of the piano is imbued with intelligence. The playing itself "involves right reason"; it is not "in accord with right reason" because right reason is not something that can be separated from the playing and deduced independently.

"Concerning practical judgment," Aristotle tells us, "the way we might get hold of it is by considering whom we speak of as people with practical judgment." Practical judgment belongs to someone who is "able to deliberate beautifully about...the sort of things that are conducive to living well as a whole."[60] The point is, once again, circular, but still illuminating and completely consistent with Aristotle's wish to understand our existing ethical discourse from within rather than to ground it in, or reduce it to, something else. The best way to understand in what excellent piano playing consists is not to develop an abstract theory but to listen to Glenn Gould and other pianists who are commonly recognized as excellent. So, too, the best way to understand the exercise of practical judgment is to learn from the example of those who are commonly regarded as possessing that quality in the highest degree.

As Martha Nussbaum has explained, the best such exemplar may be a novelist such as Henry James, who is exquisitely attuned to nuances of circumstance and behavior and ruthlessly exposes every attempt to disguise selfishness and cruelty behind moral platitudes.[61] Henry James and, one might add, George Eliot, and other such authors all recognize, with Aristotle, "that it is not possible to be good in the governing sense without practical judgment,"[62] and the overarching moral narrative of *The Ambassadors* or *Middlemarch* is one of the growing refinement and exercise of such judgment by its principal characters. In reading these books one struggles along with Lambert Strether and Dorothea Brooks in their attempts to set aside hypocrisy, to recognize wherein virtue lies, and to align their characters and actions with their increasingly sophisticated judgment of what is right and just.

Aristotle is surely correct when he tells us that "there is no such thing as doing well" without intellect and thinking and character.[63] Aristotle stresses the need for long experience and careful meditation both upon the general nature of each virtue and the concrete particulars of individual situations as a means of bringing disposition, feeling, and right reason into harmony with one another and with the beautiful in human character. It is no easy matter, but the man of excellent character will through proper training and experience learn to exercise his virtues in the right way, at the right time, for the right reasons, and with the right feelings.

Is it, then, possible to teach virtue? Aristotle would say yes, but only with significant qualifications. "Discourses appear to have the power to encourage and stimulate open-natured young people, and would make a well-born character that loves what is truly beautiful be inspired with virtue, but they are unable to encourage most people toward what is beautiful and good."[64] A child with a naturally vicious or degraded disposition will not be inspired with virtue, however powerful the discourse. "It is necessary for a character to be present in advance that is in some way appropriate for virtue, loving what is beautiful and scorning what is shameful."[65] He must be inclined by nature to love what is right simply because it is right and just, and that is the exception rather than the rule. Furthermore, "it is difficult to hit upon a right training toward virtue from youth..., for living temperately and with endurance is not pleasant to most people, and especially not to the young."[66] Once a disposition becomes fixed through habit and indulgence, moreover, it becomes extremely difficult to change. "It is not possible, or not easy, to change by words things that have been bound up in people's characters since long ago."[67]

In limited and sometimes fitful ways, we do try to teach virtue to the young. The preschool my children attended has a fourfold motto: Honest, Kind, Respectful, Responsible. In all ways, big and small, the school seeks to encourage and inculcate those values. We have drug and alcohol programs in our schools designed to teach our children temperance and to think about the consequences of their actions. The military fashions basic training to inculcate courage and a sense of teamwork and responsibility for one another. To what extent these various ways of teaching virtue actually work is open to debate, but their persistence would indicate at least some belief in their efficacy.

The key point for Aristotle, as for Nietzsche, is that it is possible to learn virtue if one is disposed to do so. It is possible to work on and perfect one's character just as one can work on and perfect a work of art. One could apply Nietzsche's metaphor of the "three metamorphoses of the spirit" to Aristotle as well. In the initial stage, the stage of the camel, the young person struggles to adopt and abide by existing moral standards, training his feelings, building his character, and developing his practical reason. In the lion stage, the man who has assimilated the values of his society can begin to question and refine them, exposing inconsistencies, rejecting platitudes, and shunning hypocrisy in favor of a deeper understanding of living and faring well. In the final stage, these hard-won lessons have created a stable equilibrium in which disposition, feeling, and judgment form a uni-

fied, consistent, and spontaneous whole. The man of excellent character is an exemplar for his community; he does not abide by virtue
but rather embodies and defines virtue for others.

THE GREAT-SOULED MAN

Possessing an excellent character is the critical component in living
and faring well. But, important as it is, it is not everything. One must
still decide how to direct one's energies in life. One must decide, in
Nietzsche's terms, who one wants to become. For Aristotle, living
among aristocrats in a society supported by slavery, only two genuine
choices present themselves: the life of public affairs and the more private life of contemplation. Aristotle himself considers the latter
superior. But he never loses his fascination with the former. As a
result, he paints a detailed and quite modern portrait of those "great-
souled" men for whom "it is honor most of all of which they consider
themselves worthy."[68]

Greatness of soul is a particular virtue of the public man. Like
the other virtues, it is a mean between extremes of vice, and at the
same time itself an extreme of virtue. "While the great-souled person
is an extreme by reason of magnitude, he is a mean by reason of
doing things the way one ought, for he assesses himself in accord with
his worth, while the others exceed or fall short of theirs."[69] The great-
souled person "is one who considers himself worthy of great things,
and is worthy of them."[70] The person who considers himself worthy
of great things but is not is vain and foolish, while the person who
underestimates his worth is small souled or unduly humble.

Aristotle, it should be stressed, does not consider humility to be a
virtue. His ethics is pre-Christian and focuses on recognizing and
valuing excellence of character as part of a rich and flourishing life.
Humility may be appropriate in some circumstances—recall
Churchill's remark about Clement Atlee: "a modest man who has
much to be modest about"—but a worthy person of undue humility
"deprives himself of the things he deserves, and seems to have something bad about him from his not considering himself worthy of what
is good, or to be ignorant of himself, since he would have reached out

for the things he was worthy of if they were good."[71] Surprisingly, Aristotle even suggests that "smallness of soul is positioned more opposite to greatness of soul than vanity is, since it both occurs more and is worse." In that single remark, we see how far Aristotle is from us: he celebrates greatness and would rather see someone pretend to greatness and end up appearing ridiculous than adopt more modest aspirations. As Michelangelo was to say, "The greater danger for most of us lies not in setting our aim too high and falling short; but in setting our aim too low, and achieving our mark."[72]

The great-souled man, like Michelangelo (who was as much a public figure in his day as any general or pope), has an outsized personality. He expects, as a reflection of his talents and worth, to be honored and respected in the public sphere. Such a man, "if in fact he is worthy of the greatest honors, must be the best human being; for the one who is better is always worthy of more, and the one who is best is worthy of what is greatest."[73] Honor is allotted to those who excel in any endeavor; but the greatest honors are properly reserved for those who combine success with excellence of character. In this sense, greatness of soul is not so much a virtue in itself as "a certain kind of adornment of the virtues, since it makes them greater, and does not come about without them. For this reason it is difficult to be great-souled in truth, for it is not possible without the beauty that belongs to goodness."[74]

In our own cynical, post-Nietzschean age, virtue is in fact the last thing we would expect from a politician or other public figure. We have seen too many puffed up, arrogant self-promoters whose pretensions to virtue have been exposed as lies. In public affairs, Thrasymachus may well be right that virtue is an obstacle to, rather than a requirement of, success. Certainly, those obsessed with honor and power and wealth are rarely virtuous in their efforts to reach those ends.

Aristotle is fully aware of this, however. He himself finds "completely ridiculous" the pretensions of those vain and foolish people who "stake a claim to things that are held in honor when they are not worthy of them."[75] Even those with wealth, power, and high birth are not worthy of honor unless they have excellent characters. Such goods are honored "by some people, but in accordance with truth, only someone good is honorable."[76] Those who have such goods from fortune, but have not virtue, "are not rightly called great-souled, since there is no worth or greatness of soul without complete virtue." Indeed, for most people, the goods of fortune are an impediment to virtue. They are likely to become "arrogant and insolent, for without virtue it is not easy to carry off one's good fortune harmoniously, but not being able to carry it off, and believing that they are superior to others, they look down on them, even while they themselves act in whatever way they happen to."[77] They seek to mimic the great-souled person in the ways they can without first having mastered and perfected their own characters.

The great-souled person will in fact comport himself moderately toward wealth and power and every sort of good and bad fortune. He "will be neither overjoyed when in good fortune nor overly distressed when in bad fortune."[78] Even honor, which he most values and deems his due, he will take only on his own terms and will treat it as a small thing. "That is why great-souled people seem to be arrogant."[79] Such a person will not curry favor or seek help from others, though he will assist others eagerly. He will be "highhanded toward those of high station or good fortune," easy and moderate toward those of a middle station, and gentle and gracious to the weak.[80] He will speak and act openly, caring only for the truth, and will disdain to conceal his feelings and beliefs. He will also disdain those things held in popular esteem, reserving himself for great and notable deeds. Aristotle even describes the physical mannerisms of the great-souled person: "a great-souled person seems to have a slow way of moving, a deep voice, and a steady way of speaking, since a person who takes few things seriously is not anxious, and one who thinks nothing is great is not intense."[81]

Thus portrayed, it is difficult to view the great-souled man as anything other than insufferable. All his life seems to be a stage play in which each action is carefully orchestrated to enhance his own stature and realize his own vision of himself as a great man. Yet, as Shakespeare has told us, we all play out our lives on a stage; we all fashion our characters for good or ill. The whole point of the *Nicomachean Ethics* is to discuss how we can fashion them for good; how, through accustoming ourselves to act in certain ways, we can bring our dispositions and feelings in line with an ideal of excellent character. Certainly, there have been great men in history, among artists (Michelan-gelo, Goethe), nation builders (Washington, Simon Bolivar), and even modern politicians (Churchill, T. Roosevelt). Shakespeare was himself a believer in great men (as well as a ruthless exposer of their flaws). Perhaps there is something faintly ridiculous about these men who insist upon their greatness and their destiny. Yet they are great for all that and we properly admire them in proportion to their excellence of character and their accomplishments.

CONTEMPLATIVE MAN

It is with some relief that the modern reader turns from the great-souled man—vividly conscious of his own dignity and awaiting his moment to strut across the stage of world affairs—to Aristotle's alter-native model of living and faring well, the quiet, largely private life of contemplation. It is a life, he tells us, of complete happiness: serious, self-sufficient, pleasurable, richly fulfilling, and as close to the divine as human beings can attain.

There is a certain amount of special pleading here. Certainly, one would have a hard time recognizing Aristotle's portrait of contempla-tive man in the stereotype of modern-day academics, with their cul-ture wars and their bitter internal politics. We would not be inclined to grant to such a life any more inherent claim to excellent character than we would to the life of public affairs. But neither would Aris-totle. Again, excellence of character is the base point from which he starts. He assumes an excellent character but then asks how that char-acter might best be exercised in living and faring well.

The key point for Aristotle is that life is activity, and each person is properly active "in connection with those things and by means of those capacities that satisfy him most."[82] Aristotle believes that plea-sure is a positive good and completes each activity. "The pleasure brings the activity to completion not as an active condition present within it all along, but as something that comes over it, like the bloom of well-being in people who are at the peak of their powers."[83] Without the activity, there will be no pleasure, and without the plea-sure the activity will not be complete. But whether the pleasure is for the sake of the activity or the activity for the sake of the pleasure is not a question worth pursing "for these appear to be joined together and incapable of separation."[84]

It is natural then for people to seek out activities that bring them pleasure. Some love music, some sports, others food and wine, still others thinking and contemplation. The activities differ in kind from one another "and so too with the pleasures that complete them."[85] Each of the pleasures is bound up with the activity in a different way and "the appropriate pleasure contributes to the growth of the activity" since those who experience pleasure "discern each sort of thing better and are more precise about it; for example, people who enjoy doing geometry become skilled at geometry, and understand each part of it more, and likewise those who love music or architecture or each of the other pursuits become better at their particular work because they enjoy it."[86]

Activities and the pleasure that brings them to completion, Aristotle tells us, also bring living to completion. Aristotle, however, believes that some activities have more inherent worth and hence are more complete than others. Living and faring well is in accord with excellence and virtue, "and this involves seriousness and does not consist in play."[87] Relaxation is not itself an end but rather for the sake of activity. Such activity should engage the best part of man, which is "intellect or some other part that seems by nature to rule and lead and have a conception about things that are beautiful and divine, and to be either divine itself or the most divine of the things in us."[88] A life of contemplation, then, is the best, the most complete, and the most conducive to living and faring well.

Even the most casual reader will notice the gaps in Aristotle's argument. Why is seriousness better than play? Why is reason to be valued more highly than emotion? Nietzsche, in his revaluation of values, would raise both questions and answer them quite differently than Aristotle. Aristotle's own brief in favor of the life of contemplation contains two arguments. The first is based on the inherent features of such a life, the other on the nature of the faculties so engaged. Both are intriguing, but neither is ultimately convincing.

First, Aristotle argues that the life of contemplation is "as self-sufficient, leisured, and unwearied as possible for a human being."[89] It is self-sufficient because it does not require others for its enjoyment, because it has no aim beyond itself, and because, although any sort of life has need of some external prosperity, "since nature is not self-sufficient for contemplating," the person absorbed in such a life will not need "many things or grand ones."[90] It is leisured because it is not scrambling for any external gain, but is loved for its own sake "for nothing comes from it beyond the contemplating, while from things involving action we gain something for ourselves, to a greater or lesser extent, beyond the action."[91] It is unwearied because it is susceptible to more sustained enjoyment than other activities, for "we are more able to contemplate continuously than to act in any way whatever."[92] Philosophy in particular, he notes, "seems to have pleasures that are wonderful in their purity and stability."[93] Accordingly, the life of contemplation "would be the complete happiness of a human being, if it takes in a complete span of life, for none of the things that belong to [living and faring well] is incomplete."[94]

This lifestyle argument will appeal to some but not to others. Certainly, your average sixteen-year-old studying pre-calculus would beg to differ on whether sustained intellectual labor is unwearied or not. Nor will the pleasures of philosophy appeal to all. Aristotle's first argument will be persuasive only to those whose tastes already run toward a life of contemplation.

His second argument attempts to place the life of contemplation on firmer ground based on the inherent superiority of the faculties involved. Aristotle argues that intellect is what distinguishes man from the other animals; it is our highest and most powerful faculty and hence activity that engages the intellect will also be the highest and most powerful activity of man. Indeed, Aristotle suggests that "if the intellect is something divine as compared with a human being, the life that is in accord with the intellect is divine as compared with a human life."[95] By contrast, "the life in accord with the rest of virtue is happy in a secondary way, since the activities that result from it are human ones."[96]

It is unclear to what extent this last argument about the divine in man is intended to be metaphorical rather than literal. I prefer to read it in the former light, but the basic point is the same regardless. Aristotle properly urges us to "strain every nerve to live in accordance with the best thing in us."[97] But whether that "best thing in us" is really the intellect or whether it is spirituality or love or something else is a question to which Aristotle does not provide a convincing answer. In fact, his own discussion of friendship offers a more balanced view of human nature than the ideal of the self-sufficient contemplative man.

FRIENDSHIP

Aristotle's *Nicomachean Ethics* is largely concerned with public virtue. The virtues of character that Aristotle discusses—courage, generosity, justice, truthfulness, sociability, and even temperance—are usually presented as the virtues of a public man in a public setting. Those virtues, moreover, are themselves publicly derived; that is, they follow (even as they refine) accepted norms of right conduct.

The man of excellent character—almost as much as the great-souled man—is thus a man on display before his fellow man. His conduct is beautiful and correct, but the element of personal affection, of genuine intimate relations with his fellows seems lacking. The man of excellent character has grown so fully into his part that everyone else tends to be reduced to props. The distance at which others are kept may be moderate (a mean between extremes of overinvolvement and indifference) but it seems nonetheless chilling for that.

It is worth stressing, then, that Aristotle spends two of his ten books in the *Nicomachean Ethics* talking about friendship. In fact, he states that friendship is "necessary for life," for "no one would choose to live without friends, despite having all the rest of the good things" that life has to offer, including riches and power.[98] Aristotle does not discuss romantic love, but his analysis of friendship is deeper and more profound than anything ever written on the subject. Enjoying true friendship—which for Aristotle presupposes virtue on both sides—is the culmination of living and faring well.

As befits the man who invented biology, Aristotle begins his discussion with taxonomy. Friendship is of three kinds. First, there are friendships of utility. Such persons "do not love one another for themselves, but insofar as something good comes to them from one another."[99] These are friendships where one or both parties has an eye on his own advantage and his own advancement and is friendly insofar as he expects to gain thereby. These relationships of convenience are based on the perceived goods (wealth, power, influence) that the other party has to bestow.

Second, there are friendships of pleasure. Such persons "are fond of charming people not for being people of a certain sort, but because they are pleasing to themselves."[100] These are friendships that seem to value the other person for their charm or wit or brilliant conversations, but are really just a variation on friendships of convenience. They are friendships in which one or both parties is primarily interested in being entertained or amused.

These two types of friendship can of course be mixed and matched, with one person seeking advantage and the other entertainment, or each party seeking a mixture of the two. But Aristotle does not consider either to be a true form of friendship. They are "friendships of an incidental kind," which are "easily dissolved."[101] They are essentially bartered-for exchanges and once the terms of the bargain change, the relationship itself is unlikely to survive. If one party no longer seems useful (perhaps having already served as a stepping stone) and/or the other no longer seems charming (whether due to age or circumstances or changing tastes), there is no core of genuine affection to keep the relationship going. "So when that through which they were friends has departed, the friendship is dissolved, since the friendship was a consequence of that."[102]

The third sort of friendship, and the only one that really counts for Aristotle, is "a friendship for virtue."[103] It is a relationship between equals in which each person is concerned most for the welfare of the other. It is the only "complete sort of friendship," because it is "between people who are good and are alike in virtue."[104] Such friendships are both beneficial and pleasant, but each person strives most to give benefit and pleasure to the other. Such persons "wish for good things for their friends for their own sake," rather than for whatever good things those friends can bestow upon them.[105]

"Such friendships," Aristotle tells us, "are likely to be rare, for such people are few."[106] Moreover, they need time and intimate acquaintance with one another for friendship to develop, for it is not possible for people to know one another until "each shows himself to each as loveable and is trusted." Once formed, however, "there is a trusting, and a never doing each other wrong, and everything else people consider worthy of friendship in its true sense."[107] Such a friendship is not only "beautiful," but it will not easily be dissolved due to passing time or changing needs and tastes.[108] It will last "as long as [the two friends] are good, and virtue is enduring."[109]

A critical aspect of such friendship is a shared taste in activities. For "whatever it is for the sake of which they choose to be alive—this is what they want to be engaged in with their friends."[110] Some friends will drink together, others will exercise together, or hunt together, or even "engage in philosophy together, each sort spending their days together in whatever it is, out of all things in life, that they are most contented by; for since they want to share their lives with their friends, they do those things and share those things that they believe living together consists in."[111] In the course of these shared activities, the friendship itself will ripen and the friends will benefit from their association with one another, becoming even better people as each strives to live in harmony with the other. "The friendship of decent people is decent, and grows along with their association, and they seem to become even better people by putting the friendship to work and by straightening one another out, for they have their rough edges knocked off by the things they like in one another."[112]

One can readily imagine Aristotle's contemplative man with one or even a few such friends, knocking off his rough edges and giving his quiet, scholarly life a vitality and richness and meaning that it would not otherwise have. It is harder to imagine the great-souled man with any true friends. Friendship is not a one-sided relationship, and the great-souled man is too conscious of his own significance to be on equal terms with others. He may have loyal lieutenants and he may dispense bounty as if he were the most generous of friends, but always with an eye to his own glory.

Interestingly, though, Aristotle paints even true friends as vying with one another in beautiful gestures of friendship for the sake of "something great" in themselves.[113] They wish for and do good things for the sake of their friends, without seeking anything in return. But such behavior is not wholly altruistic. Aristotle notes that when a person distributes the greater good to his friend—whether it be money or honors or office—"he will give up all these things to a friend, since this is a beautiful thing for him, and something to be praised."[114] In this way, although he distributes more goods to his friend, he "distributes to himself the greater share of the beautiful."[115]

Such a person, Aristotle tells us, will be eager to invite friends into his good fortunes, "since it is a beautiful thing to do good for others," but be hesitant to invite them into his misfortunes.[116] He will "go uninvited" to friends who need assistance and find ways to benefit them. At the same time, he will be reluctant to ask others for help and slow to take favors, "since it is not a beautiful thing to be eager to get benefits."[117] Ever the pragmatist, however, Aristotle recognizes that friendship is a two-way street and that only giving, never receiving, can itself seem a form of selfishness and grandiosity. Thus, accepting benefits from a friend and, letting the friend do "a beautiful thing," is also a critical component of true friendship.

Friendship, in short, is necessary for life and beautiful in itself. It is both a reward of virtue and a spur to greater virtue. It makes of each activity, through being shared with a friend, richer, fuller, and more vibrant. A man with good friends is truly living and faring well.

This is philosophy at its best: practical, thoughtful, nuanced, enlightening, and even inspiring. Ethics, in Aristotle, is not reduced to a single dimension, whether it be utility, or the categorical imperative, or even the Nietzschean drama of self-overcoming. The *Nicomachean Ethics* takes account of the full variety of life. Somehow at the end of reading Aristotle one feels more completely human and alive, more open to the possibilities of excellence, and even, one hopes, a better person.

CHAPTER SIX
HEIDEGGER AND AUTHENTICITY

The sentence, "Language is language," leaves us to hover over an abyss as long as we endure what it says.[1]

I
t is easy not to like Martin Heidegger, whether as a man or as a writer. His enthusiastic support of National Socialism, as well as his post-war effort to conceal that support, is repugnant. The willful obscurity of his prose, with its compound Germanic neologisms, is famously off-putting.

Yet Martin Heidegger may have had more influence on twentieth-century intellectual life than any thinker besides Freud and Einstein. He stands with Wittgenstein as one of the two greatest philosophers since Nietzsche, and his prose, once deciphered, is strangely and deeply moving. Indeed, one feels that Heidegger, better than any other philosopher, has penetrated to the most basic characteristics of what it is to be alive in the world. He was, moreover, a man with many devoted students and colleagues, including many Jews (such as his longtime friend and lover Hannah Arendt) who deeply admired him. Close inspection reveals that his early involvement with National Socialism was, without excusing it, more naive than venal.

Heidegger is an ambiguous character, a man poised, as a recent biography was entitled, "between good and evil." As such he is a fitting symbol both of his philosophy—which attempts to come to grips with the inherent ambiguity of everyday life—and of the twentieth century, in which the certainty, clarity, and sense of progress of earlier ages were finally and irrevocably lost. Heidegger himself ultimately quailed in the face of the ambiguity that he so forcefully portrayed as the essential condition of man, fleeing first into the arms of the German *volk* and later into a quasi-mystical reunion with the foundational essence of Being, which he claimed to perceive, however dimly, in the fragmentary writings of the pre-Socratic Greeks. But his initial analysis of man's being-in-the-world and being-with-others—an analysis that spurns all false foundations and is content to travel within a circle of ever deeper interpretations—is the final triumph and self-immolation of philosophy.

Heidegger was born in Messkirch on September 26, 1889. Messkirch is in the southeastern corner of Germany near Lake Constance and not far from Ulm, where Einstein had been born ten years earlier. His family on his mother's side had farmed in the area for many generations. His father, a master cooper (maker of casks and barrels), was also a sexton at the Church of St. Martin, and the family lived in a small house opposite the church. They were a deeply Catholic family, and Heidegger later explained that the rhythms of his life revolved around the daily ringing of the bells, the rituals of the church feasts, and the passing seasons. In words reminiscent of Wordsworth, he spoke of a "splendor then hardly visible" that lay on all things.[2] Much of his philosophy was an attempt to recapture that forgotten splendor.

Heidegger, a promising student, was supported by the church in the expectation that he would become a priest. He attended a Catholic boarding school in Constance starting in 1903. For the next thirteen years, Heidegger was wholly dependent upon the church for his education and maintenance, even as he grew increasingly estranged from its beliefs.

In 1909, Heidegger entered the Jesuit order as a novice but lasted only two weeks, withdrawing ostensibly for medical reasons. Later that year, he entered the Freiburg Theological Seminary with the avowed intention of becoming a theologian. Again, however, his health intervened. He suffered from heart pains, and in February 1911 he left the seminary for a period of rest at Messkirch. Once free of theology, his heart ceased to trouble him (though the pains flared up again during World War I when he was faced with induction into the military).

Heidegger changed his course of study to philosophy, focusing on medieval scholasticism and in particular the work of Thomas Aquinas. He completed his doctorate at Freiberg in 1913, but managed to retain the support of the Catholic Church until 1916. He wrote for Catholic periodicals, even as he struggled not to be pigeonholed as a Catholic philosopher. Heidegger fell increasingly under the influence of Hegel, Nietzsche, Kierkegaard, and above all the great Jewish philosopher Edmund Husserl, who had a chair at Freiburg. Husserl, though resistant at first because of Heidegger's ties to the Catholic Church, eventually accepted Heidegger as his protégé.

Like Kant before him, Heidegger became a Privatdozent in 1915. That same year, he married Elfride Petri, a young economics student, in a Catholic ceremony performed by his friend and sponsor, Engelbert Krebs. The marriage lasted until Heidegger's death, sixty-one years later, and seems to have been remarkably contented, despite Heidegger's multiple infidelities.

With Husserl's patronage and support, Heidegger felt sufficiently emboldened to abandon Catholicism "officially," which he did in a January 1919 letter to Krebs. Heidegger explained that his study of philosophy "made the *system* of Catholicism problematic and unacceptable for me."[3] Yet he was quick to reassure Krebs of his belief in a higher power guiding his actions. "I believe that I have an inner calling for philosophy, and that by answering the call through research and teaching I am doing everything in my power to further the spiritual life of man—that and *only* that—thereby justifying my life and work in the sight of God."[4] As Elfride explained in a follow-up letter, they still believed in a "personal God," but without any "dogmatic ties."[5]

Husserl made great efforts to obtain posts for his protégé. Ultimately, those efforts resulted in a professorship at Marburg, which Heidegger assumed in 1923. It was there that he met and began his love affair with a young, brilliant, and beautiful Jewish student named Hannah Arendt, who became a fixture in his life. Heidegger himself was an attractive figure in those years. He was small but extremely athletic and had very intense, piercing eyes. His lecture style was said to be mesmerizing, although few claimed to understand him fully.

Elfride used a small inheritance to purchase some land and build a hut for Heidegger in Todtnauberg, on the edge of the Black Forest. Heidegger spent much of his time there, reading, skiing, thinking, and writing. The hut in Todtnauberg became another fixture, a place where, he explained, life "appears to the mind as something pure, simple and immense."[6] It was there that he composed most of his masterpiece, *Being and Time*. Neither parent lived to read the book. His father died in 1924, the year Heidegger began his affair with Arendt. His mother died in 1927, the year *Being and Time* was published. He placed a copy of the book on her deathbed. The contents would have given her little consolation; the book argues that confronting the nothingness and inevitability of death is what gives authenticity to life. There is no sign in it of any belief in a personal God.

Heidegger dedicated the book to Husserl, inscribing it as follows:

EDMUND HUSSERL
in friendship and admiration
Todtnauberg in Baden, Black Forest
8 April 1926.

When Husserl retired in 1928, Heidegger was appointed to his Freiberg chair at Husserl's urging.

The years between 1928 and 1933 were quiet ones for Heidegger, if not for Germany. He published little but gave his lectures and sought to deepen and extend the insights of *Being and Time* under the ever-growing shadow of Hitler and National Socialism. Heidegger did not view this movement with alarm; far from it. He thought that only National Socialism could deal with the grave problems of mass unemployment and unrest, while preventing a collapse into communism. More bizarrely, he saw National Socialism as a collective philosophical movement that would, somehow, lead to a more authentic existence for the German people, through a reconnection with its deepest roots. Heidegger harbored a deep suspicion of modernism and wanted to preserve German folk life, the idealized life of Messkirch and Todtnauberg. He romanticized National Socialism and in particular its mass-appeal aspects: the bonfires, the rallies, and the symbols. He thought that National Socialism was promoting the importance of "nature, history, language; the Volk, custom, the state."[7] As he later explained, he thought he was vouchsafed a vision of "the inward truth and greatness" of the Nazi movement.[8]

Yet the ugliness of the Nazi movement was certainly there for him to see. Jews were increasingly harassed and banned from public employment. In April 1933, Husserl (whose sons had fought for Germany in World War I) was officially suspended from any ability to teach—an unnecessary indignity, since he had already retired. Elfride sent flowers and a bland note of regret to Husserl's wife, suggesting that the suspension was a bureaucratic mistake. Heidegger himself sent not a word to his former teacher and mentor who had worked so hard to promote his career.

It was partly due to the suspension of Husserl that the rector of the University of Freiberg resigned his post. Heidegger willingly and eagerly took his place. In his rectoral address, given on April 22, 1933, he sought to place the university itself at the service of the German state and "German destiny . . . in its most extreme distress."[9] He even insisted on everyone raising his or her right hand in the "Sieg Heil!" salute during the singing of the Nazi anthem, the "Horst-Wessel Lied." Heidegger formally joined the Nazi party on May 1, two months after Hitler became chancellor and began his ruthless suppression of all opposing parties. In an "Appeal to German Students," given in November of that year, Heidegger argued that "[t]he Führer himself and alone is the present and future German reality and its law."[10]

As rector, however, Heidegger proved more of an embarrassment than an aid to the Nazi party. His ham-fisted efforts to ensure uniform support for National Socialism within the university led to angry dissension among those colleagues who valued academic freedom. Perhaps more important, his attempt to give philosophical underpinnings to the Nazi movement was met with utter incomprehension. The thugs in the party could grab hold of a dime-store version of Nietzsche's slogan, "the will to power," but they did not know what to make of Heidegger's speeches about authenticity and nothingness, given at bonfire rallies that Heidegger attended dressed in the folk garb of his native region. The Nazi press became increasingly critical and even mocking of the Freiberg rector. Heidegger quietly resigned his position on April 23, 1934, just one year and one day after assuming it.

From that point on, Heidegger ceased to play any active role in the Nazi party. Indeed, some of his writings were sufficiently critical of racism and biological determinism that the Gestapo placed him under surveillance. But he retained his party membership until the end of the war. His most dedicated students—Hannah Arendt, Elisabeth Blochmann (with whom he also had an affair), and Karl Lowith—were forced to flee Germany without a word of public protest from Heidegger (although he did provide private assistance, at least to Blochmann). His silence continued throughout the brutal attacks on Jewish students and the establishment of the first concentration camps. He even removed the dedication to Husserl from a subsequent edition of *Being and Time*, allegedly at the insistence of the publisher, who feared Nazi censorship. When Husserl died in 1938, Heidegger failed to attend his cremation, pleading indisposition.

Following the war, Heidegger was himself banned from teaching by the de-nazification committee, despite his acrobatic efforts simultaneously to minimize, to disguise, and to justify his role in the party. He plausibly claimed to know nothing about the murder of millions of Jews and, as for the daily acts of violence that he could not but have seen, he called them shameful but said that "one was powerless to prevent" them.[11] Perhaps that was true, but his statement—cast in impersonal terms in an attempt to spread the blame of nonaction—is deeply ironic. The word "one" here is a translation, "man," which preceded by a definite article was a critical term in Heidegger's philosophy, "das Man." As we shall see, in *Being and Time*, Heidegger argues that "das Man" is the source of norms and practices into which the inauthentic man flees for comfort and justification.

Thanks to the interest of French intellectuals in his work, Heidegger was gradually rehabilitated and allowed to resume his university lectures in 1951. He received regular visits from a forgiving (and now famous) Hannah Arendt up to the time of his death in 1976. He also managed several trips to Greece, which was a transformative experience for him. He felt there a sense of divine mystery that brought him ever closer, he thought, to the origins of philosophy and the essence of Being. He increasingly focused his attention on poetry and art, which he said were produced from a direct, unmediated experience of Being.

Heidegger died on May 26, 1976, at the age of eighty-six. He is buried in Messkirch. His descendants still own the little hut in Todtnauberg. His failings as a man have been consigned to history. But his writings have forever changed our understanding of being-in-the-world.

REMEMBERING BEING

Heidegger is ludicrously and infuriatingly difficult to read. You can pick almost any sentence at random from *Being and Time* and read it aloud for comic effect. For example: "Ontically, 'letting something be involved' signifies that within our factical concern we let something ready-to-hand *be* so-and-so *as* it is and already and *in order that* it be such."[12] That sentence is relatively clear compared to others I might have chanced upon. The same might be said, however, of Joyce's *Ulysses* (though there the effect, when comic, is almost always deliberate). Joyce is trying to do something that he cannot do in any other way than through his experiments with form and language. So, too, in his more ponderous manner is Heidegger. Indeed, they are both trying to do something very similar, which, in Heideggerian terms, we would call "remembering Being." Joyce, at least the early Joyce, would call it "epiphany" (from the Greek, meaning "appearance" or "revelation").

Heidegger believes that we in the Western philosophical tradition have forgotten Being. Being does not appear to us; it does not reveal itself to us. Our very language, in its manner of representing the world, disguises and conceals Being from us. Just what Heidegger means by that remains to be seen. But it does give us some sense of why his style is so difficult. First, he uses the entire professorial apparatus of German metaphysics—with its arcane, abstract vocabulary and its muddy prose—in his effort to show that the Western philosophical tradition self-destructs. Second, he invents an entirely new vocabulary as a replacement for, and as a means of escape from, that tradition in order to obtain a closer understanding of Being. As Heidegger himself explains, with regard to the awkwardness and "inelegance" of expression in the analyses to come, we may remark that it is one thing to give a report in which we tell about *beings*, but another to grasp beings in their *Being*. For the latter task we lack not only most of the words but, above all, the "grammar."[13]

Thus, reading Heidegger is like learning a foreign language. At first one must rely upon crude translations into terms one understands. Ultimately, one becomes comfortable with the terminology and the "grammar," which has its own internal coherence and sheds its own fitful illumination. Heidegger wrote a late essay called "Building Dwelling Thinking." One can eventually dwell within the thinking that Heidegger so painstakingly builds. As with Joyce, it repays the effort.

The fundamental question of philosophy, for Heidegger, concerns the nature of Being. What is it for things "to be"? For a chair to be means I can sit on it. For a table to be means I can write at it. Like Socrates, however, Heidegger is not interested in such specific examples. He is not interested in particular physical objects or thoughts or processes. "*What is asked about* is Being—that which determines beings as beings, that on the basis of which beings are already understood."[14] We must engage in a close study of "not just this being or that, but rather the *Being* of beings."[15] Heidegger considers Being to be the most general, and at the same time the most elusive of concepts, one that cannot be reduced to, or defined in terms of, entities or substances or processes or events.

This fundamental question as posed by Heidegger seems—after Wittgenstein—to be deeply confused and mistaken. It is rather like St. Augustine's "What is time?" (see p. 92), which Heidegger also asks. But Heidegger is not asking the question under the grip of the Augustinian picture of language. He is not seeking some metaphysical substance or crystalline, uniform meaning that corresponds to the words "being" and "is" and "to be" in our language. To the contrary, like Wittgenstein, he is trying to break the hold of such a picture. "If we are to understand the problem of Being, our first philosophical step consists in not 'telling a story'—that is to say, in not defining beings as beings, by tracing them back in their origin to some other beings, as if Being had the character of some possible being."[16]

Philosophy has been telling such stories since its inception. Plato tells us that the essence of Being lies in the eternal, immutable, immaterial Forms to which all beings imperfectly aspire. Christianity tells us that the essence of Being is God, the eternal, immutable, and immaterial first cause and highest good of all beings. Hegel tells us that Being is Absolute Spirit revealing itself in History. In each case, philosophy offers us a "metaphysical" explanation, an explanation that goes beyond the merely physical world and reveals the hidden essence that is the ground of all transitory beings. All beings are presented as but a by-product or mere appearance of that essence. This tradition continues, Heidegger suggests, down to Nietzsche's contention that the essence of all things is the will to power. (This is in fact a willful, one-sided reading of Nietzsche—turning the great antimetaphysician into the "last metaphysician"—but that is neither here nor there for the point Heidegger is trying to make.)

Like Wittgenstein, Heidegger thoroughly rejects this tradition. But his main objection is not so much Wittgenstein's point that the tradition traffics in nonsense because it takes "language on holiday," outside the context in human life that gives language meaning. Heidegger does agree that traditional metaphysics is nonsense, and he does agree that we must both start and remain within the context of everyday human life. But his more urgent objection is that these "stories" distract us from what is truly important. By seeking some entity or substance to explain Being, they distract us from the amazing and primordial fact that Being reveals itself to us at all. To borrow Wittgenstein's phrase, "we fail to be struck by what, once seen, is most striking and most powerful."[17] Heidegger wants to recapture a sense of wonder and astonishment at the sheer Being of beings, at the fact that there is *something* rather than nothing. That sense of wonder should not be dissipated in false and nonsensical explanations about the grounds and essence of Being. The fact of existence, in the midst of the possibility of nothingness, is itself what is so astonishing.

It is this feeling of wonder and amazement that Heidegger calls "remembering Being" and which he believes is the source (and goal) of all true philosophy. Why is there something rather than nothing? The question never receives, and is not meant to receive, an answer—not a scientific answer and certainly not a theological or metaphysical answer.

It is the question itself that is the beginning and end of all meditation about Being. It is a question of attitude, of openness to Being.

"To work out the question of Being adequately," Heidegger introduces the term *Dasein*, which is traditionally left untranslated in English versions of his writing. Dasein means, literally, "being there." Heidegger uses it to refer to our human existence, our "being-in-the-world."[18]

Dasein is the clearing in which phenomena (objects, thoughts, feelings, other people) disclose themselves to us. Heidegger uses here the term *lichtung*, which means literally a glade or clearing in a forest. It is an open space in which "the Being of beings stand[s] out in full relief" against a background of nothingness.[19] Like a Hopper painting, light emerges from shadow, creates a clearing in which Being reveals itself, and returns into shadow. Dasein is "the horizon within which something like Being in general becomes intelligible."[20]

We will discuss Dasein in much greater detail in the next section. For present purposes, it is important to recognize that Heidegger is building on, while altering in critical respects, the phenomenology of Husserl's *Logical Investigations*. Husserl wanted to study the essential structure of consciousness by focusing on the thoughts, sensations, and desires present to consciousness. He starts with Descartes' *cogito* ("I think") and brackets the question of the existence of anything outside consciousness so as to focus exclusively on the nature of our inner experience. Husserl wants to avoid any "commitments" as to the metaphysical status of the objects of consciousness.

In some ways, Dasein serves a function similar to that of the Cartesian "self" in Husserl. In his analysis of Dasein, Heidegger focuses solely on what discloses itself to us in experience. Heidegger's phenomenology resists any attempt to go beyond or behind Dasein's absorption in the world of things and other people. Heidegger too avoids any metaphysical commitments. "Least of all can the Being of being ever be anything such that 'behind it' stands something else 'which does not appear.'"[21] "'Behind' the phenomena of phenomenology there is essentially nothing else."[22] There are only the "stories" of the metaphysicians, which must be thoroughly rejected and scrubbed from our language.

At the same time, however, Heidegger rejects the entire Cartesian tradition, which treats the "I" as itself an entity that precedes experience. "One of our first tasks will be to prove that if we posit an 'I' or subject as that which is proximally given, we shall completely miss the phenomenal content of Dasein."[23] Dasein always, already finds itself "thrown" into a world of physical objects and other people. Dasein exists in a particular place at a particular point in time with a web of relations to things and to other people. "Dasein is never 'proximally' a being which is, so to speak, free from Being-in, but which sometimes has the inclination to take up a 'relationship' towards the world."[24] Nor is Dasein an isolated subject that enters only indirectly and contingently into relations with others. "By 'Others' we do not mean everyone else but me—those over against whom the 'I' stands out. They are rather those from whom, for the most part, one does *not* distinguish oneself—those among whom one is too."[25]

In treating Dasein as always embedded in the world, Heidegger sidesteps the subject-object dualism of the Cartesian tradition. By bracketing the outside world, the Cartesian ego/subject becomes trapped in its own consciousness. Our primary experience of the world is reduced to isolated thoughts and sense impressions (sights, sounds, smells), and philosophers since Descartes have had an impossible time working their way from that starting point to an external world of objects and "other minds" that exists independently of our perceptions. Some, like Bishop Berkeley, happily embrace that dilemma and conclude that tables and chairs and the like have no existence separate and apart from our sensations. Others, like Kant, bridge the gap only by reducing the tables and chairs to "mere appearances" and confessing man's fundamental incapacity to know things as they are in themselves.

But that entire epistemological tradition is in fact a falsification of experience. Dasein "does not dwell proximally alongside 'sensations'; nor would it first have to give shape to the swirl of sensations to provide the springboard from which the subject leaps off and finally arrives at a 'world.'"[26] We don't experience sense impressions. We sit at chairs, we write at tables, we smell coffee, we hear sirens, and we speak with other people. "A bare subject without a world" is never given; nor is "an isolated 'I' without Others."[27] Dasein is always a "being there," that is, being somewhere or other in a concrete setting. "The compound expression 'Being-in-the-world' indicates in the very

214 THREE QUESTIONS WE NEVER STOP ASKING

way we have coined it, that it stands for a *unitary* phenomenon. This primary datum must be seen as a whole."[28] What is primary is not the isolated subject of Cartesian philosophy but the already-immersed-in-the-world, Dasein. That is our starting point. That is our ending point. Dasein is always, already "in" the world of objects and people.

There is a certain *ipse dixit* quality to Heidegger's phenomenology. It calls to mind Samuel Johnson, who kicked a stone and stated, "Thus, I refute Berkeley." Johnson was affirming common sense, in the simplest terms, against philosophical sophistry. Heidegger is essentially doing the same thing in the jargon of phenomenology. He is focusing on what actually shows itself to Dasein. Phenomenology, he tells us, takes us not to a world of appearances but "to the things themselves."[29]

Another way to look at Heidegger's phenomenology is through the lens of Wittgenstein's private language argument. Wittgenstein shows that it is misleading to treat the language of thoughts, emotions, and sensations as if it refers to "objects" in some inherently private picture show of the immaterial, Cartesian subject. For Wittgenstein, language is a shared, social tool that takes its meaning from our behavior and our practices. Language is inherently and necessarily shared. Heidegger concurs: "communication is never anything like a conveying of experiences...from the interior of one subject into the interior of another."[30] Or, as he later explains, "in talking, Dasein *expresses* itself not because it has, in the first instance, been encapsulated as something 'internal' over against something outside, but because as Being-in-the-world it is already 'outside' when it understands."[31]

Thus, just as he rejects the metaphysical tradition from Plato to Nietzsche, so, too, Heidegger rejects the epistemological tradition from Descartes to Husserl. The former fosters an illusion of transcendence. The latter fosters an illusion of a crystalline center of consciousness to which all experience is directly given. Neither is an adequate account of our being in the world and our being with others. We cannot view the world from the standpoint of eternity. Nor can we reduce the world to our own consciousness. There is no premise-free beginning from which we can analyze either self or object. Self and object are themselves understandings of Dasein.

To replace these traditions, Heidegger seeks to recapture an authentic prephilosophical understanding of Being. For Heidegger, all inquiry about Being must start, as does Aristotle's inquiry on ethics, *in media res*. Dasein dwells in the world of shared social practices and skills. That is our fundamental reality: we find ourselves amid people and objects that matter to us in certain ways; we have goals and are immersed in particular activities. We know our way about in this world. We interpret it and relate to it. We have an existing language in which we speak about it. Our inquiry must take our language and our commitments—the ways in which people and things matter to us—as a starting point, because there is no detached perspective that frees us from our existing interpretations of the world.

As in Aristotle, the best we can do is find a starting point for an inquiry that circles back upon itself in an increasingly layered and illuminating way. Heidegger admits to this "manifest circularity."[32] In order to get straight on the question of Being, he tells us, we have to make Dasein "transparent in [its] own Being."[33] That is, we must explain Being in terms of the being of Dasein and the various terms that relate to that Being. But "if we see this circle as a vicious one and look out for ways of avoiding it, even if we just 'sense' it as an inevitable imperfection, then the act of understanding has been mis-understood from the ground up."[34] We always find ourselves in an interpretive relationship with the world.

The focus of Heidegger's inquiry, then, is on what he calls an "existential analytic" of Dasein. Despite the formal structure and difficult language, the inquiry is very similar to Aristotle's analysis of human flourishing. It introduces key terms that are interdefined, circumscribing an area of discourse. The goal is not to break out of that circle, but to deepen our understanding of the circumscribed space. "We must… endeavor to leap into the 'circle,' primordially and wholly, so that even at the start of the analysis of Dasein we make sure that we have a full view of Dasein's circular Being."[35] The goal is to reach a clearing in which our forgotten understanding of Being shows itself and is illumined.

EXISTENTIAL DASEIN

"The 'essence' of Dasein," Heidegger tells us, "lies in its existence."[36] This statement (altered to "existence precedes essence") becomes the rallying cry of Jean-Paul Sartre (1905–1980) and the French existentialists. They understand Heidegger to mean that man has no inherent nature; he defines himself solely through his actions and, at each moment, enjoys a terrible freedom of choice of which he cannot unburden himself by relying on any moral or spiritual authority.

There are certainly significant elements of this existentialist view in Heidegger's work. But it does not at all reflect what Heidegger means when he says that "the 'essence' of Dasein lies in its existence." Heidegger means, quite literally, that Dasein ("being there") has an essence that is inextricably tied to its existence. The connection itself is made in language. "That kind of Being towards which Dasein can comport itself in one way or another, and always does comport itself somehow, we call '*existence*.'"[37] As discussed, Dasein is not a Cartesian subject. It is not a fixed point from which the world is explored. "We cannot define Dasein's essence by citing a 'what' of the kind that pertains to a subject-matter"; "its essence lies rather in the fact that in each case it has its Being to be."[38] Dasein can only understand itself in terms of the ways in which it comports itself in the world. Dasein "finds" itself in what it does.

That last statement does sound rather like Sartre. But Heidegger is not suggesting that Dasein enjoys complete freedom in what it does. Heidegger is much closer to Wittgenstein and Aristotle in terms of the embeddedness of Dasein in human life and practices than he is to Sartre. Dasein finds itself "thrown" into a world and relationships. Things and people matter to Dasein in certain ways, and Dasein understands itself in understanding how the world and relationships matter to it.

Dasein is not writing on a blank slate. The "understanding" upon which Dasein depends has "already been 'deposited' in the way things have been expressed."[39] Dasein is constantly interpreting itself according to interpretations that it finds "ready to hand" in the world. "Any interpretation which is to contribute understanding, must already have understood what is to be interpreted."[40] That is because we need a language in which to express our understanding, and language itself takes its meaning (in circular fashion) from our way of being-in-the-world, from the ways in which people and things matter to us.

Heidegger's point—echoing Aristotle and prefiguring Wittgen-stein—is that you cannot disengage Dasein from its context in mean-ingful human life and activity. Dasein just *is* its absorption in the world and other people; any rebellion against social conventions (broadly understood to include not just behavioral mores but the entire "grammar" of our existence) is itself defined by those conven-tions. We don't have complete, radical freedom because we act against this background. Our choices are never arbitrary and ungrounded. They are embedded in our forms of life, our background under-standing and ways of dealing with the world. Even our reactions and rejections occur against this defining background.

Aristotle sees this embeddedness as a positive thing. He contends that our human nature determines what is meaningful to us and what constitutes the good life for man. Our human nature is the essential background against which our life can unfold and be fruitful. Hei-degger takes a darker view. Each culture understands its own inter-pretation of Dasein to be human nature. Dasein feels at home in that interpretation. But this feeling of being "at home" is an illusion. Dasein has no fixed nature that antedates its engagement in the world. Where Aristotle sees human flourishing, Heidegger sees an inau-thentic understanding of the basic condition of Dasein. The purpose of philosophy, for Heidegger, is not to live and fare well consistent with one's preexisting cultural norms, but to obtain a better under-standing of, and hence a more authentic existence for, Dasein.

Such an inquiry, Heidegger tells us, is "one of the possibilities"[41] of Dasein. But given that our "understanding" has "already been 'deposited' in the way things have been expressed,"[42] how is such a second-level understanding possible? Wittgenstein seeks only to dis-solve philosophical confusion. Heidegger seeks what Wittgenstein calls an *übersicht* (perspicuous overview)—and what Heidegger calls a *lichtung* (clearing)—not just of particular philosophical confusions, but of our essential way of being-in-the-world. In the process, he coins neologisms and uses words in bizarre ways in an effort to get us to see what we don't ordinarily notice because it is so close to us. Wittgenstein of course does the same—with coinages such as "lan-guage games," "forms of life," "family-resemblance concepts," and his own particular use of the term "grammar." But Heidegger's ambition is much grander: he wants an *übersicht* of the essential features of Dasein's engagement with the world and with others so that we can somehow transcend that engagement and see it as a limited whole.

Just how well Heidegger succeeds with his "existential analytic of Dasein" is open to debate. But no one can dispute that his discussion is full of provocative insights. I want to focus here on four interrelated points. The points are so interrelated that they could be taken in almost any order; they are points in a circle, not stages in an argument. The goal is not any sort of syllogism, but "a full view of Dasein's circular Being."[43]

First, "the primordial Being of Dasein itself" is "care."[44] Dasein always finds itself in relations and situations that matter to it in certain ways. Dasein is not abstractly disengaged. "Things always already matter" to Dasein.[45] Dasein is disposed toward things and people, and it is out of that disposedness that "we can encounter something that matters to us."[46] "In everyday terms, we understand ourselves and our existence by way of the activities we pursue and the things we take care of."[47] Our disposedness "determines what and how one 'sees.'"[48] We understand people and things insofar as they affect us and matter to us.

Second, "Dasein always has understood itself and always will understand itself in terms of possibilities."[49] Dasein understands itself in terms of what it can do, not in terms of some preexisting essence. Dasein finds itself "thrown" into a particular culture and particular relationships that define its ways of being human.[50] Dasein finds various interpretations of its being "ready to hand" (son, father, boss, worker, lover). These interpretations have established (if flexible) norms of behavior. The gravitational force of those established norms is tremendously powerful, but we are free to act either in accordance with them or against them. Either way, the norms themselves create the "potentiality-for-Being"[51] of Dasein, and Dasein finds itself "in its possibilities." "Freedom... *is* only in the choice of one possibility—that is, in tolerating one's not having chosen the others and one's not being able to choose them."[52]

Third, "Dasein has been *dispersed* into the One, and must first find itself."[53] Heidegger uses the pronoun "das Man" in this passage, which is rendered as "the They" in the standard translation by Macquarrie and Robinson. That is misleading, however, since it sets up an apparent opposition between the inherent integrity of Dasein and the demands of the They. Such a translation plays into an existentialist account of Dasein as struggling for freedom against external impositions. Heidegger's point is somewhat different, which is why he derives "das Man" from the impersonal singular pronoun "man," which is better rendered as "one" in English. The being of Dasein, Heidegger tells us, is dissolved into the One and largely indistinguishable from it. "In this inconspicuousness and unascertainability, the real dictatorship of the One is unfolded."[54]

Heidegger's point, again, is that Dasein can interpret itself and its world only in terms of interpretations that it finds in the world. Dasein accordingly interprets itself as One interprets oneself. "Dasein is constantly delivered over to this interpretedness, which controls and distributes the possibilities of average understanding and of the state-of-mind [disposedness] belonging to it."[55]

> We take pleasure and enjoy ourselves as *one* takes pleasure; we read, see, and judge about literature and art as *one* sees and judges; likewise we shrink back from the "great mass" as *one* shrinks back; we find "shocking" what *one* finds shocking.[56]

Heidegger doesn't just mean that we are naturally conformists; even nonconformity is an interpretation of the One, an interpretation that we find ready-to-hand in the world. This interpretedness levels down the possibilities of everyday Being. "In this averageness with which the One prescribes what can and may be ventured, it keeps watch over everything exceptional that thrusts itself to the fore."[57] The One, which presents every judgment and decision as its own, deprives Dasein of its answerability. "The particular Dasein in its everydayness is *disburdened* by the One."[58]

Fourth, there is "a basic kind of Being which belongs to everydayness: we call this the *'falling'* of Dasein."[59] Heidegger quite deliberately uses the religious metaphor of "the fall." But the falling of Dasein is not a "'fall' from a purer and higher 'primal status.'"[60] It is a state of original sin that is part of the basic everyday absorption of Dasein in the world. This fallenness signals our absorption in the One, and it is marked by idle talk, curiosity, tranquility, and forgetting.

Idle talk is the form of discourse in which our everyday understanding is deposited. It not only "releases one from the task of genuinely understanding, but develops an undifferentiated kind of intelligibility, for which nothing is closed off any longer."[61] Idle talk glosses over the mystery of the world. In place of wonder, we have curiosity, which "seeks novelty only in order to leap from it anew to another novelty."[62] Such curiosity does not tarry observantly, "but rather seeks restlessness and the excitement of continual novelty and changing encounters. In not tarrying, curiosity is concerned with the constant possibility of *distraction*. Curiosity has nothing to do with observing entities and marveling at them."[63]

Together, idle talk, for which there is nothing that is not understood, and curiosity, for which nothing is closed off, lead Dasein to feel "at home." They minimize our "distantiality," our feeling of uneasiness and uncanniness, our feeling of *not* being at home in the world. They support the supposition "that one is leading and sustaining a full and genuine 'life,'" a supposition that brings tranquility.[64] "Falling Being-in-the-world, which tempts itself, is at the same time *tranquillizing*."[65] It is also a forgetting of the true Being of being. Dasein by its absorption in the One has always, already lost itself and a proper understanding of its relationship to Being. Dasein has been disburdened of its responsibility, and it leads an inauthentic life by fleeing into a world of distraction and idle talk.

As with Aristotle, understanding Heidegger depends as much on a glossary of terms as it does on a discursive discussion. If anything, it is more important in Heidegger's case. Despite his generally muddy prose, these terms—care, absorption, thrownness, the One, leveling down, disburdening, falling, tranquillizing, fleeing, forgetting, inauthenticity—have in their context in his work a resonance and a power that is itself uncanny. But Heidegger is the anti-Aristotle. Aristotle sees our shared values—which he considers reflective of our human nature—as a means to a rich and fulfilling life. Heidegger has no interest in living and faring well in Aristotle's sense. He sees our shared values as oppressive, as restricting "the possible options of choice to what lies within the range of the familiar, the attainable, the respectable—that which is fitting and proper."[66] Our shared values disburden Dasein of responsibility and tranquilize it. They lead to a "dimming down of the possible as such."[67] Inauthentic Dasein "not only forgets the forgotten but forgets the forgetting itself."[68]

This theme of an inauthentic existence dissipated in idle talk and curiosity is also the subject of Proust's great masterwork, *In Search of Lost Time*. "We live with our gaze averted from ourselves," Proust says, smothered beneath a "whole heap of verbal concepts and practical goals which we falsely call life."[69] For Proust, as for Heidegger,

> we have to rediscover, to reapprehend, to make ourselves fully aware of that reality, remote from our daily preoccupations, from which we separate ourselves by an ever greater gulf as the conventional knowledge which we substitute for it grows thicker and more impermeable, that reality which it is very easy for us to die without ever having known and which is, quite simply, our life.[70]

Proust seeks that rediscovery in art, which he sees as a constant struggle "to discern beneath matter, beneath experience, beneath words, something that is different from them,"[71] fragments of existence liberated by a metaphor from the contingencies of time and shown in their pure state: "life at last laid bare and illuminated."[72]

As with Proust, Heidegger's only interest is in "remembering Being." Any life that falls short of that goal is to him inauthentic. "The particular Dasein has been *dispersed* into the One, and must first find itself."[73] Dasein must discover the world in its own way and bring it close by clearing away concealments and obscurities and "breaking up ... the disguises with which Dasein bars its own way."[74]

But how is that to happen if "everyone is the other, and no one is himself"?[75] How does Dasein become authentic in its own Being when "Dasein has in every case already gone astray and failed to recognize itself"?[76] How does Dasein cut through the concealments and obscurities in order to reach the clearing in which the nature of its own Being becomes illumined?

Before Odysseus could return to his true home and reclaim his rightful, authentic place as husband, father, and king, he had to visit the land of the dead. So, too, did Aeneas and Dante and, in his own way, Leopold Bloom. And so, too, Heidegger tells us, must we.

BEING-TOWARDS-DEATH

We will all die. It is part of the essence of Dasein that existence is a movement in time, stretched out between birth and death.[77] I will die and you will die. Yet your death is fundamentally different from my own. I can experience and objectify *your* death. But, as Wittgenstein noted in the *Tractatus*, death is not an event in my life.[78] When I die, Dasein is extinguished. My "being there" will no longer *be* anywhere. Death is "the possibility of the impossibility of every way of comporting oneself towards anything."[79] It is the definitive end of "being-in-the-world" and of "being-with-others." The light cast by Dasein goes out and nothing is left.

Dasein, understood as "being-towards-death," finds itself alone, face to face with this nothingness. Dasein, we might say, floats in a sea of nothingness, like Odysseus buffeted by the ocean waves, fighting against submersion and oblivion. Dasein is "held out into the nothing."[80] Only against the background of that nothingness does Being shine forth. "The nothing does not merely serve as the counterconcept of beings; rather it originally belongs to their essential unfolding as such. In the Being of beings the nihilation of the nothing occurs."[81] This is a deeply troubling image. Nothing is not just the absence of Being; Being itself is the absence of nothing. The nothing is more primordial, more fundamental than Being itself, which in its essence comes from and returns to nothingness. (Recall, again, the light and shadow of the Hopper paintings, or Hamlet's remark that death is a "positive negation.")[82] Man is, in Heidegger's striking phrase, "a placeholder of the nothing."[83]

Heidegger would say with some justice that we spend our lives fleeing from this very realization. We wholly absorb ourselves in everydayness and dissipate our energies in idle talk and curiosity. Or, through philosophy and religion, we attempt to define ourselves in terms of something fixed and eternal. Either way, we tranquilize ourselves. We not only forget the true fragility of Dasein; we forget the forgetting.

The nothing for which Dasein is a placeholder, however, cannot be an object of direct thought. Thinking "is always essentially thinking about something," whereas "the nothing is the negation of the totality of beings."[84] We grasp nothingness not as an object but in the way people and things lose their significance for us in the face of death. The possibility of death "makes manifest that all Being-alongside the things with which we concern ourselves, and all Being-with Others, will fail us when our ownmost potentiality-for-Being is the issue."[85] As people and things recede from us, we no longer feel at home in the world. "We can get no hold on things."[86] Heidegger calls this unsettledness "anxiety." "Being-towards-death is essentially anxiety."[87]

Anxiety is a pivotal concept for Heidegger. It is a feeling of vertigo as Dasein realizes that it is in movement on a high wire stretched between birth and death, between nothing and nowhere, with only nothingness as its ground. Anxiety is "the abandonment of Dasein to itself" in the face of death.[88] In this abandonment, "everyday familiarity collapses."[89] The world is not absent, but entities within the world fail us, they lose their importance. "Anxiety discloses an insignificance of the world; and this insignificance reveals the nullity of that with which one can concern oneself."[90] Anxiety confronts Dasein with "the simplicity of its *fate*."[91]

This confrontation can occur at any time. Anxiety lies in wait for us and overtakes us in the midst of our absorption in the world. "It needs no unusual event to rouse it. Its sway is as thoroughgoing as its possible occasionings are trivial."[92] W. H. Auden captures the sudden intrusion of anxiety in a beautiful line: "[T]he crack in the tea-cup opens / A lane to the land of the dead."[93] Everyday familiarity suddenly collapses and we are face to face with nothingness. Milan Kundera, a writer steeped in Heidegger, articulates the same point:

> It takes so little, so infinitely little, for someone to find himself on the other side of the border, where everything—love, convictions, faith, history—no longer has meaning. The whole mystery of human life resides in the fact that it is spent in the immediate proximity of, and even in direct contact with, that border, that it is separated from it not by kilometers but by barely a millimeter.[94]

By detaching Dasein from its absorption in the world, anxiety makes it impossible for Dasein to continue to understand itself "in terms of the 'world' and the way things have been publicly interpreted."[95] Heidegger, unlike Aristotle, considers this detachment a virtue; indeed, for Heidegger it may be the only virtue. Heidegger considers the public understanding of living and faring well to be a threat to the authenticity of Dasein. Inauthentic Dasein "can dwell in tranquillized familiarity."[96] But "not-being-at-home" is the more primordial, more fundamental condition of Dasein.[97] Anxiety, by unsettling Dasein, brings Dasein closer to a proper understanding of its essential, existential nature.

Anxiety, then, is not the fear of this or that thing. Anxiety is deeper and more formless. In anxiety, Dasein confronts "the pure 'that-it-is' of one's ownmost individualized thrownness."[98] As Rüdiger Safranski explains, "Dasein experiences itself as homeless, unguarded and unguided by any objective Being."[99] Naked Dasein peers into the abyss, for as long as it can endure to do so, and finds nothingness as the only ground of its nature.

AUTHENTICITY

Dasein returns from its encounter with nothingness changed and yet the same. Dasein continues to engage with the world, and that world "does not become another one 'in its content,' nor does the circle of Others get exchanged for a new one."[100] Any "for-the-sake-of-which" Dasein might choose is still provided by the One. It is already there as a choice within our culture, and in choosing (or rejecting) it we do not in any way break out of this circle. "In no case is a Dasein, untouched and unseduced by this way in which things have been interpreted, set before the open country of a 'world-in-itself.'"[101]

And yet, Heidegger tells us, Dasein can achieve authenticity by resolutely and self-consciously embracing its attachment to the world and others in the face of nothingness. Meaning depends upon our sharing the world with others. All meaning is provided by the One. Only death frees Dasein from that context. But Dasein may, in the face of Death, choose its life.

Here, we circle back to the point where we began in our discussion of Dasein. Dasein's only essence is existence. Dasein has no fixed nature that unfolds itself in time and against which the validity of our choices can be gauged. We exist in a range of possibilities (possible

moods, possible projects, possible self-interpretations) and in acting
we choose among these possibilities. Our Being is our becoming; it is
the set of decisions and choices that we make in our lives. Dasein
simply *is* its unfolding in time. All meaning for Dasein is found in
time, but time itself does not bring meaning; it brings death and nothingness. Precisely that recognition, however, allows Dasein to transcend its "thrownness" and achieve a resoluteness and authenticity
that gives form and shape to one's life.

Authenticity is not a matter of this or that action or any particular
"for-the-sake-of-which." Authentic Dasein achieves "constancy of the
Self," by neither fleeing from the contingent nature of existence into
the noncontingent nor completely losing itself in the contingent.[102]
Authentic Dasein pulls itself together "from the *dispersion* and *discon-
nectedness*"[103] of everydayness by recognizing that one can never "have
power over one's own most Being from the ground up."[104] By
accepting its thrownness and holding itself out into the nothing,
Dasein lets "itself be summoned out if its lostness in the One."[105]

Aristotle, as we saw, accepts the circle of self-interpretations in
which man is contained (though he calls it "human nature") and by
embracing that circle achieves a vision of living and faring well
within the mores and social practices of his time and culture. Heidegger recognizes the same self-contained circle and that any conception of living and faring well will inevitably be defined by the
mores and social practices of one's time and culture. But Heidegger
believes that living and faring well according to a set of inherited
values is exposed as hollow and empty when Dasein faces the nothingness in which it is grounded, when "the crack in the teacup opens
/ A lane to the land of the dead." Hence, Heidegger wants authentic
Dasein to view this circle as a whole, suspended over the void, and to
understand Dasein's choices within it from that perspective.

Heidegger believes that such a vision is liberating and even a
source of deep, lasting joy. In the clearing of Being, we recognize that
there is an authentic counter-possibility to the dispersion and discon-
nectedness of the self that are characteristic of irresolute falling. This
authentic mode of being-in-the-world does not "stem from 'idealistic'
exactions soaring above existence and its possibilities; it springs from a
sober understanding of what are factically the basic possibilities for

Dasein."[106] Dasein can achieve a constant sense of self by freeing itself for its own death. By coming face to face with the one possibility "which is not to be outstripped," Dasein is liberated from its "lostness" in those everyday possibilities which are thrust upon it by the One.[107] Without such a "forerunning" of Death, neither selfhood nor freedom is possible. Only in "an impassioned freedom towards death—a freedom which has been released from the illusions of the One"—is Dasein able to live authentically and deliberately.[108] With that impassioned freedom, moreover, "there goes an unshakable joy."[109]

There is no one, definitive way for authentic Dasein to unfold its life. There is no fixed human nature against which Dasein can gauge the validity of either its short-term choices or its long-term plans. There is only the One, which already encompasses all the ways in which Dasein might interpret and develop its own being. But the One is itself autonomous and ungrounded and will not save Dasein from its existential essence as a placeholder for the nothing. The most Dasein can do is choose deliberately and authentically in the clearing of Being and in the face of the anxiety occasioned by its Being-towards-death. Dasein may, in the Nietzschean phrase adopted by Heidegger, "choose its hero."[110] That is, through a hard-won constancy of the self in the face of Death, Dasein may make a particular path through the world—coming out of nothingness and passing into nothingness—its own. In this always incomplete process of becoming a self, Dasein realizes "the possibility of taking over from itself its ownmost Being."[111]

The most important aspect of authenticity for Heidegger, however, is not the choice of a path through life, which is nothing but one particular way of being. What is critical is to reach the clearing in which Being itself and hence the being of Dasein can be seen. Dasein must open itself into the clearing of Being "in order to be more authentically 'there' in the 'moment.'"[112]

In his memorable phrase, Heidegger insists that in everydayness we have forgotten Being. We tend to treat things and even other people as "equipment ready-to-hand," not as beings in themselves but as "something in-order-to."[113] As Hubert Dreyfus, the only truly indispensable commenter on Heidegger, explains, "Dasein is always in the process of using equipment *in-order-to* obtain some end *towards-which* the activity of Dasein is oriented, and . . . all this is *for-the-sake-of* some self-interpretation of Dasein."[114] For Heidegger, this equipmental focus ignores the Being of beings. It is a form of enslavement to the equipmental that alienates Dasein from its world. Other people are not "equipment ready-to-hand; they are themselves Dasein."[115] Even things participate in Being in a manner not captured by their equipmental uses. Our freedom from the equipmental, our authentic dealing with one another and with the world, reveals itself in "letting beings be."[116] "To let be is to engage oneself with beings," to become that clearing "into which every being comes to stand."[117]

Heidegger seems close here to the Kantian notion that moral freedom lies in a lack of self-interest, in treating others as ends in themselves rather than as means to one's own ends. But Heidegger's thrust is really quite different and not at all focused on morality in the Kantian sense. For Heidegger, remembering Being is an end in itself because only in remembering Being is Dasein authentically "there" in the moment. "Only this clearing grants and guarantees to us humans a passage to those beings that we ourselves are not, and access to the being that we ourselves are."[118] Only authentic Dasein transcends the uses to which beings may be put and illuminates the Being of beings. Walt Whitman captured the same point in a beautiful line: the authentic human being (which is a key concept for Whitman, though he expressed it as the man who "is complete in himself") "judges not as the judge judges but as the sun falling round a helpless thing."[119]

Authentic Dasein does not judge according to fixed, inherited categories. Authentic Dasein suspends judgment; it lets beings be and shines the light of its understanding on all beings as the sun falling round a helpless thing. Only thereby does Dasein understand its own existential condition as a placeholder of the nothing, as an evanescent clearing into which every being may come to stand. Only then does Dasein experience unshakeable joy and gratitude at the sheer "that it is" of Being.

POETICALLY MAN DWELLS

Following the completion of *Being and Time*, Heidegger took what he would call a "turn" in his thought. Whether that "turn" was simply a continuation around the circle of self-interpretations or whether it tries somehow to break out of that circle (by claiming a perspective that is not simply one more interpretation) is itself a matter of interpretive dispute. But the nature of the turn is clear. Heidegger was left dissatisfied by the radical individualism and existential rootlessness of Dasein, as presented in *Being and Time*. Heidegger wanted the very sort of connection to a broader culture and system of values that he had disdained as "fleeing" and "tranquillizing" and "the tyranny of the One." Much of his later work is an effort to offer "a vision of a new autochthony," or rootedness.[120]

It is important to recognize, though, that Heidegger is still not particularly interested in ethics, as we would understand that term. He is not concerned with the homely virtues of kindness and decency and tolerance and compassion that allow men and women to live together in society. Heidegger always focuses on the primacy of authenticity over decency. For him, as for Nietzsche, good or correct action pales in significance beside the intense and spontaneous creativity of Dasein.

What Heidegger recognizes, however, is that without shared concerns to undergird them, our chosen values lose their authority and fail to give any intrinsic meaning to our lives. Authentic Dasein needs commitment, but as long as all values are simply posited and without grounding, we are well on our way to nihilism (and French existentialism) in which any commitment is purely arbitrary; so-called values simply become a reflection of power relationships (as Nietzsche already alleged). Heidegger continues to reject the idea of a "true self" or human nature against which values can be gauged. He continues to reject the idea of a common humanity that might form the basis for meaningful relations with one another. Yet, paradoxically, he wants Dasein to feel connected and at home in the world and increasingly believes that such a connection is possible if we recover a more primordial relationship to Being. In this vein, Heidegger begins to reinterpret anxiety so that it is no longer an inherent and inescapable condition of Being-towards-death but rather a symptom of modern rootlessness.

I do not find myself altogether sympathetic to this turn in Heidegger's thought. As we will see, it leads him into mythology and a lyricism that borders on mysticism. It is also, I think, partially this turn that makes Heidegger so susceptible to the barbarity of National Socialism. Dasein in its lonely struggle in the face of nothingness becomes the German nation in its own collective struggle in a hostile world. The mass-appeal aspects of the movement—the bonfires, the rallies, the swastika, the Sieg Heil!—become for Heidegger symbols of the spiritual mission of the German Volk, which he thinks will lead to a more authentic, collective connection with nature and with its own history, language, and customs. Heidegger chooses his hero and it is, for a time, Adolf Hitler.

After the war, and in the wake of the de-nazification process, an ostensibly repentant Heidegger reinterprets National Socialism as itself a symptom of the flight of Being into nihilism and the will to power. He seeks a new vision of rootedness in the ancient Greeks. But to some extent the stink of Nazism still hangs over that quest and it makes one rightly suspicious of Heidegger's new mythology, which he sums up in a late interview with the assertion: "only a god can save us."[121] Note that he does not say only God can save us. His point is not that we need divine intervention or any particular religious belief, but that we need a sense of the sacred mystery of Being as a counter to the centrifugal forces of modern life.

The later Heidegger is a strong critic of the rational/scientific/technological focus of modern life and thinking, which he believes has changed our relationship with nature and with one another. Our feeling for nature has withered as our ability to manipulate nature has grown. In words that resonate strongly today, he argues that we cannot treat nature as "a gigantic gasoline station, an energy source for modern technology and industry."[122] His point is not to condemn technology as the work of the devil. He admits that would be shortsighted and foolish. Scientific and technological advances have exponentially increased material welfare (although they have also been enlisted in the horrors of modern warfare). But, he suggests, "we can affirm the unavoidable use of technical devices, and also deny them the right to dominate us, and so to warp, confuse, and lay waste our nature."[123]

What Heidegger advocates is openness to the mystery of Being, such as that evinced by the pre-Socratic Greeks, whom he thought experienced the "presencing of the divine in the world."[124] Our lives today are "harassed by work, made insecure by the hunt for gain and success, bewitched by the entertainment and recreation industry."[125] If we are to escape this frenetic, inauthentic existence, we need to relearn, in the words of Heidegger's favorite poet, Friedrich Hölderlin, how to dwell poetically in the world. Hölderlin is dedicated to re-creating in poetry the spirit of "Holy Greece! Home of all the gods."[126] Hölderlin wants to re-enchant the world with a new poetic mythology that will bring meaning and fulfillment to our lives so that "the fire of the gods drives us to set forth by day / And by night."[127] Heidegger is deeply sympathetic to this approach. In Heidegger's view, if we obtain a simpler, unfiltered relationship to the earth, to the sky, to divinities, and to other mortals—what he calls the primordial Four-fold—we can "recapture the old and now rapidly disappearing autochthony in a changed form."[128] Dwelling in the divine mystery of Being offers us a new foundation "upon which we can stand and endure in the world of technology without being imperiled by it."[129]

It is difficult to take this sentimental nostalgia for an older, simpler time altogether seriously. The exuberant mythology of ancient Greece makes for fascinating study and certainly has something to say about the wellsprings of our being. And Heidegger's emphasis on setting aside manipulation in favor of openness to nature and to other human beings has considerable resonance. But any suggestion that we should supplement our modern rational/scientific viewpoint with a quasi-mystical array of new or rediscovered divinities is either a badly strained metaphor or nothing short of silly.

Still, there are two serious points that Heidegger is making. The first point concerns the critical role of art in defining (and redefining) what it means to be human and how our lives may be ordered and given meaning. Heidegger portrays art as allowing each entity "to stand in the light of its being."[130] Poetry, Heidegger tells us, is a form of "letting-dwell."[131] The same point can be applied to the other arts. Novels, paintings, music all step into the clearing of Being, shed their light and help us to see, to hear, to understand, and to appreciate the great mystery of human life and the sheer "that it is" of the world. Art in all its forms lets Being be; it gives us, as Proust said, fragments of existence "liberated from the contingencies of time."[132] It celebrates and creates a dwelling for Being. In the process art can change our sense of the possibilities of being-in-the-world. A major work of art is, literally, a world-defining event. Great artists develop what has hitherto been unheard, unsaid, and unthought and project it upon the world, thereby unconcealing an aspect of Being that has lain in darkness. This conception of art has been enormously and justifiably influential, though its origins in Plato, Kant, the early Nietzsche, and others hardly make it novel, except in its terminology.

The second, much more controversial, point to be derived from Heidegger's later work is that great thinkers, like great artists, can also change our relationship to and understanding of Being and, in the process, give our lives coherence and meaning. Here, Heidegger appears to be advocating a conception of philosophy that brings us back, full circle, to Plato, where language is not merely a tool for use in everyday life, but a gateway to Being, and where certain words develop talismanic significance in bringing us closer to (helping us recollect) the true essence of the beings that surround us. This conception of philosophy has been widely dismissed as a regress to the philosophical tradition Heidegger demolished in his youth. Yet there is a core of what Heidegger is saying that warrants our closest attention and our deepest respect.

THE END OF PHILOSOPHY AND THE TASK OF THINKING

In the line quoted at the beginning of this chapter, Heidegger states, "The sentence, 'Language is language,' leaves us to hover over an abyss as long as we endure what it says." What I take Heidegger to be affirming here is what Wittgenstein calls the autonomy of grammar. Language is a man-made creation without any fixed essence that anchors it to the world in a predetermined way. Thus, we cannot by means of a study of language determine anything about the essential or necessary structure of the world. Our language is intimately connected with and a critical part of our evolving way of being-in-the-world. But all talk about the world presupposes a language, which is always, already "ready-to-hand." In recognizing language as language we "hover over an abyss" because the sort of ahistorical, noncontingent Platonic grounding that we have been taught to expect is a mirage. Language is not a gateway to metaphysical insight. In the sentence, "Language is [only] language," philosophy as traditionally conceived comes to an end.

Yet, Heidegger insists, there is a "task of thinking" that can fill the space of traditional philosophy and fulfill some of the same intellectual and spiritual needs that led us to philosophy in the first place. It is a task very much akin to that of the poet and involves "the liberation of language from grammar into a more original essential framework."[133] Language, Heidegger tells us, is the house of Being in which man dwells. "Those who think and those who create with words are the guardians of this home."[134] To serve that function, the thinker must first "let himself be claimed again by Being."[135] That is, he must "learn to exist in the nameless" in order to "find his way once again into the nearness of Being."[136] Being discloses itself to man via language. But the thinker, like the poet, must go beyond and behind language to Being itself. He must exist in the nameless in order to remember Being in its primordial originalness. "Only thus will the preciousness of its essence be once more bestowed upon the word, and upon man a home for dwelling in the truth of Being."[137]

This account sounds very Platonic: man uses language as a step ladder to go beyond language and obtain a direct apprehension (or recollection) of Being. He then uses his recollection of Being to refashion language into a "more essential framework" for the House of Being. Mixed up in this Platonism is Heidegger's sense that ancient Greek thinkers were closer to Being than we are ourselves and that through a close study of particular terms in their language, we too can come closer to the essence of Being.

Many philosophers attracted to *Being and Time* are highly critical of this "turn" in Heidegger's thought, calling it a failure of nerve and an unwillingness to accept the radical implications of the sentence, "Language is language." They believe that Heidegger has no right to his nostalgia for an older form of speech that supposedly disclosed Being more directly and accurately than does our modern chatter. If there is no more to Being than its interpretations by Dasein, they contend, then it makes no sense to suggest that some interpretations are closer to Being than others. Thus, Richard Rorty objects to the later

Heidegger's attempt to use words (both his own neologisms and ancient Greek terms), not just as tools, but as "hints" and "signs" of the true but ineffable essence of Being that lies behind language. All such attempts, he says, are just "one more language-game" in "a long series of self-conceptions. Heideggerese is only Heidegger's gift to us, not Being's gift to Heidegger."[138] It is a "vain hope," concludes Rorty, that "there is still the possibility of something called 'thinking' after the end of philosophy."[139]

I disagree with this criticism on two levels. First, and less significantly, it is unfair to read Heidegger's later writings as a complete repudiation of his most fundamental point in *Being and Time*, which is that there is and can be no ahistorical, noncontingent grounding for our language and our social practices. Nor is it necessary to do so. The later Heidegger can be readily interpreted as offering a new self-conception that is grounded on nothing more than his own reenvisioning of the philosophical tradition. When the later Heidegger talks of "a more essential framework" and being "claimed by Being," it is perfectly reasonable to read those references consistently with his lifelong view that the only essence of Being is its existence in time and that explaining Being in terms of some other, hidden beings is a fool's errand.

Second, and much more important, it is not a "vain hope" to believe that some sort of "thinking" can take the place of traditional philosophy, and that this thinking is different from, and a worthwhile supplement to, art and science. Even if all Heidegger offers us in the end is "Heideggerese," that is a great deal. Choosing the right words and the right metaphors to help us see what he wants us to see is philosophical thinking of the highest order.

Heidegger, through his close study of the philosophical tradition, reaches certain conclusions that allow him to reenvision that tradition and attain a new set of insights about our being-in-the-world. As Heidegger notes, "every attempt to gain insight into the supposed task of thinking finds itself moved to review the whole history of philosophy."[140] What Heidegger attains at the end of this process is a fresh way of speaking about Being and, hence, a new way of being-in-the-world. Heidegger gives us a different sort of illumination from that provided by art, or at least a different path to that illumination.

That does not mean that Heidegger claims for himself that he has "finally gotten language right" and aligned it with metaphysical reality. It simply means that Heidegger has found a mode of expressing his philosophical insights about being-in-the-world that he believes encompasses and goes beyond any other in the philosophical tradition. Heideggerese is the best means of expressing the truth as Heidegger sees it.

We can say of Heidegger's truth that it is just "one more in a long series of self-conceptions." Fair enough: but Heiddeger could justifiably respond that it is all right to privilege one form of discourse over another. We must do that in order to speak and think at all. If you have a better way of characterizing our being-in-the-world, please do so. Until then, this is what I believe. This is where I stand, in the light of Being as I understand it.

The question whether there is something called philosophy that is still worthwhile pursuing as an active endeavor—or whether like lovers of opera we are reduced to replays of the standard repertoire—turns on whether Heidegger is right when he says that we can never conclusively capture the elusive nature of reality, that something significant eludes us whenever we speak or write and spurs us to improve our mode of expression, to search out new metaphors and new words. Wittgenstein characterizes this feeling as getting to the point "where one would just like to emit an inarticulate sound." But he thinks, in the end, that the feeling is just one more illusion, a shadow cast by language. "Such a sound is an expression only as it occurs in a particular language-game, which should now be described."[141]

What Heidegger believes is that we must constantly reengage with Being—"learn to exist in the nameless"—in order to create a new self-conception, a new vocabulary in which we can dwell and feel at home. (Nietzsche's fable of the three metamorphoses of the spirit makes a similar point.) This new vocabulary becomes our very own "house of the truth of Being."[142] For Heidegger, human beings will never feel at home in their language when "for them language becomes a mere container for their sundry preoccupations."[143] This feeling of not being at home is not an illusion. It is a fundamental characteristic of being-in-the-world and the inevitable source of philosophy.

What Heidegger wants is a kind of thinking that constantly reconstructs the house of the truth of Being in ways that open us more fully to the mystery of life. Heidegger wants to jettison all the metaphors of transcendence and return philosophy to its origins in questioning and wonder. Traditional philosophical doctrines, theories about the nature of being, are just more ways of treating beings instrumentally in terms of other beings (whether those other "beings" are Platonic forms, the Christian God, or Cartesian sense impressions). What is needed is not a new theory, but a new engagement, a new openness to Being. What is needed is a new piety of thinking that focuses with gratitude and jubilation on the sheer miracle of the "here" and the "that," the miracle that there is something rather than nothing. Philosophy, for Heidegger, is a constant attempt to remain open to that miracle and then find ways of proclaiming it in words that are so fresh and so striking that they leave us breathless and change our way of being-in-the-world.

We return yet again to the most enduring and important metaphor in the history of philosophy: Plato's myth of the cave. To retell that myth in "Heideggerese" is readily done, although it took the whole history of philosophy to arrive at his account. Indeed, the whole history of philosophy really is nothing more than a retelling of that myth in ever new ways. We dwell in a cave of inherited ideas and values given us by the One. We have ceased to hear our most common words. We have ceased to be struck by what they reveal. We can use them; they are tools or equipment ready to hand. But we have lost their poetic force and hence their direct connection with Being. We have lost the sense of mystery and wonder that lies beyond language. We can manipulate beings to our own benefit, but we have forgotten Being.

Through a study of philosophy we can regain that sense of mystery and wonder. We can, slowly and painstakingly, emerge into the "open clearing" of Being. In reaching that clearing we have not discovered a new metaphysical foundation for Dasein. But we have come to recognize Dasein as itself the clearing in which Being shows itself. We are vouchsafed a vision of Being upon which the creativity of Dasein—holding itself out into the Nothing—ultimately rests. A philosopher of genius, like Heidegger, can return from that encounter with Being and give an account that helps the rest of us to see and to understand.

In Heidegger, then, Western philosophy comes full circle and is ready to begin again. He is not the end of the story, but only another of many beginnings. "Philosophizing ultimately means nothing other than being a beginner."[144] Heidegger has passed through T. S. Eliot's "unknown, remembered gate / When the last of earth left to discover / Is that which was the beginning."[145] He beckons us to follow.

EPILOGUE

In the very first class of the very first philosophy course I ever took, the revered Stanford teacher Robert Mothershead told a joke. A student goes to a guru and asks, "On what does the earth rest?" The guru responds, "A great rock." The student goes off and thinks about this for some time and returns: "On what does the rock rest?" "Another rock," is the answer. This exchange is repeated several times before the exasperated guru finally answers, "It's rocks all the way down."

Little did I realize then that much of what I needed to know about philosophy was contained in that joke. The main tradition of philosophy since Plato has been a search for rocks on which our lives, our language, and our social practices are to rest secure. For Plato, the rock is the eternal forms. For Descartes, the rock is the "I" of consciousness. For Kant, the rock is pure reason, which itself rests uneasily on the unknown and unknowable "thing in itself." Despite their undeniable beauty and sophistication, all the attempts of the philosophers to find a noncontingent, ahistorical grounding for our being-in-the-world are ultimately little better than the guru's "great rock." They are variations on a single theme.

But there is an alternate tradition that traces to Aristotle and culminates in Nietzsche, Wittgenstein, and Heidegger. These thinkers teach us, each in his own way, that the search for such foundations is

237

a history of illusions. It brings us no new knowledge. It gives us no greater understanding. To the contrary, it sets up expectations and standards of certainty and security that cannot be realized and hence leaves us feeling uncertain and insecure, with our lives stripped of all apparent value and meaning. With all the rocks taken away, we hover over the abyss.

For many, religion provides a *deus ex machina* to rescue us from this abyss. But for others, myself included, traditional religious belief is simply no longer a possibility. It is another of the guru's great rocks, part of the same mythology as Plato's form of the good, but with a darker hue. Even in its most benign manifestations, religion is too often a force for willful ignorance and an apologist for intolerance. *Pace* Heidegger, a god will not save us. Plato recognized that fact two thousand five hundred years ago, when he asked, Do the gods love piety because it is pious or is it pious because the gods love it? In convincingly arguing the former, Plato made the gods irrelevant. A naked appeal to authority cannot and should not satisfy us.

Here in the twenty-first century, we enjoy amazing advances in science and technology, advances that are improving the quality of life for hundreds of millions of people. These same advances allow us to kill our fellow human beings with the utmost efficiency, to degrade our environment, and to reduce the diversity of life on earth. The need for moral and spiritual guidance is great. Yet we sit amid the ruins of philosophy and theology.

The great Czech writer Milan Kundera suggests that today we have only the novel to turn to for moral and spiritual guidance. "In the modern world, abandoned by philosophy and splintered by hundreds of scientific specialties," Kundera writes, "the novel remains to us as the last observatory from which we can embrace human life as a whole."[1] The novel is the true Heideggerian genre in which we can fully explore man's existential nature. European philosophy "could not think out man's life, think out his 'concrete metaphysics'"; it is "the novel that is fated finally to take over this vacant terrain."[2] The novel's whole reason for being, he tells us, is to say "what only a novel can say."[3]

Fair enough. We can cede the novel its invaluable territory; we can let it say what only a novel can say, and yet still insist that there are some things only philosophy can say. We can still insist that there is a task of thinking and a manner of writing that is neither metaphysical nor concrete, that steps outside the framework of traditional philosophy without trying to compete with literature, and that employs abstractions that clarify rather than falsify our experience.

We have ceased to believe in the stories of the great philosophers. Philosophical theories and explanations have been relegated to the realm of myth. Current academic philosophers have either become museum curators or, to the extent they are doing "new work," custodians of grammar, trying to tidy and tighten our concepts, without daring actually to use them for anything that seems remotely worthwhile. By keeping their analytical aspirations small, contemporary philosophers hope to escape the fate of their predecessors. But, writ small or large, philosophy is still chasing the same illusory clarity first posed as an ideal by Plato. Contemporary philosophy has simply added irrelevance and mind-numbing boredom to the list of charges.

Why, then, do I think that philosophy is still a worthwhile endeavor? Part of the answer lies in Socrates' original injunction that the beginnings of wisdom lie in the recognition of ignorance. As Wittgenstein showed, the human mind has a natural tendency to seek absolute clarity and secure foundations. This tendency manifests itself in so many ways, direct and indirect, that exposing the various illusions to which it leads has inherent value. If nothing else, it can save us from dogmatism.

But if philosophy is to be worthwhile, there has to be more to it than recognizing what we don't know but are inclined to think we do. Otherwise, we should, as Wittgenstein urged (and I once did), stop doing philosophy once we think we have mastered the art of dissolving so-called philosophical puzzles. That would leave us still hovering over the abyss, longing for value and meaning in a world in which our ingrained standards of certainty and security cannot be met.

What the study of philosophy offers us is the chance to fashion our own answers to the three questions posed by Kant: What can I know? What may I hope? What ought I to do? Or as Bertrand Russell's cab driver more pithily put it, "What's it all about?" For the cab driver's question is really Kant's three questions, none of which can ultimately be considered in isolation and none of which can ultimately be ignored.

By clearing away the houses of cards constructed by their predecessors, Nietzsche, Heidegger, and Wittgenstein lay open to view the intellectual, spiritual, and moral space in which our lives unfold and allow us to chart its shape as never before. They give us, in the process, a deeper appreciation of what it means to be human. Yet, it is an appreciation that can only be garnered in juxtaposition to the thoughts of their great predecessors and as part of a continuing dialogue. The secret to understanding our present is to live "as if the centuries were nothing."

In living with the six thinkers discussed in this book, I have come away with six ideas that I think are the tools with which to forge a sort of philosophical wisdom. They are more fully developed above, but I want to summarize them briefly here.

Autonomy. There are no metaphysical, epistemological, or theological rocks on which to ground our most basic practices. Philosophy, as a search for foundations and explanations and justifications that lie outside our practices, is dead. All explanation and justification is immanent, not transcendent. If we want to know whether a particular proposition of physics is true, only physics can tell us. The thought that the philosopher can step outside a practice and find an Archimedean point of reference from which to evaluate it is simply an illusion. There are no guarantees of knowledge other than those we ourselves have developed in the various disciplines that make up our knowledge of the world and one another. There are no guarantees of the moral values and obligations that determine what we owe to one another other than those we ourselves have developed through the centuries. There are no guarantees of the aesthetic values that inform our appreciation of art, literature, and music that lie outside the evolving practice of those arts. That is not to say there is no such thing as knowledge or morality or aesthetic value. Quite the contrary; the point is rather that all these concepts have meaning within evolving language-games that set their own "grammatical" standards for their application. Language is not laid over reality in a fixed and predetermined way, and we cannot penetrate through language to a hidden realm, a realm reserved for philosophers, in which the essential nature of truth, virtue, and beauty are revealed. Our grammar is autonomous.

Rootedness. Despite their autonomy, there is a naturalness, almost a feeling of inevitability, about our social, moral, and artistic practices that makes them, in broad outlines, feel right to us. Indeed, if they did not feel right to enough people we would change them. We have, we might say, internalized their grammar. Aristotle puts this point in terms of a common human nature. Wittgenstein makes the same basic point by saying that we have agreement not just in judgments but in forms of life. Heidegger refers to "the One" which "disburdens" Dasein by making every decision and judgment its own. Even Nietzsche cites a developmental phase in which the strong, reverent spirit absorbs existing values and the tradition they represent. The point of all these metaphors is that there is a preexisting background against which, for better or worse, human flourishing occurs. Living and faring well at least to some extent consists in recognizing, internalizing, and realizing the values and ideals of the communities in which we live. Without some such connection, we will never feel at home.

Ambiguity. The Socratic insistence on strictly defined terms—with sharp boundaries that either clearly include or clearly exclude any given example—is a fatal first step in philosophy. As Wittgenstein convincingly shows us, words are tools used in a variety of ways, and various applications of the same word may bear only a family resemblance to one another. There is no common thread (or "form") that determines in every instance whether something is a "game" or a "virtue" or a "thing of beauty." Our ordinary language is much looser than the philosophers can bear, particularly when it comes to moral, political, and aesthetic concepts, the very concepts that matter most to us. The trend of modern analytic philosophy is to try to sharpen these tools, to make them more exact and precise. But that is as much a distortion of human life as are the sweeping theories of the philosophical tradition. Drawing a sharp boundary where none previously existed changes the concept in question. The ambiguity of moral, political, and aesthetic judgments is a key feature of our language, and coping with that ambiguity is a critical aspect of being human. In ambiguity lies the flexibility for change and for growth.

Anxiety. The early Heidegger emphasizes the anxiety of being-towards-death, the "crack in the teapot" that exposes our fragile existence as a placeholder for the nothing. Anxiety, for the early Heidegger, is a function of our recognition that the norms and values of the One are artificial bulwarks that will abandon us in our wholly personal encounter with Death. The later Heidegger, in my view more soundly, emphasizes anxiety as a feeling of not being fully "at home" among the norms and values of the One. But his cure for that anxiety is to find a new rootedness that is altogether too close to Orwell's learning to love Big Brother. Anxiety has no cure. It is a function of both the fragility of life and the ambiguity of our norms and values. In anxiety lies freedom. Not the existential freedom completely to remake ourselves with every choice, but the freedom to choose within a background of values and norms that does not fully determine our path through life. Kant traces morality to this freedom, and I think he is right to do so. In freedom lies the dignity of each individual. We don't need a Cartesian "soul" or even an enlightenment ideal of rationality on which to base our morality, but simply a very human recognition of a shared anxiety and a shared fate that warrants consideration and respect.

Creativity. Freedom allows for creativity and change. T. S. Kuhn, in studying the history of the sciences, argues that there are two sorts of change: incremental change and paradigm shifts. Incremental change occurs within the interstices of existing norms and assumptions. Incremental change shifts ambiguous concepts in gradual, almost imperceptible ways. It is the product of many small choices, like the hidden hand of economics or the gradual accretions of the common law. We are all participants in this process insofar as we speak and write and participate in the evolution of our language (and hence in our forms of life). But there are also more seismic changes, wrought by the vision of individual geniuses—the Nietzsche, the Einstein, and the Picasso—who fundamentally alter our ways of seeing and understanding the world. They forge for us a new truth that seems to come out of nowhere, but for which the ground has in fact been carefully prepared. As Nietzsche explains, in his wonderful parable of the three metamorphoses of the spirit, only someone who has mastered and internalized the tradition within which he or she works and then rebelled against its limitations can make a fresh beginning and provide us with a new paradigm within which to dwell.

Wonder. Philosophy begins in wonder. Traditionally, however, it ends in theories and explanations designed to redirect that wonder into a worship of false gods. Plato and his successors dismiss everyday life and practices as the merest of appearances and offer us the higher comfort, in one version or another, of the forms. Wittgenstein and Heidegger, by contrast, reject theories and explanations in favor of an *übersicht* (overview) or a *lichtung* (clearing) in which our everyday wonder and amazement at being-in-the-world and being-with-others is not dissipated but heightened to a fever pitch. Our study of the history of philosophy is itself a metamorphosis of the spirit in which the tradition is mastered and then rejected in favor of a new beginning and a sacred "Yes." We have toiled through the philosophical underbrush to reach a clearing in which Being is made luminous and an object of wonder. Spinoza and Einstein would call that a religious feeling. Nietzsche and Heidegger would not. Whatever vocabulary one chooses, we have left dogmatism far behind in favor of an openness and receptivity that transforms our experience.

If, then, I had to answer Lord Russell's cabbie in a single sentence, I would say: We must replace worship with wonder,[4] and fashion our own meaning by engaging creatively with ambiguity and anxiety to forge new and ever better connections with the world and the people among whom we live and love.

This is the truth as I see it. This is the shape of the intellectual, spiritual, and moral space in which I believe our lives unfold. Note, I do not with Nietzsche say that this is "my truth," as if each person's truth were just one perspective among many. I think it is "the" truth, so far as I understand it, and when Nietzsche says "the truth does not exist," I accept his statement only insofar as it implies with Socrates that we are never finished inquiring, that our views are always subject to refinement, and even wholesale revision, based on our continuing engagement with life.

Would my answer satisfy Lord Russell's cabbie? Almost certainly not. Will it satisfy me tomorrow? Probably not. Do I expect it to satisfy others? I hope not. We can and should listen to the debates of the great philosophers. We can and should ponder their answers. But in the end we must each struggle in our own way with the three questions posed by Kant. Only through our own strenuous efforts can we break the intellectual, spiritual, and moral blinders that limit our vision. Only thus can we finally take a good look around the cave in which we exist and move upward toward the light, knowing that we are not abandoning everyday concerns but rather learning to see them in a new way.

> We shall not cease from exploration
> And the end of all our exploring
> Will be to arrive where we started
> And know the place for the first time.[5]

SUGGESTIONS FOR
FURTHER READING

PLATO

The Hackett Publishing Company commissioned a new set of translations of the dialogues, which are now gathered together in a four-volume, leather-bound edition published by Easton Press in 2001. See John M. Cooper, ed., *Plato: Complete Works*, 4 vols. (Norwalk, CT: Easton Press, 2001). There are also several single-volume editions of the complete dialogues, and individual dialogues or sets of dialogues are ubiquitously available in paperback.

Among the dialogues that everyone should undertake to read are *Euthyphro, Apology, Crito, Phaedo, Symposium, Phaedrus, Meno,* and *The Republic.* For those interested in some of the more intricate and problematic aspects of Plato's theory of the forms, I would also recommend *Parmenides* and *Theaetetus.*

Biographical details, many of questionable reliability, may be found in Diogenes Laertius, *Lives of the Eminent Philosophers*, Book III, Loeb Classical Library, translated by R. D. Hicks (Cambridge, MA: Harvard University Press, 1972). The two most fruitful and accessible secondary sources are Gregory Vlasto, *Socrates: Ironist and Moral Philosopher* (Ithaca, NY: Cornell University Press, 1991), and Alexander Nehamas, *Virtues of Authenticity: Essays on Plato and Socrates* (Princeton, NJ: Princeton University Press, 1999). I also recommend

Allan Bloom's commentary to his translation of *The Republic* (New York: Basic Books, 1968); Martha Nussbaum, *Plato's Republic: The Good Society and the Deformation of Desire* (Washington, DC: Library of Congress, 1998); Gregory Vlastos, ed., *Plato: A Collection of Critical Essays*, vols. 1 & 2 (Garden City, NY: Anchor Books, 1971); Gregory Vlastos, ed., *The Philosophy of Socrates: A Collection of Critical Essays* (Garden City, NY: Anchor Books, 1971); and Julius Moravcsik, *Plato and Platonism* (Oxford: Blackwell, 1992). For a brilliant and fresh perspective on Plato's theory of forms (in which ancient conceptions of light and vision are explored to suggest that Plato envisioned a much more active, constitutive engagement with the forms than the passive one we usually encounter), see Peter Pesic, "Seeing the Forms," *Journal of the International Plato Society* (2007), available online at http://www .nd.edu/~plato/plato7issue/Pesic,%20Seeing%20the%20Forms1 .pdf (accessed April 28, 2009).

WITTGENSTEIN

The *Philosophical Investigations* is not an easy book to understand. But everyone interested in Wittgenstein should read at least the first 184 sections, which give a full flavor of the whole and a remarkably compact overview of Wittgenstein's thinking, particularly on the nature of philosophy. The best secondary source is the four-volume *Analytical Commentary* written by P. M. S. Hacker and published by Blackwell. (The first two volumes were written with G. P. Baker.) Volume 1 tracks the first 184 sections of the *Investigations* and can be read with great profit in conjunction with them. See G. P. Baker and P. M. S. Hacker, *Wittgenstein: Understanding and Meaning* (Oxford: Blackwell, 1980).

There is an excellent biography written by Ray Monk, *Ludwig Wittgenstein: The Duty of Genius* (New York: Free Press, 1990), as well as a fascinating exploration of the cultural milieu that helped form Wittgenstein's early preoccupations by Allan Janik and Stephen Toulmin, *Wittgenstein's Vienna* (New York: Touchstone, 1973). The best single-volume commentaries are Anthony Kenny, *Wittgenstein* (Harmondsworth, UK: Penguin Books, 1973) and P. M. S. Hacker, *Insight and Illusion* (New York: Oxford University Press, 1972). An intriguing exploration (or, more accurately, extrapolation) of Wittgenstein's views on ethics is made by James C. Edwards, *Ethics without Philosophy: Wittgenstein and the Moral Life* (Tampa: University Press of Florida, 1985).

KANT

It is too much to expect the general reader to tackle *The Critique of Pure Reason* in its entirety, but Kant's two prefaces and the introduction give a nice overview. Kant also wrote shorter works on metaphysics, *Prolegemena to Any Future Metaphysics*, and morals, *Foundations of the Metaphysics of Morals*, which are much more accessible.

The best account of Kant's life is by Manfred Kuehn, *Kant: A Biography* (Cambridge: Cambridge University Press, 2001). The secondary literature is vast, but two short books that provide an overview of Kant's life and works are Roger Scruton, *Kant: A Very Short Introduction* (New York: Oxford University Press, 1982) and S. Korner, *Kant* (Harmondsworth, UK: Penguin Books, 1955). An extremely clever and engaging study of Kant's first critique, from the perspective of analytic philosophy, is P. F. Strawson, *The Bounds of Sense* (London: Metheun, 1975).

NIETZSCHE

Reading Nietzsche is exhilarating and requires no special background. Start with *The Gay Science*, particularly books IV and V. After that, *Thus Spoke Zarathustra*, *Twilight of the Idols*, and *The Antichrist* are all lively, highly provocative, and beautifully written (often beautifully overwritten). *The Genealogy of Morals* is the most like a traditional work of philosophy in that it is a sustained discussion on a single topic, whereas most of Nietzsche's work is aphoristic. *Ecce Homo*, his intellectual biography, is an acquired taste. All are available in paperback in Walter Kaufmann's excellent translations.

There are two good, recent biographies of Nietzsche, one by Curtis Cate (Woodstock, NY: Overlook Press, 2005) and one by

Rüdiger Safranski (New York: W. W. Norton, 2002). The latter book is more impressionistic than thorough, but contains many brilliant insights about Nietzsche's thought in relation to his life. Among the best secondary sources are Alexander Nehamas, *Nietzsche: Life as Literature* (Cambridge, MA: Harvard University Press, 1985); Walter Kaufmann, *Nietzsche: Philosopher, Psychologist, Antichrist*, 3rd ed. (Princeton, NJ: Princeton University Press, 1968); and Brian Leiter, *Nietzsche on Morality* (London: Routledge, 2002).

ARISTOTLE

Aristotle's *Complete Works*, edited by Jonathan Barnes, are available in two volumes as part of the Bollingen Series published by Princeton University Press (4th printing 1991). Individual editions of the *Nichomachean Ethics* are readily available.

Some biographical details may be found in Diogenes Laertius, *Lives of the Eminent Philosophers*, book V, Loeb Classical Library, translated by R. D. Hicks (Cambridge, MA: Harvard University Press, 1972). Among the standard secondary works are G. E. R. Lloyd, *Aristotle: The Growth & Structure of His Thought* (Cambridge: Cambridge University Press, 1968); J. O. Urmson, *Aristotle's Ethics* (Oxford: Blackwell, 1988); and Sarah Broadie, *Ethics with Aristotle* (New York: Oxford University Press, 1991). For the general reader, however, I would recommend Martha C. Nussbaum, *The Fragility of Goodness: Luck and Ethics in Greek Tragedy and Philosophy* (Cambridge: Cambridge University Press, 1986), and Alasdair MacIntyre, *After Virtue*, 2nd ed. (Notre Dame, IN: University of Notre Dame Press, 1984). Both of these brilliant books deal with the critical role of Aristotle's thought in the broader debate about moral issues.

HEIDEGGER

The standard translation of *Being and Time* is by John Macquarrie and Edward Robinson (San Francisco: HarperSanFrancisco, 1962). An easier place to start, though, is with *Basic Writings*, David F. Krell, ed.

(New York: Harper & Row, 1977), which includes a number of key essays and the introduction to *Being and Time*. Another, even more accessible book, which provides a sense of the later Heiddeger, is *Poetry, Language, Thought*, translated by Albert Hofstadter (1971; repr., New York: HarperCollins, Perennial Classics, 2001).

The indispensable secondary work is Hubert L. Dreyfus, *Being-in-the-World: A Commentary on Heidegger's "Being and Time," Division I* (Cambridge, MA: MIT Press, 1991). The best biography is Rüdiger Safranski, *Martin Heidegger: Between Good and Evil*, translated by Ewald Osers (Cambridge, MA: Harvard University Press, 1998). For those interested in Heidegger's controversial connections with the Nazi party, there is Hugo Ott, *Martin Heidegger: A Political Life*, translated by Allan Blunden (New York: Basic Books, 1993). Other helpful secondary works include the first four essays in Richard Rorty, *Essays on Heidegger and Others: Philosophical Papers*, vol. 2 (Cambridge: Cambridge University Press, 1991); George Steiner, *Martin Heidegger* (Chicago: University of Chicago Press, 1976); Mark Wrathall, *How to Read Heidegger* (New York: W. W. Norton, 2005); and Charles Guignon, ed., *The Cambridge Companion to Heidegger* (Cambridge: Cambridge University Press, 1993).

EPILOGUE

In the epilogue, I try to sketch the shape of the moral, spiritual, and intellectual space in which our lives unfold, using ideas from all six thinkers studied in this book, but without seeking either to provide foundations for or to transcend our everyday existence. Various contemporary writers are already far advanced on this task. Among the books I most highly recommend are Alexander Nehamas, *The Art of Living: Socratic Reflections from Plato to Foucault* (Berkeley and Los Angeles: University of California Press, 1998); Martha C. Nussbaum, *Love's Knowledge: Essays on Philosophy and Literature* (New York: Oxford University Press, 1990); Peter Pesic, *Labyrinth: A Search for the Hidden Meaning of Science* (Cambridge, MA: MIT Press, 2000); James C. Edwards, *The Authority of Language: Heidegger, Wittgenstein, and the Threat of Philosophical Nihilism* (Tampa: University of South Florida Press,

1990); and everything by Stanley Cavell, but particularly *Must We Mean What We Say?* (Cambridge: Cambridge University Press, 1976), *The Senses of Walden* (San Francisco: Northpoint Press, 1981), *This New Yet Unapproachable America: Lectures after Emerson after Wittgenstein* (Albuquerque, NM: Living Batch Press, 1989), and *Cities of Words* (Cambridge, MA: Harvard University Press, 2004). I also recommend, although I disagree in critical respects with, the late Richard Rorty, *Consequences of Pragmatism* (Minneapolis, MN: University of Minneapolis Press, 1982). For an effective critique of Rorty's "social constructivism" and relativism, see Paul Boghossian, *Fear of Knowledge: Against Relativism and Constructivism* (New York: Oxford University Press, 2006).

NOTES

PREFACE

1. Plato, *Apology* 38a, trans. G. M. A. Grube, in *Plato: Complete Works*, ed. John M. Cooper (Norwalk, CT: Easton Press, 2001; first published 1997 by Hackett), 1:17.

2. *Apology* 36c.

3. *Apology* 17c.

4. *Apology* 29a.

5. Plato, *Euthyphro, Apology, and Crito, and the Death Scene from Phaedo*, trans. Frederick J. Church, rev. Robert D. Cumming, 2nd rev. ed. (Indianapolis, IN: Bobbs-Merrill, 1956), p. 49.

6. *Apology* 29e.

7. Ludwig Wittgenstein, *Philosophical Investigations*, trans. G. E. M. Anscombe, 3rd ed. (New York: Macmillan, 1973), sec. 133.

8. The anecdote about the cab driver, originally published in the London *Times*, is quoted in Annie Dillard, *Pilgrim at Tinker Creek* (1974; repr., New York: HarperCollins, HarperPerennial, 1998), p. 171. It also forms the centerpiece of a more recent book by Julian Baggini, *What's It All About? Philosophy and the Meaning of Life* (New York: Oxford University Press, 2005).

9. *Selected Letters of Friedrich Nietzsche*, trans. and ed. Christopher Middleton (1969; repr., Indianapolis, IN: Hackett, 1996), p. 174.

10. See Charles Taylor, *A Secular Age* (Cambridge, MA: Harvard University Press, 2007), p. 5 ("We all see our lives, and/or the space wherein we live our lives, as having a certain moral/spiritual shape.").

11. Leo Strauss, *Studies in Platonic Political Philosophy* (Chicago: University of Chicago Press, 1983), p. 147.

CHAPTER ONE

1. Alfred North Whitehead, *Process and Reality*, ed. David Ray Griffin and Donald W. Sherburne (New York: Free Press, 1979), p. 39.
2. Plato, *Euthyphro* 4e, trans. G. M. A. Grube, in *Plato: Complete Works*, ed. John M. Cooper (Norwalk, CT: Easton Press, 2001; first published 1997 by Hackett), 1:1.
3. *Euthyphro* 4a–b.
4. *Euthyphro* 4e–5a.
5. *Euthyphro* 5d–e.
6. *Euthyphro* 6d–e.
7. *Euthyphro* 9e.
8. *Euthyphro* 15c.
9. *Euthyphro* 11b.
10. *Euthyphro* 11d–e.
11. *Euthyphro* 15e.
12. *Euthyphro* 15e–16a.
13. See Alexander Nehamas, *The Art of Living: Socratic Reflections from Plato to Foucault* (Berkeley and Los Angeles: University of California Press, 1998), p. 41.
14. Plato, *Charmides* 159a, trans. Rosamond Kent Sprague, in Cooper, *Plato: Complete Works*, 2:639.
15. Plato, *Laches* 191d–e, trans. Rosamond Kent Sprague, in Cooper, *Plato: Complete Works*, 2:664.
16. Plato, *Phaedo* 76b, trans. G. M. A. Grube, in Cooper, *Plato: Complete Works*, 1:49.
17. Plato, *Theaetetus* 146c–e, trans. M. J. Levett, rev. Myles F. Burnyeat, in Cooper, *Plato: Complete Works*, 1:157.
18. *Charmides* 166c–d.
19. Plato, *Gorgias* 458a, trans. Donald J. Zeyl, in Cooper, *Plato: Complete Works*, 2:791.
20. Plato, *Apology* 38a, trans. G. M. A. Grube, in Cooper, *Plato: Complete Works*, 1:17.
21. Plato, *Euthyphro, Apology, and Crito, and the Death Scene from Phaedo*, trans. Frederick J. Church, rev. Robert D. Cumming (New York: Liberal Arts Press, 1948), p. 68.

22. Plato, *Meno* 71b, trans. G. M. A. Grube, in Cooper, *Plato: Complete Works*, 2:870.

23. *Meno* 72c–d.

24. *Meno* 72c, 73d, 74a.

25. *Meno* 80b.

26. *Meno* 80c–d.

27. *Meno* 81a.

28. *Meno* 81c–e.

29. *Meno* 84a–b.

30. *Meno* 84b–c.

31. *Meno* 85c–d.

32. *Meno* 86b.

33. *Meno* 89a, 89c.

34. *Meno* 89e.

35. *Meno* 94d–e.

36. *Meno* 99b.

37. *Meno* 99e–100a.

38. *Meno* 100b.

39. Ibid.

40. Plato, *Republic* 344e, trans. G. M. A. Grube, rev. C. D. C. Reeve, in Cooper, *Plato: Complete Works*, 3:971.

41. *Republic* 338c.

42. *Republic* 343d.

43. *Republic* 348c.

44. *Republic* 344c.

45. *Republic* 345a.

46. *Republic* 365b–c.

47. *Republic* 367e.

48. *Republic* 370c.

49. *Republic* 465c.

50. *Republic* 377c.

51. *Republic* 401c–d.

52. *Republic* 379a.

53. *Republic* 424c–d.

54. *Republic* 424d–e.

55. See, e.g., Karl R. Popper, *The Open Society and Its Enemies*, vol. 1, *The Spell of Plato*, 5th rev. ed. (Princeton, NJ: Princeton University Press, 1971).

56. See Martha Nussbaum, *Plato's Republic: The Good Society and the Deformation of Desire* (Washington, DC: Library of Congress, 1998).

57. *Republic* 377b (emphasis added).

58. *Republic* 430e.

59. *Republic* 439d, 581a.

60. *Republic* 443c–d.

61. *Republic* 443d–e.

62. *Republic* 444b.

63. *Republic* 473c–d.

64. *Republic* 510d.

65. *Republic* 511c.

66. *Republic* 511b–c.

67. *Republic* 476b.

68. *Republic* 511b.

69. *Republic* 515c.

70. *Republic* 517c.

71. *Republic* 520c.

72. *Republic* 540a–b.

73. *Republic* 496c.

74. *Republic* 527b.

75. *Republic* 561c–d.

76. *Republic* 586a–b.

77. *Republic* 532c, 533d.

78. *Phaedo* 79d.

79. Plato, *Letter VII* 341c–d, trans. Glenn R. Morrow, in Cooper, *Plato: Complete Works*, 4:1646.

80. *Phaedo* 67a.

81. *Phaedo* 66a.

82. *Republic* 534b–c.

83. Plato, *Cratylus* 386d–e, trans. C. D. C. Reeve, in Cooper, *Plato: Complete Works*, 1:101.

84. *Cratylus* 386e.

85. *Phaedo* 79d.

86. Plato, *Parmenides* 135b–c, trans. Mary Louise Gill and Paul Ryan, in Cooper, *Plato: Complete Works*, 1:359; Kenneth Dorter, *The Theory of Forms and "Parmenides I,"* in *Essays in Ancient Greek Philosophy*, ed. John P. Anton and Anthony Preus, vol. 3, *Plato* (Albany: State University of New York Press, 1989), p. 183.

CHAPTER TWO

1. Ludwig Wittgenstein, *Philosophical Investigations*, trans. G. E. M. Anscombe, 3rd ed. (New York: Macmillan, 1973), sec. 126.

2. Ray Monk, *Ludwig Wittgenstein: The Duty of Genius* (New York: Free Press, 1990), p. 272.

3. Ludwig Wittgenstein, preface to *Tractatus Logico-Philosophicus*, trans. David F. Pears and Brian F. McGuiness, rev. ed. (Atlantic Highlands, NJ: Humanities Press, 1974), p. 4.

4. *Tractatus*, 6.41.

5. *Tractatus*, 6.42.

6. Ibid.

7. *Tractatus*, 5.6.

8. *Tractatus*, 6.41.

9. *Tractatus*, 5.632.

10. *Tractatus*, 6.4312.

11. *Tractatus*, 6.54.

12. *Tractatus*, 7.

13. *Investigations*, sec. 133.

14. *Investigations*, sec. 109.

15. *Investigations*, sec. 124.

16. *Investigations*, sec. 1 n. 1.

17. *Investigations*, sec. 1.

18. Ibid.

19. *Investigations*, sec. 2.

20. See Stanley Cavell, *Notes and Afterthoughts on the Opening of Wittgenstein's "Investigations,"* in *The Cambridge Companion to Wittgenstein*, ed. Hans D. Sluga and David G. Stern (New York: Cambridge University Press, 1996), pp. 261–95.

21. *Investigations*, sec. 1 n. 1.

22. *Investigations*, secs. 19, 23.

23. *Investigations*, sec. 25.

24. *Investigations*, sec. 199.

25. *Investigations*, sec. 65.

26. *Investigations*, sec. 66.

27. Ibid.

28. *Investigations*, sec. 67.

29. *Investigations*, sec. 40.

30. *Investigations*, sec. 44.

31. *Investigations*, sec. 432.

32. *Investigations*, pt. 2, p. 212.

33. *Investigations*, sec. 78.

34. *Investigations*, sec. 71.

35. *Investigations*, sec. 75.

36. *Investigations*, sec. 76.

37. Plato, *Cratylus* 386d–e, trans. C. D. C. Reeve, in *Plato: Complete Works*, ed. John M. Cooper (Norwalk, CT: Easton Press, 2001; first published 1997 by Hackett), 1:101.

38. *Investigations*, sec. 580.

39. *Investigations*, sec. 354.

40. *Investigations*, sec. 290.

41. *Investigations*, sec. 246.

42. *Investigations*, sec. 244.

43. *Investigations*, sec. 288.

44. *Investigations*, sec. 289.

45. *Investigations*, sec. 293.

46. *Investigations*, sec. 303.

47. *Investigations*, pt. 2, p. 222.

48. *Investigations*, sec. 256.

49. *Investigations*, sec. 293.

50. *Investigations*, sec. 258.

51. *Investigations*, sec. 257.

52. Ibid.

53. *Investigations*, sec. 261.

54. Ibid.

55. *Investigations*, sec. 293.

56. *Investigations*, sec. 304.

57. *Investigations*, sec. 281.

58. *Investigations*, pt. 2, p. 178.

59. *Investigations*, sec. 496.

60. *Investigations*, sec. 32.

61. *Investigations*, sec. 28.

62. *Investigations*, sec. 30.

63. *Investigations*, sec. 50.

64. Ibid.

65. *Investigations*, sec. 314.

66. *Investigations*, sec. 325.

67. *Investigations*, sec. 481.

68. *Investigations*, sec. 120.

69. *Investigations*, pt. 2, p. 224.

70. *Investigations*, pt. 2, p. 226.

71. *Investigations*, sec. 374.

72. *Investigations*, sec. 217.

73. *Investigations*, sec. 123.

74. See *Investigations*, sec. 89. ("Augustine says in the *Confessions* 'quid est ergo tempus? si nemo ex me quaerat scio; si quaerenti explicare velim, nescio.'")

75. *Investigations*, sec. 115.

76. *Investigations*, sec. 435.

77. *Investigations*, sec. 92.

78. *Investigations*, sec. 89.

79. *Investigations*, sec. 116.

80. *Investigations*, sec. 109.

81. *Investigations*, sec. 90.

82. *Investigations*, sec. 255.

83. *Investigations*, sec. 98.

84. *Investigations*, sec. 38.

85. *Investigations*, sec. 133.

86. *Investigations*, sec. 97.

87. *Investigations*, sec. 134.

88. *Investigations*, sec. 120.

89. *Investigations*, sec. 119.

90. *Investigations*, sec. 118.

91. *Investigations*, sec. 77.

92. *Investigations*, sec. 124.

93. *Investigations*, sec. 217.

94. *Investigations*, sec. 122.

95. *Investigations*, sec. 129.

CHAPTER THREE

1. Immanuel Kant, *Critique of Pure Reason*, trans. Norman Kemp Smith, unabridged ed. (New York: St. Martin's Press, 1965), Bxxx (italics omitted). Standard pagination for the *Critique of Pure Reason* gives A cites (to the first German edition) and/or B cites (to the second German edition, to which Kant added substantial new material).

2. Immanuel Kant, *Critique of Practical Reason*, trans. Lewis White Beck (Indianapolis, IN: Bobbs-Merrill, 1956), p. 166.

3. *Critique of Pure Reason*, Axvii.

4. *Critique of Pure Reason*, A51, B75.

5. Ibid.

6. *Critique of Pure Reason*, Bxviii.

7. *Critique of Pure Reason*, A107 (emphasis added).

8. *Critique of Pure Reason*, B131–32.

9. *Critique of Pure Reason*, A116.

10. *Critique of Pure Reason*, B277.

11. *Critique of Pure Reason*, A111.

12. Ludwig Wittgenstein, *Philosophical Investigations*, trans. G. E. M. Anscombe, 3rd ed. (New York: Macmillan, 1973), sec. 304.

13. *Critique of Pure Reason*, B224.

14. *Critique of Pure Reason*, A246, B303 (italics omitted).

15. *Critique of Pure Reason*, A287, B344.

16. *Critique of Pure Reason*, Avii.

17. *Critique of Pure Reason*, A5, B8–9.

18. See Walter Isaacson, *Einstein: His Life and Universe* (New York: Simon & Schuster, 2007), p. 4.

19. Brian Greene, *The Fabric of the Cosmos: Space, Time, and the Texture of Reality* (New York: Knopf, 2004), p. 473.

20. Ibid., p. 487.

21. Ibid., p. 472.

22. Ibid., p. 20.

23. Ibid., p. 5 (italics omitted).

24. *Investigations*, sec. 38.

25. *Investigations*, sec. 107 (italics omitted).

26. *Critique of Pure Reason*, A805, B833.

27. *Critique of Pure Reason*, Bxxxi.

28. *Critique of Pure Reason*, A595, B623.

29. *Critique of Pure Reason*, A600, B628.

30. *Critique of Pure Reason*, A620, B648.

31. *Critique of Pure Reason*, A622, B650.

32. *Critique of Pure Reason*, A623, B651.

33. *Critique of Pure Reason*, A630.

34. Immanuel Kant, *Critique of Judgement*, trans. James Creed Meredith (Oxford: Clarendon Press, 1952), pt. 2, p. 125.

35. *Critique of Pure Reason*, A569, B597 (italics omitted).

36. *Critique of Practical Reason*, p. 4.

37. Immanuel Kant, *Foundations of the Metaphysics of Morals*, trans. Lewis White Beck (Indianapolis, IN: Bobbs-Merrill, 1959), p. 16.

38. *Metaphysics of Morals*, p. 15.

39. *Metaphysics of Morals*, p. 6.

40. *Metaphysics of Morals*, p. 29.

41. *Metaphysics of Morals*, p. 31.

42. *Metaphysics of Morals*, p. 39.

43. *Metaphysics of Morals*, p. 47.

44. *Metaphysics of Morals*, p. 46.
45. *Metaphysics of Morals*, p. 71.
46. *Metaphysics of Morals*, p. 65.
47. *Critique of Practical Reason*, p. 4.
48. *Critique of Practical Reason*, p. 130.
49. *Critique of Practical Reason*, p. 118.
50. *Critique of Practical Reason*, p. 127.
51. *Critique of Practical Reason*, p. 123.
52. *Critique of Practical Reason*, p. 129.
53. *Critique of Practical Reason*, p. 134.
54. Immanuel Kant, *Religion and Rational Theology*, trans. and ed. Allen W. Wood and George di Giovanni (Cambridge: Cambridge University Press, 1996), p. 190.
55. *Religion and Rational Theology*, p. 264 (italics omitted).
56. *Religion and Rational Theology*, p. 267.
57. *Religion and Rational Theology*, p. 186.
58. *Religion and Rational Theology*, p. 198.
59. *Religion and Rational Theology*, p. 193.
60. *Religion and Rational Theology*, p. 210 (italics omitted).
61. *Religion and Rational Theology*, p. 211n.
62. *Religion and Rational Theology*, p. 272.
63. *Religion and Rational Theology*, pp. 180–81.
64. *Religion and Rational Theology*, p. 199.
65. See *Critique of Judgement*, pt. 2, p. 54.
66. Isaacson, *Einstein*, p. 393.
67. Ibid., pp. 384, 387.
68. Ibid., pp. 384–85, 389.
69. Ibid., p. 385.

CHAPTER 4

1. Friedrich Nietzsche, *Thus Spoke Zarathustra*, in *The Portable Nietzsche*, trans. Walter Kaufmann (New York: Viking Press, 1968), p. 144.
2. See Curtis Cate, *Friedrich Nietzsche* (Woodstock, NY: Overlook Press, 2005), p. 72. It has long been a subject of speculation as to where and how Nietzsche contracted syphilis, with most commenters opting for the local brothel. Lately, however, the assumption that Nietzsche suffered and ultimately died from syphilis has itself been challenged. See Richard Schain, *The Legend of Nietzsche's Syphilis* (Westport, CT: Greenwood Press, 2001).

3. Friedrich Nietzsche, *Ecce Homo*, trans. Walter Kaufmann, in *On the Genealogy of Morals / Ecce Homo* (New York: Vintage Books, 1969), p. 326 ("Why I Am a Destiny," sec. 1).

4. Friedrich Nietzsche, *The Gay Science*, trans. Walter Kaufmann (New York: Vintage Books, 1974), p. 307 (sec. 357).

5. *Gay Science*, p. 279 (sec. 343).

6. Ibid.

7. *Gay Science*, p. 182 (sec. 125).

8. *Gay Science*, p. 307 (sec. 357).

9. *Gay Science*, p. 279 (sec. 343).

10. *Gay Science*, p. 181 (sec. 125).

11. *Gay Science*, p. 280 (sec. 343).

12. *Gay Science*, p. 191 (sec. 143).

13. *Gay Science*, p. 280 (sec. 343).

14. Friedrich Nietzsche, *On the Genealogy of Morals*, trans. Walter Kaufmann and R. J. Hollingdale, in *On the Genealogy of Morals / Ecce Homo*, p. 18 (preface, sec. 4).

15. *Ecce Homo*, pp. 236–37 ("Why I Am So Clever," sec. 1).

16. *Gay Science*, p. 307 (sec. 357).

17. *Genealogy of Morals*, p. 156 (Third Essay, sec. 25).

18. Friedrich Nietzsche, *The Antichrist*, in *The Portable Nietzsche*, p. 585 (sec. 17).

19. Friedrich Nietzsche, *Twilight of the Idols*, in *The Portable Nietzsche*, p. 481 ("'Reason' in Philosophy," sec. 4).

20. *Genealogy of Morals*, p. 156 (Third Essay, sec. 25).

21. *Twilight of the Idols*, p. 484 ("'Reason' in Philosophy," sec. 6).

22. *Thus Spoke Zarathustra*, p. 198.

23. *Twilight of the Idols*, p. 481 ("'Reason' in Philosophy," sec. 2).

24. Friedrich Nietzsche, *Daybreak: Thoughts on the Prejudices of Morality*, trans. R. J. Hollingdale (Cambridge: Cambridge University Press, 1982), p. 32 (sec. 49).

25. *Daybreak*, p. 32 (sec. 49).

26. *Antichrist*, p. 627 (sec. 47).

27. *Gay Science*, p. 307 (sec. 357).

28. Friedrich Nietzsche, *Human, All Too Human: A Book for Free Spirits*, trans. R. J. Hollingdale (Cambridge: Cambridge University Press, 1986), p. 66 (vol. 1, sec. 113) (emphasis added).

29. *Gay Science*, p. 76 (sec. 2).

30. *Antichrist*, p. 632 (sec. 50).

31. *Thus Spoke Zarathustra*, p. 428.

32. *Ecce Homo*, p. 334 ("Why I Am a Destiny," sec. 8).
33. Friedrich Nietzsche, *The Will to Power*, trans. Walter Kaufmann and R. J. Hollingdale (New York: Vintage Books, 1968), p. 91 (sec. 141).
34. *Thus Spoke Zarathustra*, p. 143.
35. *Thus Spoke Zarathustra*, p. 292.
36. *Antichrist*, p. 627 (sec. 47).
37. *Ecce Homo*, p. 244 ("Why I Am So Clever," sec. 3).
38. *Will to Power*, p. 16 (sec. 18).
39. *Twilight of the Idols*, p. 524 ("Skirmishes of an Untimely Man," sec. 16).
40. *Gay Science*, p. 265 (sec. 335).
41. *Antichrist*, p. 577 (sec. 11).
42. Ibid.
43. *Gay Science*, p. 265 (sec. 335).
44. Friedrich Nietzsche, *Beyond Good and Evil*, in *Basic Writings of Nietzsche*, trans. and ed. Walter Kaufmann (New York: Modern Library, 1968), p. 275 (sec. 108).
45. *Thus Spoke Zarathustra*, p. 203.
46. *Beyond Good and Evil*, p. 327 (sec. 212).
47. *Antichrist*, p. 612 (sec. 38).
48. *Antichrist*, p. 613 (sec. 39).
49. *Gay Science*, p. 185 (sec. 128).
50. *Genealogy of Morals*, p. 17 (preface, sec. 3).
51. *Genealogy of Morals*, p. 39 (First Essay, sec. 10).
52. *Genealogy of Morals*, pp. 33–34 (First Essay, sec. 7).
53. *Genealogy of Morals*, p. 34 (First Essay, sec. 7).
54. *Genealogy of Morals*, p. 40 (First Essay, sec. 11).
55. *Genealogy of Morals*, p. 40 (First Essay, sec. 11).
56. *Genealogy of Morals*, p. 36 (First Essay, sec. 10).
57. *Genealogy of Morals*, p. 33 (First Essay, sec. 7).
58. *Genealogy of Morals*, p. 85 (Second Essay, sec. 16).
59. *Ecce Homo*, p. 312 ("Genealogy of Morals").
60. Ibid.
61. *Genealogy of Morals*, p. 84 (Second Essay, sec. 16).
62. *Will to Power*, p. 33 (sec. 53) (italics omitted).
63. *Genealogy of Morals*, p. 36 (First Essay, sec. 10).
64. *Antichrist*, p. 621 (sec. 44).
65. *Antichrist*, p. 615 (sec. 40).
66. *Antichrist*, p. 623 (sec. 45).
67. *Thus Spoke Zarathustra*, p. 206.

68. *Genealogy of Morals*, p. 85 (Second Essay, sec. 16).

69. *Ecce Homo*, pp. 332–33 ("Why I Am a Destiny," sec. 7).

70. *Twilight of the Idols*, p. 487 ("Morality as Anti-Nature," sec. 1).

71. *Thus Spoke Zarathustra*, p. 204.

72. *Genealogy of Morals*, p. 93 (Second Essay, sec. 23).

73. *Antichrist*, p. 589 (sec. 21).

74. *Twilight of the Idols*, p. 501 ("The 'Improvers' of Mankind," sec. 1).

75. *Genealogy of Morals*, p. 91 (Second Essay, sec. 20).

76. *Will to Power*, p. 12 (sec. 12).

77. *Gay Science*, p. 283 (sec. 344).

78. *Will to Power*, p. 282 (sec. 521).

79. *Twilight of the Idols*, p. 479 ("'Reason' in Philosophy," sec. 1).

80. *Gay Science*, p. 300 (sec. 354).

81. *Twilight of the Idols*, p. 483 ("'Reason' in Philosophy," sec. 5).

82. *Antichrist*, p. 579 (sec. 12).

83. *Thus Spoke Zarathustra*, p. 191.

84. *Twilight of the Idols*, p. 485 ("How the 'True World' Finally Became a Fable").

85. *Will to Power*, pp. 10–11 (sec. 7).

86. *Will to Power*, p. 9 (sec. 4).

87. *Will to Power*, p. 12 (sec. 12).

88. *Beyond Good and Evil*, p. 200 (sec. 2).

89. *Will to Power*, p. 19 (sec. 28).

90. *Will to Power*, p. 13 (sec. 12).

91. *Will to Power*, p. 146 (sec. 253).

92. *Will to Power*, p. 35 (sec. 55).

93. Matthew Arnold, "Dover Beach," st. 4.

94. *Will to Power*, p. 11 (sec. 7).

95. *Will to Power*, pp. 16–17 (sec. 20).

96. *Will to Power*, p. 32 (sec. 51).

97. *Thus Spoke Zarathustra*, p. 228.

98. *Thus Spoke Zarathustra*, p. 188.

99. *Ecce Homo*, p. 326 ("Why I Am a Destiny," sec. 1).

100. *Thus Spoke Zarathustra*, p. 171.

101. *Gay Science*, p. 286 (sec. 346).

102. *Thus Spoke Zarathustra*, p. 199.

103. *Twilight of the Idols*, p. 554 ("Skirmishes of an Untimely Man," sec. 49).

104. Ibid. (italics omitted).

105. *Genealogy of Morals*, p. 96 (Second Essay, sec. 24).

106. Ibid.

107. *Portable Nietzsche*, p. 441 (Notes).

108. *Will to Power*, pp. 220–21 (sec. 409).

109. *Gay Science*, p. 122 (sec. 58).

110. *Beyond Good and Evil*, p. 206 (sec. 9).

111. *Thus Spoke Zarathustra*, p. 308.

112. *Thus Spoke Zarathustra*, p. 196.

113. *Human, All Too Human*, pp. 14–15 (vol. 1, sec. 6).

114. *Gay Science*, p. 122 (sec. 58).

115. *Beyond Good and Evil*, p. 326 (sec. 211).

116. *Gay Science*, p. 79 (sec. 4).

117. Ibid.

118. *Thus Spoke Zarathustra*, p. 137.

119. Ibid.

120. *Thus Spoke Zarathustra*, p. 138.

121. *Thus Spoke Zarathustra*, p. 139.

122. Ibid.

123. Ibid.

124. *Beyond Good and Evil*, p. 291 (sec. 188).

125. *Gay Science*, p. 247 (sec. 310).

126. Saul Bellow, *Henderson the Rain King*, Viking Compass ed. (New York: Viking Press, 1965), p. 267.

127. Ibid., p. 328.

128. Ibid., p. 340.

129. Ibid., p. 341.

130. *Thus Spoke Zarathustra*, p. 351.

131. *Gay Science*, p. 191 (sec. 143).

132. *Gay Science*, p. 233 (sec. 290).

133. Friedrich Nietzsche, *Schopenhauer as Educator*, trans. James W. Hillesheim and Malcolm R. Simpson (South Bend, IN: Regnery/Gateway, 1965), p. 60.

134. *Gay Science*, p. 266 (sec. 335).

135. *Portable Nietzsche*, p. 40 (Notes [1873]).

136. Friedrich Nietzsche, *The Use and Abuse of History*, trans. Adrian Collins, 2nd rev. ed. (Indianapolis, IN: Bobbs-Merrill, 1957), p. 72.

137. *Gay Science*, p. 232 (sec. 290).

138. Ibid.

139. Bellow, *Henderson the Rain King*, pp. 297–98.

140. Ibid., p. 271.

141. *Ecce Homo*, p. 254 ("Why I Am So Clever," sec. 9).

142. *Thus Spoke Zarathustra*, p. 218.

143. *Gay Science*, p. 232 (sec. 290).

144. *Gay Science*, p. 289 (sec. 347).

145. *Will to Power*, p. 33 (sec. 53) (italics omitted).

146. *Twilight of the Idols*, p. 554 ("Skirmishes of an Untimely Man," sec. 49) (italics omitted).

147. See *Human, All Too Human*, p. 9 (vol. 1, preface, sec. 6).

148. *Use and Abuse of History*, p. 61.

149. *Gay Science*, p. 228 (sec. 283).

150. See *Gay Science*, p. 255 (sec. 324).

151. Friedrich Nietzsche, *The Birth of Tragedy*, in *Basic Writings of Nietzsche*, p. 26 ("Attempt at a Self-Criticism," sec. 7).

152. *Birth of Tragedy*, p. 17 ("Attempt at a Self-Criticism," sec. 1).

153. *Gay Science*, p. 38 (preface, sec. 4).

154. See *Genealogy of Morals*, pp. 93–94 (Second Essay, sec. 23).

155. *Thus Spoke Zarathustra*, p. 435.

156. *Gay Science*, p. 273 (sec. 341).

157. *Ecce Homo*, p. 258 ("Why I Am So Clever," sec. 10).

158. *Thus Spoke Zarathustra*, p. 307.

159. *Thus Spoke Zarathustra*, p. 153.

160. *Use and Abuse of History*, p. 61.

161. *Thus Spoke Zarathustra*, p. 156.

CHAPTER 5

1. Aristotle, *Ethics* 3.5.1113b6–14. For the most part, I use the translation of the *Nicomachean Ethics* by Joe Sachs (Newburyport, MA: Focus Publishing, 2002). In a few instances, however, I prefer the translation of W. D. Ross, as revised by J. O. Urmson, in the *Complete Works of Aristotle: The Revised Oxford Translation*, ed. Jonathan Barnes (Princeton, NJ: Princeton University Press, 1984), 2:1729. Those instances are noted in parentheses, following the citation.

2. The quotations from canto IV of Dante's *Inferno* are taken from two different translations: John D. Sinclair (1939; repr., New York: Oxford University Press, 1981) and Allen Mandelbaum (Norwalk, CT: Easton Press, 2001).

3. *Ethics* 1.6.1096a16 (Ross/Urmson translation).

4. *Ethics* 1.6.1096a27–29.

5. *Ethics* 5.1.1129a26–29.

6. *Ethics* 1.3.1094b18–27.

7. *Ethics* 7.1.1145b3–8.

8. *Ethics* 10.8.1179a17–24.

9. *Ethics* 1.3.1095a8–9.

10. *Ethics* 2.2.1103b27–30.

11. *Ethics* 2.4.1105b12–16 (Ross/Urmson translation).

12. *Ethics* 3.5.1113b6–14.

13. See Alasdair MacIntyre, *After Virtue*, 2nd ed. (Notre Dame, IN: University of Notre Dame Press, 1984), pp. 109–21.

14. *Ethics* 1.13.1102a14–17 (translation amended).

15. See Aristotle, *On the Soul* 2.1.412a20–21, trans. J. A. Smith, in Barnes, *Complete Works of Aristotle*, 1:641.

16. *On the Soul* 2.1.412b5–8.

17. *On the Soul* 2.1.413a4.

18. Ludwig Wittgenstein, *Philosophical Investigations*, trans. G. E. M. Anscombe, 3rd ed. (New York: Macmillan, 1973), pt. 2, p. 178.

19. *Ethics* 1.2.1094a18–23.

20. *Ethics* 1.7.1097b1–8.

21. *Ethics* 1.7.1097b20–21.

22. *Ethics* 1.4.1095a19–20 (Ross/Urmson translation).

23. See J. O. Urmson, *Aristotle's Ethics* (Oxford: Blackwell, 1988), p. 12.

24. See Martha C. Nussbaum, *The Fragility of Goodness: Luck and Ethics in Greek Tragedy and Philosophy* (Cambridge: Cambridge University Press, 1986), p. 340.

25. For an example of an excellent glossary, see pp. 201–12 of the Sachs translation.

26. *Ethics* 7.13.1153b13–21.

27. *Ethics* 1.9.1099b25–28.

28. *Ethics* 9.9.1169b28–31.

29. *Ethics* 1.7.1098a14–24.

30. *Ethics* 1.5.1095b20 (Ross/Urmson translation).

31. *Ethics* 3.3.1112b12–13.

32. *Ethics* 3.7.1115b12–13.

33. *Ethics* 2.4.1105b5–9.

34. *Ethics* 4.1.1121a4–5.

35. *Ethics* 2.2.1104a35–1104b4.

36. *Ethics* 10.1.1172a21–24.

37. *Ethics* 2.1.1103b1–3.

38. *Ethics* 2.1.1103a31–33.

39. *Ethics* 2.1.1103a11–15.

40. *Ethics* 2.1.1103b15–18.

41. *Ethics* 2.1.1103b23–27.

42. *Ethics* 2.2.1104a12–13.
43. *Ethics* 2.6.1106b24–26.
44. See Urmson, *Aristotle's Ethics*, pp. 28–29.
45. *Ethics* 2.6.1107a1–8.
46. *Ethics* 3.11.119a13–24.
47. *Ethics* 2.6.1107a23–28.
48. *Ethics* 2.61107a25.
49. *Ethics* 2.6.1107a8–18.
50. *Ethics* 2.6.1106b28–31.
51. *Ethics* 4.5.1126a9–12.
52. *Ethics* 2.8.1108b19–31.
53. *Ethics* 2.9.1109b2.
54. *Ethics* 2.9.1109b5–9.
55. *Ethics* 2.9.1109b7–8 (Ross/Urmson translation).
56. *Ethics* 6.1.1138b22–27.
57. *Ethics* 6.13.1144b18–21.
58. *Ethics* 6.13.1145a6–9.
59. *Ethics* 6.13.1144b26–33.
60. *Ethics* 6.5.1140a25–31.
61. See Nussbaum, *Fragility of Goodness*, p. 313.
62. *Ethics* 6.13.1144b26–33.
63. *Ethics* 6.2.1139a32–38.
64. *Ethics* 10.9.1179b7–11.
65. *Ethics* 10.9.1179b29–35.
66. *Ethics* 10.9.1179b32–35.
67. *Ethics* 10.9.1179b17–19.
68. *Ethics* 4.3.1123b21–26.
69. *Ethics* 4.3.1123b14–17.
70. *Ethics* 4.3.1123b2–3.
71. *Ethics* 4.3.1125a20–24.
72. *Ethics* 4.3.1125a33–35.
73. *Ethics* 4.3.1123b26–36.
74. *Ethics* 4.3.1124a1–6.
75. *Ethics* 4.3.1123b35–36, 4.3.1125a28–35.
76. *Ethics* 4.3.1124a23–36.
77. *Ethics* 4.3.1124b1–8.
78. *Ethics* 4.3.1124a17–18.
79. *Ethics* 4.3.1124a14–24.
80. *Ethics* 4.3.1124b18–1125a3.
81. *Ethics* 4.3.1125a14–18.

82. *Ethics* 10.4.1175a13–15.
83. *Ethics* 10.4.1174b33–36.
84. *Ethics* 10.4.1175a17–25.
85. *Ethics* 10.5.1175a29–39.
86. *Ethics* 10.5.1175a29–1175b2.
87. *Ethics* 10.6.1177a2–3.
88. *Ethics* 10.7.1177a12–26.
89. *Ethics* 10.7.1177b19–22.
90. *Ethics* 10.8.1178b31–1179a3.
91. *Ethics* 10.7.1177b1–5.
92. *Ethics* 10.7.1177a20–25.
93. *Ethics* 10.7.1177a25–31.
94. *Ethics* 10.7.1177b19–27.
95. *Ethics* 10.7.1177b25–36.
96. *Ethics* 10.8.1178a9–10.
97. *Ethics* 10.7.1177b34 (Ross/Urmson translation).
98. *Ethics* 8.1.1155a2–7.
99. *Ethics* 8.3.1156a11–20.
100. Ibid.
101. *Ethics* 8.3.1156a20–25.
102. Ibid.
103. *Ethics* 8.12.1162a26.
104. *Ethics* 8.3.1156b7–8.
105. *Ethics* 8.3.1156b10–18.
106. *Ethics* 8.3.1156b25–30.
107. *Ethics* 8.4.1157a21–26.
108. *Ethics* 8.1.1155a29.
109. *Ethics* 8.3.1156b15.
110. *Ethics* 9.12.1172a1–3.
111. *Ethics* 9.12.1172a4–10.
112. *Ethics* 9.12.1172a10–14.
113. *Ethics* 9.8.1169a25.
114. *Ethics* 9.8.1169a25–34.
115. *Ethics* 9.8.1169a36–1169b3.
116. *Ethics* 9.11.1171b16–19.
117. *Ethics* 9.11.1171b18–29.

CHAPTER 6

1. Martin Heidegger, "Language," in *Poetry, Language, Thought*, trans. Albert Hofstadter (1971; repr., New York: HarperCollins, HarperPerennial, 2001), p. 189.

2. Quoted in Rüdiger Safranski, *Martin Heidegger: Between Good and Evil*, trans. Ewald Osers (Cambridge, MA: Harvard University Press, 1998), p. 7.

3. Quoted in Hugo Ott, *Martin Heidegger: A Political Life*, trans. Allan Blunden (New York: Basic Books, 1993), p. 106.

4. Quoted in ibid., p. 107.

5. Quoted in ibid., p. 109.

6. Quoted in ibid., p. 125.

7. Martin Heidegger, "The Self-Assertion of the German University," in *The Heidegger Controversy*, ed. Richard Wolin (Cambridge, MA: MIT Press, 1993), p. 33.

8. Quoted in Ott, *Heidegger: A Political Life*, p. 135.

9. Günther Neske and Emil Kettering, *Martin Heidegger and National Socialism: Questions and Answers* (New York: Paragon House, 1990), p. 10.

10. Quoted in Safranski, *Heidegger: Between Good and Evil*, pp. 232–33.

11. Quoted in Ott, *Heidegger: A Political Life*, p. 173.

12. Martin Heidegger, *Being and Time*, trans. John Macquarrie and Edward Robinson (San Francisco, CA: HarperSanFrancisco, 1962), p. 117.

13. *Being and Time*, p. 63 (translation amended). Macquarrie and Robinson translate "Seiendes" and "Seiende" as "entity" and "entities," respectively. But they acknowledge "being" and "beings" as alternative translations, which I prefer. I have amended relevant quotations accordingly.

14. *Being and Time*, pp. 25–26 (translation amended).

15. *Being and Time*, p. 59 (translation amended).

16. *Being and Time*, p. 26 (translation amended).

17. Ludwig Wittgenstein, *Philosophical Investigations*, trans. G. E. M. Anscombe, 3rd ed. (New York: Macmillan, 1973), sec. 129.

18. *Being and Time*, p. 27.

19. *Being and Time*, p. 49 (translation amended).

20. *Being and Time*, p. 274.

21. *Being and Time*, p. 60 (translation amended).

22. Ibid.

23. *Being and Time*, p. 72.

24. *Being and Time*, p. 84 (translation amended).

25. *Being and Time*, p. 154.

26. *Being and Time*, p. 207.

27. *Being and Time*, p. 152.

28. *Being and Time*, p. 78.

29. *Being and Time*, p. 50.

30. *Being and Time*, p. 205.

31. Ibid.

32. *Being and Time*, p. 27.

33. Ibid.

34. *Being and Time*, p. 194 (italics omitted).

35. *Being and Time*, p. 363.

36. *Being and Time*, p. 67 (italics omitted).

37. *Being and Time*, p. 32.

38. *Being and Time*, pp. 32–33.

39. *Being and Time*, p. 211.

40. *Being and Time*, p. 194.

41. *Being and Time*, p. 27.

42. *Being and Time*, p. 211.

43. *Being and Time*, p. 363.

44. *Being and Time*, p. 169.

45. Hubert L. Dreyfus, *Being-in-the-World: A Commentary on Heidegger's "Being and Time," Division I* (Cambridge, MA: MIT Press, 1991), p. 169.

46. *Being and Time*, p. 177 (italics omitted).

47. Martin Heidegger, *The Basic Problems of Phenomenology*, trans. Albert Hofstadter, rev. ed. (Bloomington: Indiana University Press, 1988), p. 159.

48. *Being and Time*, p. 213.

49. *Being and Time*, p. 185.

50. *Being and Time*, p. 174.

51. *Being and Time*, p. 184.

52. *Being and Time*, p. 331.

53. *Being and Time*, p. 167 (translation amended). For the reasons discussed in text, I use the translation, "the One," for the German, "das Man," rather than the Macquarrie and Robinson translation, "the They."

54. *Being and Time*, p. 164 (translation amended).

55. *Being and Time*, p. 211.

56. *Being and Time*, p. 164 (translation amended with "one" for "man").

57. *Being and Time*, p. 165 (translation amended).

58. Ibid.

59. *Being and Time*, p. 219.

60. *Being and Time*, p. 220.

61. *Being and Time*, p. 213.

62. *Being and Time*, p. 216.

63. Ibid.

64. *Being and Time*, p. 222.

65. Ibid.

66. *Being and Time*, p. 239.

67. Ibid.

68. *Basic Problems of Phenomenology*, p. 290.

69. Marcel Proust, *Time Regained*, in *In Search of Lost Time*, trans. C. K. Scott Moncrieff et al., rev. D. J. Enright (London: Folio Society, 2000), 6:474–75.

70. Ibid., 6:474.

71. Ibid.

72. Ibid.

73. *Being and Time*, p. 167 (translation amended).

74. Ibid.

75. *Being and Time*, p. 165.

76. *Being and Time*, p. 184.

77. See *Being and Time*, p. 426.

78. See Ludwig Wittgenstein, *Tractatus Logico-Philosophicus*, trans. David F. Pears and Brian F. McGuiness, rev. ed. (Atlantic Highlands, NJ: Humanities Press, 1974), 6.4311.

79. *Being and Time*, p. 307.

80. Martin Heidegger, "What Is Metaphysics?" in *Basic Writings*, ed. David F. Krell (New York: Harper & Row, 1977), p. 108.

81. Ibid., p. 106.

82. *Hamlet*, ed. Edward Hubler, in *Tragedies*, Everyman's Library, vol. 1 (New York: Knopf, 1992), p. 64 (act 3, sc. 1, line 78).

83. Quoted in Safranski, *Heidegger: Between Good and Evil*, p. 179.

84. "What Is Metaphysics?" p. 99.

85. *Being and Time*, p. 308.

86. "What Is Metaphysics?" p. 103.

87. *Being and Time*, p. 310.

88. *Being and Time*, p. 236.

89. *Being and Time*, p. 233.

90. *Being and Time*, p. 393.

91. *Being and Time*, p. 435.

92. "What Is Metaphysics?" p. 108.

93. W. H. Auden, "As I Walked Out One Evening," st. 11.

94. Milan Kundera, *The Book of Laughter and Forgetting*, trans. Aaron Asher (New York: HarperCollins, HarperPerennial, 1999), p. 281.

95. *Being and Time*, p. 232.

96. *Being and Time*, p. 234.

97. *Being and Time*, p. 233.

98. *Being and Time*, p. 394.

99. Safranski, *Heidegger: Between Good and Evil*, pp. 162–63.

100. *Being and Time*, p. 344.

101. *Being and Time*, p. 213.

102. *Being and Time*, p. 369 (italics omitted).

103. *Being and Time*, p. 441.

104. *Being and Time*, p. 330.

105. *Being and Time*, p. 345 (translation amended).

106. *Being and Time*, p. 358.

107. *Being and Time*, p. 308.

108. *Being and Time*, p. 311 (translation amended; italics and emphasis omitted).

109. *Being and Time*, p. 358.

110. *Being and Time*, p. 437.

111. *Being and Time*, p. 308.

112. *Being and Time*, p. 376.

113. *Being and Time*, p. 97.

114. Dreyfus, *Being-in-the-World*, p. 301.

115. *Being and Time*, p. 157.

116. Martin Heidegger, "On the Essence of Truth," in Krell, *Basic Writings*, p. 127.

117. Ibid.

118. Martin Heidegger, "The Origin of the Work of Art," in *Poetry, Language, Thought*, p. 51.

119. Walt Whitman, "By Blue Ontario's Shore," st. 10.

120. Martin Heidegger, *Discourse on Thinking*, trans. John M. Anderson and E. Hans Freund (New York: Harper & Row, 1969), p. 55.

121. Martin Heidegger, interview by Rudolf Augstein and Georg Wolff, September 23, 1966 (published in *Der Speigel*, May 31, 1976, pp. 193–219).

122. *Discourse on Thinking*, p. 50.

123. Ibid., p. 54.

124. Martin Heidegger, "The Thing," in *Poetry, Language, Thought*, p. 182.

125. Martin Heidegger, "'...Poetically Man Dwells...,'" in *Poetry, Language, Thought*, p. 211.

126. Friedrich Hölderlin, "Bread and Wine," in *Poems of Friedrich Hölderlin*, trans. James Mitchell, 2nd ed. (San Francisco: Ithuriel's Spear, 2007), p. 13.

127. Ibid., p. 11.

128. *Discourse on Thinking*, p. 55.

129. Ibid.

130. "Origin of the Work of Art," p. 35.

131. "'...Poetically Man Dwells...,'" p. 213.

132. Proust, *Time Regained*, in *In Search of Lost Time*, 6:468.13.

133. Martin Heidegger, "Letter on Humanism," in Krell, *Basic Writings*, p. 194.

134. "Letter on Humanism," p. 193.

135. "Letter on Humanism," p. 199.

136. Ibid.

137. Ibid.

138. Richard Rorty, *Essays on Heidegger and Others* (Cambridge: Cambridge University Press, 1991), p. 65.

139. Ibid.

140. Martin Heidegger, "The End of Philosophy and the Task of Thinking," in Krell, *Basic Writings*, p. 378.

141. *Investigations*, sec. 261.

142. "Letter on Humanism," p. 199.

143. "Letter on Humanism," p. 239.

144. Quoted in Safranski, *Heidegger: Between Good and Evil*, p. 1.

145. T. S. Eliot, "Little Gidding," *Four Quartets* 4, lines 243–45.

EPILOGUE

1. Milan Kundera, *The Curtain*, trans. Linda Asher (New York: HarperCollins, HarperPerennial, 2008), p. 83.

2. Milan Kundera, *Testaments Betrayed*, trans. Linda Asher (New York: HarperCollins, HarperPerennial, 1996), p. 163.

3. Ibid.

4. See James C. Edwards, *The Authority of Language: Heidegger, Wittgenstein, and the Threat of Philosophical Nihilism* (Tampa: University of South Florida Press, 1990), p. 241 (what makes for "an *end* to our traditional philosophical, religious and ethical questions without yet being an *answer* to them, is just the difference between wonder and worship").

5. T. S. Eliot, "Little Gidding," *Four Quartets* 4, lines 239–42.

INDEX

273